FRONTPAGE 2003

MICHAEL PRICE

In easy steps is an imprint of Computer Step
Southfield Road . Southam
Warwickshire CV47 0FB . United Kingdom
www.ineasysteps.com

Printed and bound in the United Kingdom

ISBN 1-84078-269-2

Contents

Introducing FrontPage 2003

Chapter One

FrontPage 2003 allows you to create and manage Web sites for personal or business use. This chapter will introduce the use of Web space, discuss the features of FrontPage 2003 that help you build and use Web sites and show you how to install the software.

Covers

The Internet

The Internet is a global network of networks, linking millions of computers worldwide for communication. Originally developed in 1969 for the U.S. military, it grew to include educational and research institutions, and now includes commerce, industry, corporate and residential users, using the Internet to exchange documents, emails, data, device drivers, images or audio files.

You can use the Internet in many different ways. At its simplest, it is a mechanism for exchanging documents and information with anyone else who has direct or indirect access to the Internet.

A Web page is defined using the HTML mark-up language. The page can contain many elements, including text, pictures, sound and video.

To make this easier, the Internet has evolved a format for publishing information, known as the Web page. The Internet provides access to millions of Web pages, stored on thousands of computers (Web servers). The Web pages are linked together in groups known as Web sites. Each Web site has a unique address (Universal Resource Locator or URL) that allows you to access the primary home or welcome page for the site. Web pages usually refer to other Web pages with relevant, related contents.

Use the search engines on the Internet to look for Web sites and Web pages by content, then follow links to other pages and other sites.

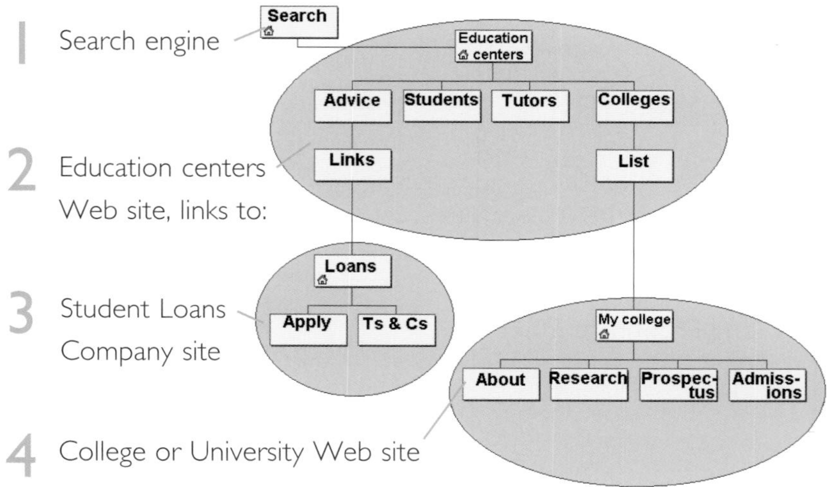

Internet access

To surf the Internet, you need an account with an Internet service provider (ISP) and the hardware and software to connect to the Internet.

You can create a dial-up connection between your PC and the Internet, using a modem and a telephone line. You make the connection when you need to transfer mail or to access information. The connection exists just for the period of the Internet session. The link is made to the Web server belonging to your ISP, but once you have dialed in, you can run Internet navigation software, such as Netscape or Internet Explorer, to view documents.

This is the most economical method for less frequent usage, since the set up costs for the modem and the telephone line rental are relatively low, and you pay only for the times when your connection is active. The telephone line is available for other purposes such as fax or voice when you are not using the Internet. You can minimize the time you spend connected, if you increase the capacity of the dial-up connection by choosing a higher speed modem (up to 56 Kbps), or by switching to the digital ISDN type of connection (for 64 Kbps or 128 Kbps).

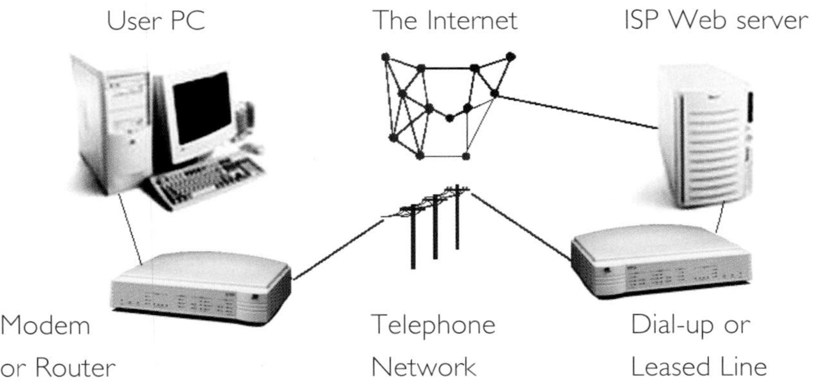

The best choice of connection depends on the way you use the Internet, but it is usually dial-up for home and small offices, or leased line for businesses. If broadband ADSL or cable modem services are available in your area, these provide always-on connections that are suitable for home or business use.

For higher rates, or when you want to make your data directly accessible from the Internet, you need a leased line. This provides a dedicated connection that is permanently available. The capacity of the line (the bandwidth) ranges from 64 Kbps to 2 Mbps or more. The leased line can be rented on a fixed fee, based on the capacity, or charged by usage – the amount of data sent over the line.

Broadband ADSL and cable modem connections are now becoming more standard, and these provide speeds of 500 Kbps to 2 Mbps, sharing a high speed link among a number of users.

Personal home pages

You can create and manage your own Web site, and be part of the information resource provided on the Internet.

You don't need a Web site to browse the Internet and search for information, but having your own Web site does allow you to make your own contribution to the Internet. You may create a personal home page, where you can store links to other Web sites and Web pages that you often want to visit. You can add information to this page or add additional pages, to share with other users on the Internet.

If you have programs, pictures or other data that you would like to share, you can also add these. Soon your home page will develop into a Web site in its own right, that other users will enjoy visiting.

The personal home page is often used to gain experience with the Internet, and help you plan how to use the Internet to support your business or service.

You can include more features such as a hit counter to record visits and a guest book to record comments. If you are in business of any type, you can use your Web site to inform others about your goods and services, and give them the opportunity to define their requirements and place their orders.

A typical home page will contain:

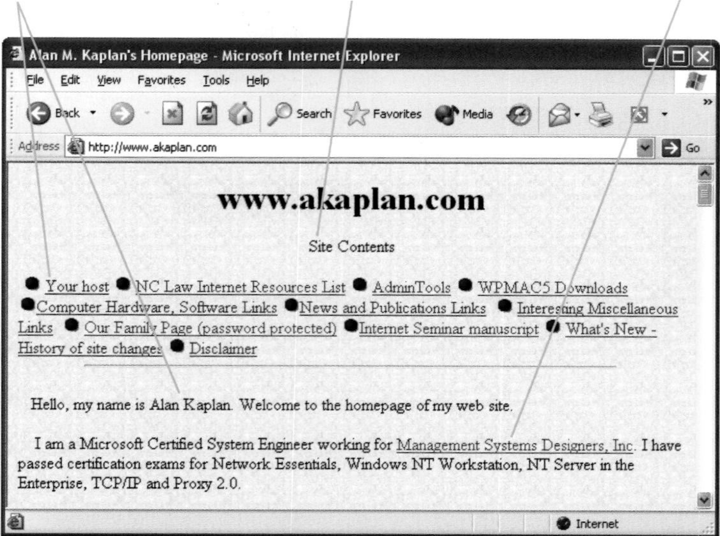

You may also find banners and pop-up windows that provide the advertisements that qualify the site for "free" Web resources.

You may find items such as date last updated or a visitor counter at the bottom of the Web page.

Web space

You can find extra free Web space, but using this means that your Web site must carry various types of adverts and banners.

The disk storage or Web space occupied by the Web site on the server may be provided by the Internet Service Provider. Most ISPs include 5 MB or 10 MB of Web space free, when you subscribe to their Internet connection service. This is sufficient for personal use, but the bigger or more complex your Web site, the more Web space you will require, so you may need to purchase additional capacity.

For individuals and smaller businesses starting out on the Internet, the ISP Web servers provide all the necessary functions.

If your ISP does not provide space, or if you have a larger business need, you may choose one of the Web hosting services with Web space and connection functions. There are also Web Presence Providers (WPPs), who specialize in Web hosting. The actual connection is provided by your ISP.

For more advanced corporate Web sites requiring larger space, dedicated servers may be required. These will be managed at a data center, with direct high speed access to the Internet.

To help find an Internet service provider, you could try The List, a directory of ISPs, Web Hosts and Web Designers in the USA and Canada. There are entries for personal and for business use. Visit the Web site http://www.thelist.com/ for details.

Your Internet address

The form that your Web site address (URL) takes will depend on the type of Internet service account that you use, and the way in which you obtain your Web space. See page 94 for information about selecting a Web Presence Provider (WPP).

Your personal home page will be identified by the server or network domain name and your account name. For example, using the FreeWebs service with the account name Queensmead, the home page URL would be:

http://www.freewebs.com/queensmead/

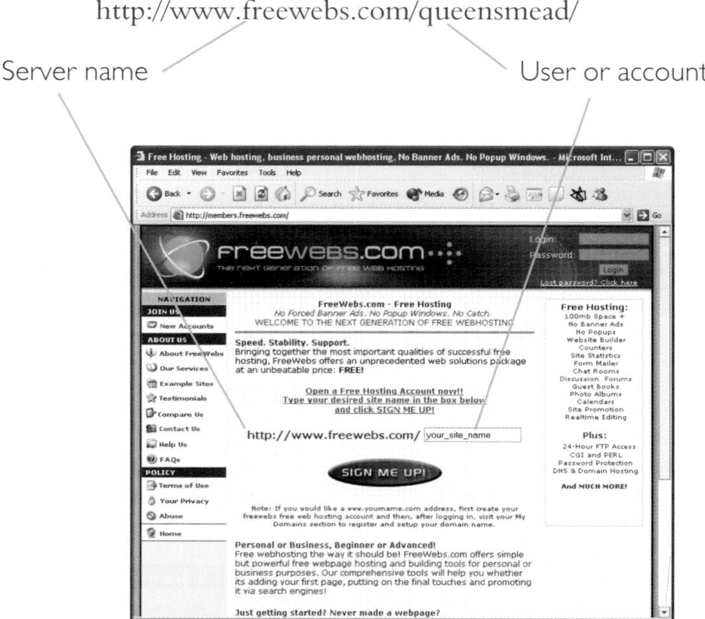

Web space is grouped to put the users of similar types in a "community" to make it easier to locate sites of possible interest.

Some services may add a Web space folder name between the server name and the Web site name. This will normally be related to the type of content, for example Music or Films.

Note that the account name Queensmead could not be used for this example – someone had already registered that name. See page 93 for details of registering domain names.

With some Internet services, the account name that you are assigned is used as a subdomain name, and is attached to the server address. So with the Hypermart.net service, the Queensmead account would have this URL:

http://queensmead.hypermart.net/

Finally, for an annual fee you can register your own domain name for Web space hosted by an Internet service, to give you a personal URL such as:

http://www.maprice.com

FrontPage 2003

FrontPage 2003 is just the tool you need to create your home page or full Web site. And it's not just for the Internet – it can be used to publish pages on your Local Area Network.

FrontPage 2003 allows you to design and build home pages and Web sites that look professional and include all the functions and features you want, without you having to deal with all the intrinsic details of the underlying HTML code. It also provides help in getting the Web pages and data files from your system to your Web space on the Internet, or onto your network server if you are designing an Intranet site for use on your Local Area Network.

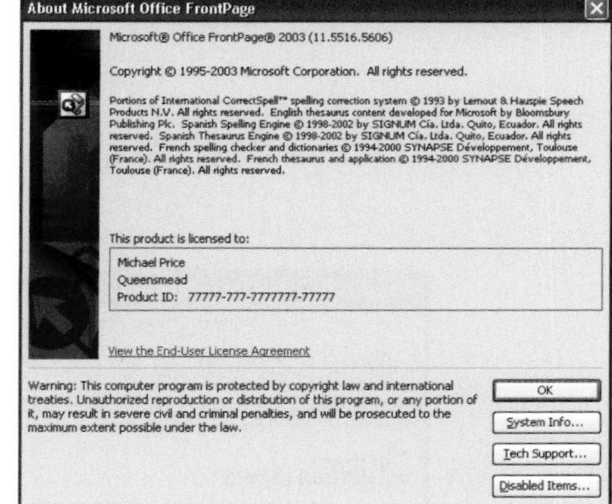

FrontPage 2003 has the flexibility of a simple HTML editor, with the professional finish you'd expect from a custom site designer, taking advantage of the latest technologies such as XML and Microsoft SharePoint.

FrontPage 2003 is a tool for both Web site creation and Web site management. With it, you can make sure that there is a consistent style and appearance applied to every page. It offers many features, including functions that reside on the server, but you are not restricted to using FrontPage facilities. You can add and change items using native HTML codes and you can incorporate advanced Web technologies. It gives you full control over the page, and you can position the items exactly where you want them.

FrontPage 2003 lets you share the task of creating and maintaining your Web site with other members of your group.

When you have created your Web site, FrontPage 2003 allows you to set up and maintain it as a unit. You can monitor the status of your site, and apply updates and changes. If you are a member of a workgroup, you can collaborate with other members who are also updating or extending the Web site.

Because FrontPage 2003 was designed as a part of the Microsoft Office Suite, you will find that the processes and procedures are familiar, and you can easily exchange documents and data with the other applications in Office 2003.

FrontPage packages

The special edition of Office 2003 Professional is an upgrade for existing users of Office 2000, and was available for a limited period only.

Unlike previous versions, FrontPage 2003 is not included as a component in any of the Microsoft Office editions, so it must be purchased as a stand-alone product. If you are a new user, you should purchase the full product. Microsoft also offers a 120 day trial, so you can confirm that the application meets your needs.

If you already have a version of FrontPage installed, you may be able to obtain the upgrade product which is available at a discount.

If you purchased a version of Office XP or FrontPage 2002 between August 15, 2003 and November 30, 2003, you may be eligible for a free upgrade to FrontPage 2003, under the Microsoft Technology Guarantee program. For details see the Web page http://www.microsoft.com/Office/howtobuy/techguarantee.mspx

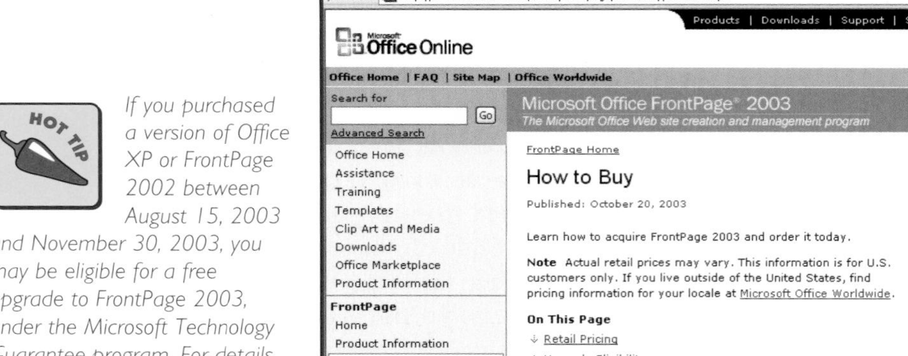

Qualifying products for the upgrade include FrontPage (the 2002, 2000, 98 or 97 versions), Office XP (the Developer, Professional with FrontPage or Professional Special editions) and Office 2000 (the Developer, or Premium editions).

Requirements

The minimum requirements are not as large, but you'll find Webs place high demands on your system, especially if you like lots of animation and video effects.

To use FrontPage 2003, the following components are recommended:

- PC with Pentium 233 MHz III processor or equivalent.
- Windows 2000 Service Pack 3 (SP3) or later, or Windows XP or later.
- 128 MB memory or greater.

FrontPage 2003 and the other applications associated with Office 2003 will not run on the Windows Me, Windows 98, or Windows NT operating systems. If your PC is currently running one of these operating systems, you must upgrade the operating system before installing FrontPage 2003.

- 180 MB available hard disk space, with an additional 200MB, 115 MB for the optional installation files cache.
- CD-ROM or DVD-ROM drive.
- Super VGA display adapter (800 x 600 or higher resolution monitor).
- Microsoft Mouse, Microsoft IntelliMouse, or compatible pointing device.

Have copies of other Web browsers, if possible, so you can check out how your site looks from other users' viewpoints.

Internet access is needed to use Internet features, so you will need a modem, a cable modem or other mechanism for connecting to the Internet. You'll need a Web browser, but it doesn't have to be Internet Explorer, since FrontPage works with any browser.

There will be other components that you need, for Windows or for multimedia applications, including printer, audio adapter, speakers, microphone, scanner or digital camera.

Windows Server 2003 running SharePoint Services is required for the advanced collaboration features.

Features of FrontPage 2003

There is an on-going debate between Web designers, with the purists preferring HTML, and the pragmatists welcoming tools to relieve the tedium. FrontPage lets you choose the best of both these approaches.

FrontPage 2003 includes many features to make it easier for you to create and manage your Web site, without having to become involved at a programmer level. It allows you to control the way your pages look, using WYSIWYG (what you see is what you get).

Among the features of FrontPage 2003 are:

Pixel-precise positioning

FrontPage allows absolute and relative positioning to place page elements such as graphics and text exactly where needed.

Tools are also provided for creating and manipulating tables that are used for layout purposes.

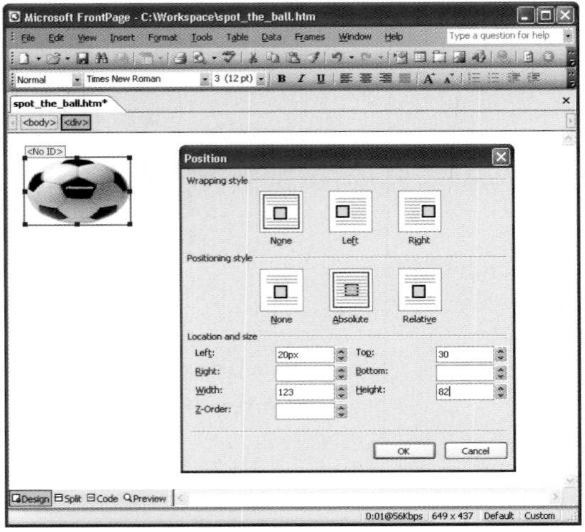

Pre-designed themes

Themes provide ready-made settings for a consistent look across the page and the Web site. You may add your own themes or customize existing themes to suit your preferences (see pages 66–67 for examples).

FrontPage 2003 uses CSS (Cascading Style Sheets) rather than HTML to apply themes, files are smaller, more transparent, and easier to control and modify than in the previous versions.

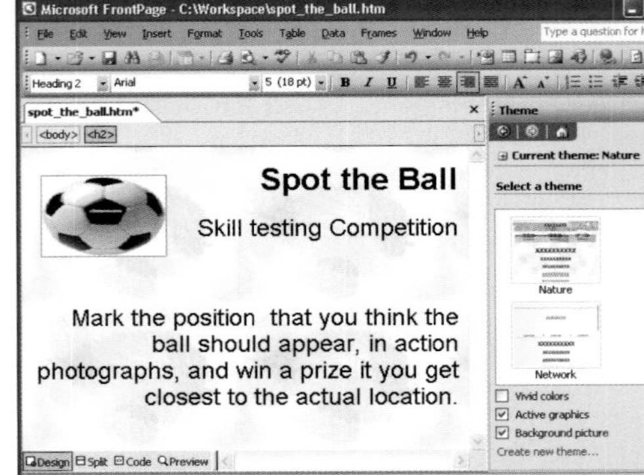

You don't need Office 2003 to use FrontPage 2003, but the two do work hand in hand, since Office applications support HTML as a native file format.

Office 2003 integration

FrontPage can integrate data from Office applications. For example, you can incorporate database queries directly into Web pages, and even update the database from Web pages. It also provides tools for handling and formatting data from XML sources.

Split view

The new Split view helps you to create and update your Web site more quickly by showing both the Code (HTML) view and the Design view at the same time. When you make changes to the design, the code updates as you work. This helps you to understand how FrontPage implements various features into the code. When you make changes to the code itself, you can update the Design view by pressing F5 to apply the changes so far.

Code view includes the IntelliSense function, to help reduce errors in code writing. IntelliSense incorporates statement completion, and shows the parameters appropriate to the code you enter. It supports HTML, XSL, JScript®, VBScript, JavaScript, and ASP.NET.

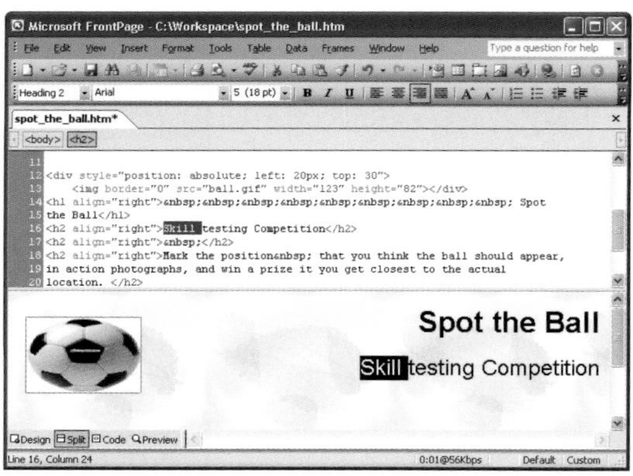

Optimize HTML

You can clean up your HTML at the time you write it, by selecting Tools, Optimize HTML, to automatically remove white space, nonessential tags and comments. You can also clean up HTML created in another program and inserted into your Web page.

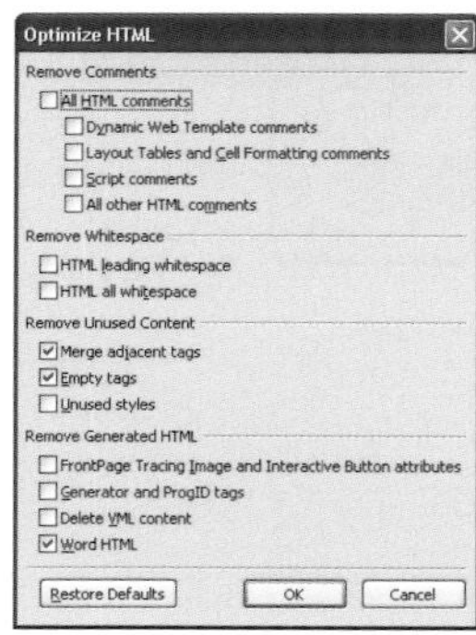

Compatibility

You can have multiple browsers installed, for example Internet Explorer, Netscape, Mozilla and Opera, and check out your Web pages on each. You can also specify which versions of browser your Web pages will display with, and enable or disallow the FrontPage and SharePoint technologies. FrontPage will restrict the features used in the site to those supported on the targeted systems.

Restricting the Web features means missing out on some effects, but will increase your potential audience.

FrontPage Webs

FrontPage manages Webs, which are Web sites that can be stored on your hard disk or on your Web server.

A FrontPage Web is like any Web site that consists of a home page plus the associated Web pages, graphics, documents, multimedia, and other files that it references. The FrontPage Web site also contains files that support the FrontPage-specific functions that allow the Web to be opened, copied, edited, and administered in FrontPage. The Web site is created in FrontPage and stored directly on a Web server or on the PC hard disk, for use on an Intranet or for later transfer to a Web server. The Web is stored in a folder or directory. The top level is known as the root or parent. There can be other folders nested within the main folder.

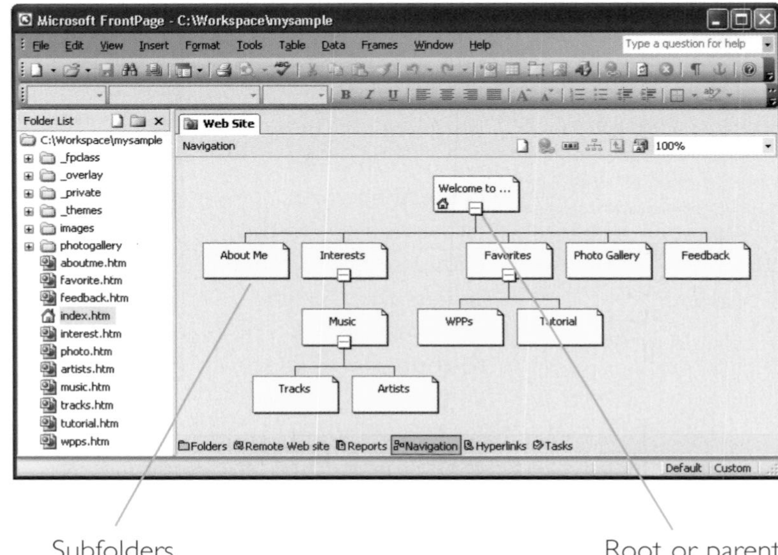

The Web server must support the FrontPage server extensions for you to use nested subwebs.

These subfolders of the root Web may themselves be complete FrontPage Webs. They are known as subwebs, and can have independent administration, authoring and browsing permissions. The subwebs can be used to organize the Web into separate sections for different departments or different groups of visitors. Searches and hyperlinks can be limited to the subweb.

For example, you could create a business Web for all users, and include a private subweb for employees and another subweb for existing customers. Each subweb could be given the authorities and permissions appropriate to the intended type of user.

Building your Web site

FrontPage 2003 is designed to handle all the tasks, with assistance from your browser and FTP (File Transfer Protocol) program.

There are a number of stages involved in creating your Web site. The exact process will vary, depending on the level of complexity in your requirements, and you may need to iterate through some of the stages a number of times, until you achieve the effect you want. However, the basic stages are as follows:

1. Defining the requirements

Decide exactly what purpose you have in mind when you establish your Web site. This may be as simple as "gaining experience with the Internet", or you may have specific aims related to your hobbies or business. Whatever the objectives, you should identify your aims and your goals before you start establishing the Web site.

2. Designing the Web site

The Web site will be a series of interconnecting Web pages, plus graphics, documents and other files and components. Choose one of the FrontPage templates to get started.

See also Chapter 12 for links to various style guides for Web sites, Web pages and HTML code.

3. Creating the components

Build the Web pages, collect data, prepare graphics, add links and put everything together to complete the site. Use your browser to preview the results.

4. Publishing the Web

Transfer the components to the Web server or LAN server that will host your Web site, and check that everything fits together the way it should, without, for example, relying on items that exist on your own hard disk. Access the site from a different PC, and try out the scenarios that your visitors will face, so that you can ensure that their visits will be effective.

You can publish updates of any size to your Web site. However, for major changes, you'd do better to repeat the whole process and build a replacement Web site.

5. Maintaining the Web

You must keep the information on the Web site up to date, respond appropriately to the feedback that you receive, and resolve and eliminate any problems or issues that arise.

FrontPage helps you carry out all these tasks. You'll also find lots of help on the Internet in the form of user group, software supplier and standards organization sites. The World Wide Web itself also provides a multitude of examples of what can be done, and you can see for yourself its impact on visitors.

FrontPage views

The Views bar that was featured in the previous version, FrontPage 2002 has been removed, but additional tabs have been provided to allow you to navigate between the views.

You can also enable the Task Pane or the Folder List (and the Navigation Pane) from this menu, or by clicking the Toggle Pane button.

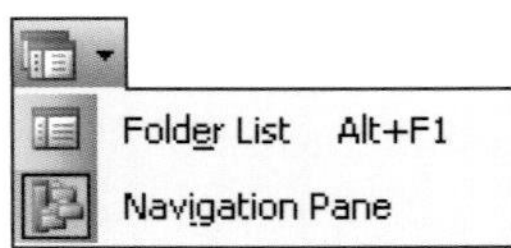

In FrontPage 2003, all the design and build tasks are carried out in the one application, with different views for the different stages and activities.

To switch to Page view:

Open the Web site and select View, then choose Page from the list.

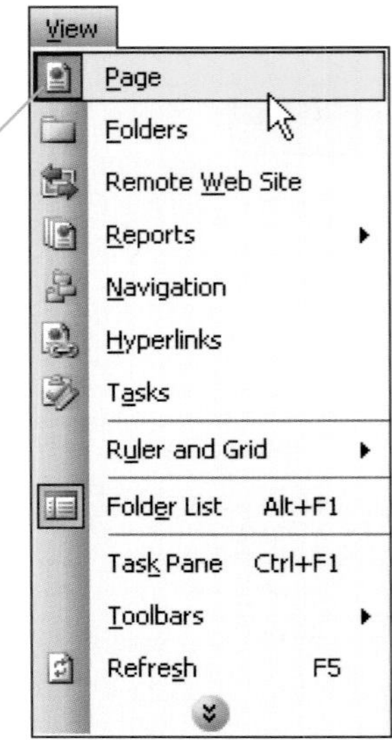

Page view

There are four different types of Page views, and you can switch between these using the tabs at the foot of the view.

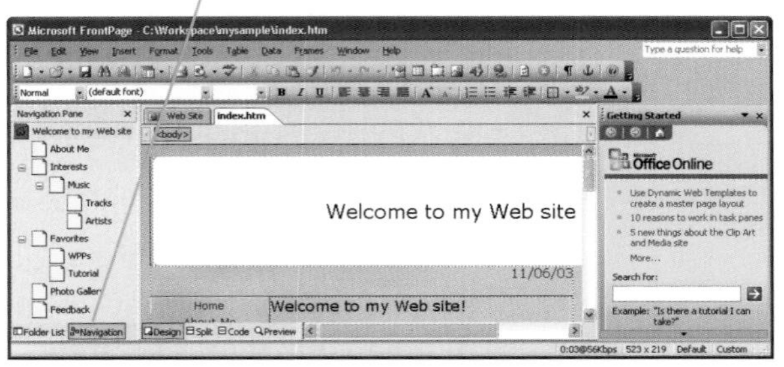

Design view: Here you design and edit Web pages visually in the WYSIWYG (What You See Is What You Get) style, where you directly edit the text, graphics, and other elements.

Code view: This shows underlying HTML code for the elements you have designed, and you can edit the HTML tags or add new code.

Split view: Combining the Design and Code views, here you can review the effect of changes immediately.

Preview view: With this you see how the page will look in the Web browser without having to save your page, allowing you to check changes before you commit to them.

Other views

There are six other views. When you select any one of these, the six views can be accessed via the tabs displayed at the foot of each.

To display these views:

2 With Page view displayed, click the Web Site tab at the top, then choose one of the six tabs at the foot.

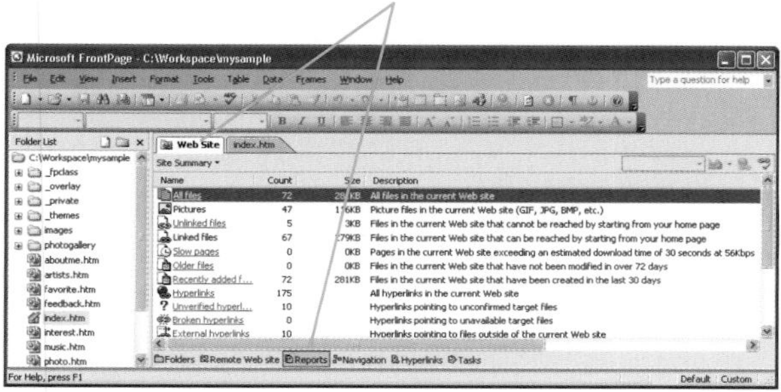

As with Page view, you can enable or disable the Task Pane and the File List. The Navigation Pane does not appear in these views.

Folders view: Work with files and folders directly, and create, delete, copy, or move folders to organize the contents of your site.

Remote Web Site view: Publish an entire Web site or selectively publish individual files, and synchronize files between two or more locations to keep them up-to-date with recent changes.

Reports view: Analyze the contents of your Web site by running report queries, allowing you to calculate the total size of the files in your site, show which files are not linked to other files, identify slow or outdated pages, and group files by task or person.

Navigation view: A hierarchical view of your Web pages, where you arrange the pages by moving them to new locations in the site.

Hyperlinks view: The status of the internal and external links in your Web site, showing you whether the hyperlinks have been verified or are broken.

Tasks view: All the tasks in your Web site displayed in a column format and providing current information about each task.

FrontPage wizards automatically generate some tasks, but you can add your own tasks and use the Tasks view to manage them.

Installing FrontPage 2003

With the 2003 version, FrontPage is no longer included in any of the Microsoft Office editions.

FrontPage 2003 must be installed as a separate, stand-alone product from its own installation CD.

1. Insert the FrontPage 2003 installation CD, and allow AutoPlay to start the installation program. If AutoPlay is not active on your system, open the CD folder and double click Setup.exe.

As with all the Office 2003 programs, you will need your setup CDs close to hand (or a copy available on a server) until you have added all the features that you want.

2. Enter the 25 character CD key provided for your copy of FrontPage, and click Next.

Microsoft Office FrontPage 2003 Setup
Microsoft Office FrontPage 2003
Product Key
In the boxes below, type your 25-character Product Key. You will find this number on the sticker on the back of the CD case or on your Certificate of Authenticity.
Product Key:
Help | < Back | Next > | Cancel

3. Enter your name, initials (and, if appropriate the organization), to personalize your copy, and click Next.

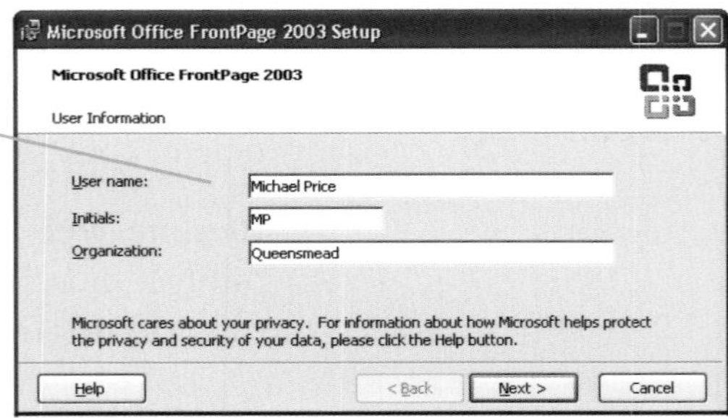

Choose Complete if you are not planning to leave the installation files on your hard disk (see page 23).

4. Choose the type of install you require, and specify the program folder, then click Next.

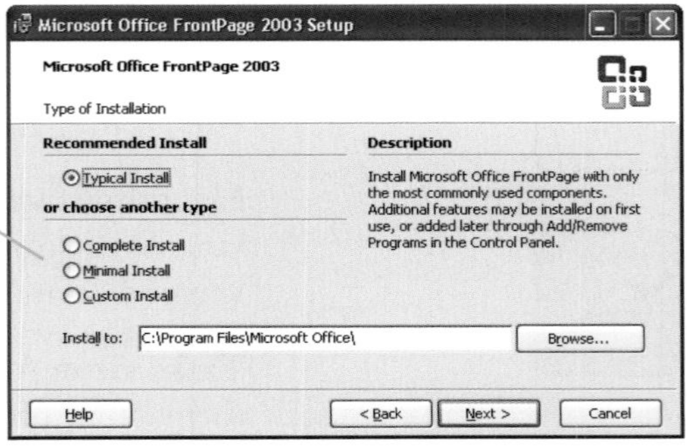

The Windows Installer will copy the necessary components to your hard disk and set them up ready for use.

This example illustrates the installation of the full version. The process for the 120 day free trial version is identical. Installation of the Upgrade version is similar but will require that you have already installed one of the qualifying products (see page 14).

When the installation has completed, you'll be offered the opportunity to save the installation files that were copied to your hard disk. You can check immediately to see if any updates have become available, if you are Internet connected.

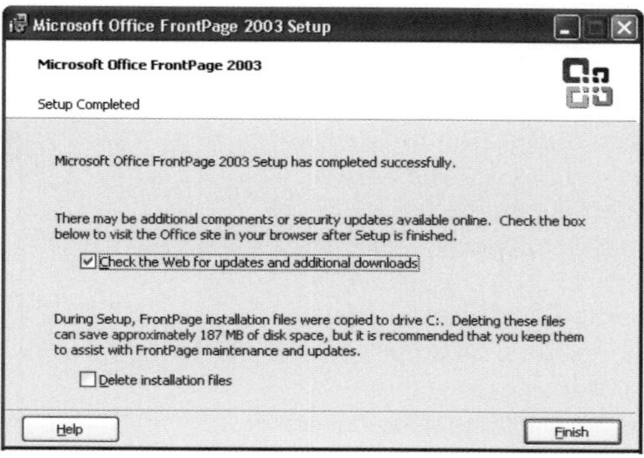

When the Office Update Web page displays, select Check For Updates to locate and apply any relevant changes.

The Office Update Web site only supports Office 2000, Office XP and Office 2003 products.

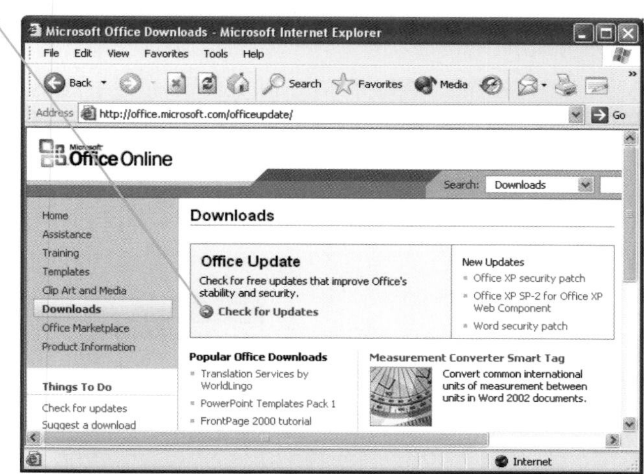

By default, the installation program places all Microsoft Office and related programs into the Microsoft Office shortcut folder in the Start menu.

When any updates have been applied, you can start FrontPage 2003 from the Start menu.

5 Select Start, All Programs, Microsoft Office, and click the Microsoft FrontPage 2003 entry.

Activating FrontPage 2003

You can start up any of the Office applications up to 50 times without activating it. After that, the functions available will be reduced and it becomes effectively read-only, until you do carry out activation. Note that with the 120 day free trial versions, activation is required immediately, since the applications start up in read-only mode, and it is available over the Internet only.

Each time you start FrontPage 2003, you'll be reminded to activate the application, either over the Internet or by telephone. You do not need to provide any personal information, since the activation is tied to the configuration of the PC.

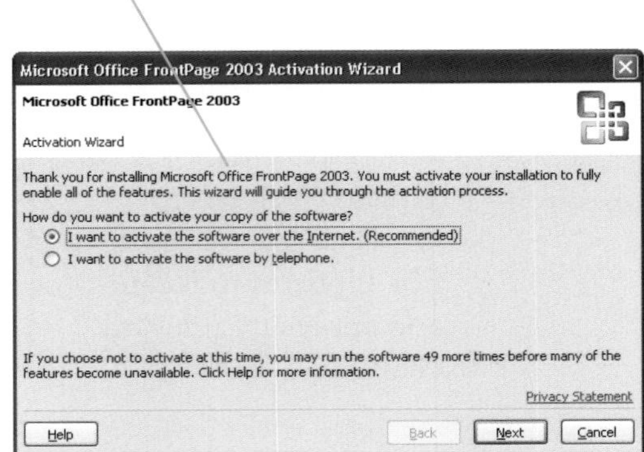

When you do complete the activation, the prompts will no longer appear, and you can make use of the full function of the application thereafter (or for the next 120 days, in the case of the free trial version). If the application has already become read-only, close and restart it to restore the full functions.

When you select to register your personal details, you'll be asked to provide your Microsoft Passport ID. Sign up for a Passport ID if you do not already have one.

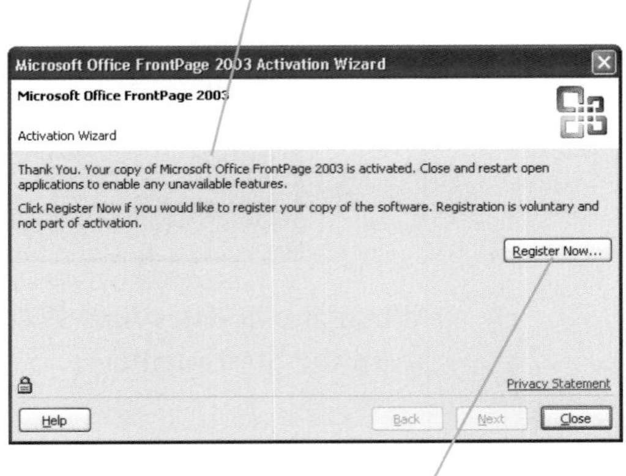

You can choose if you wish to register your personal details with Microsoft. However, this is not a mandatory requirement.

Using FrontPage 2003

This provides an introduction to FrontPage by stepping through the creation of a simple Web site. It uses image and text files downloaded from the In Easy Steps Web site, so you can concentrate on FrontPage skills and techniques.

Covers

Chapter Two

Creating a Web site

FrontPage includes a set of Web page and Web site templates, to make it possible for you to create a Web site from scratch:

1 Select File, New to display the New task pane, select More Web site templates, and choose the one nearest to your requirements.

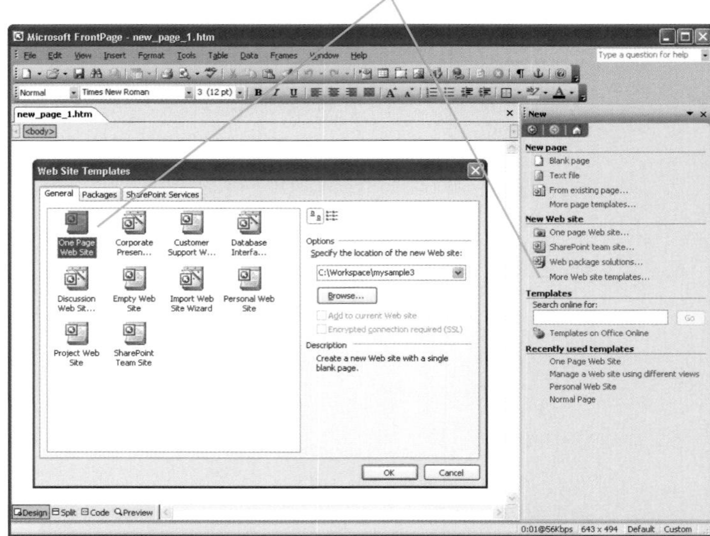

This will give you a predefined set of Web pages and components, and this is often the easiest way to build a standard Web site.

However, if this is your first Web site, you may want some instructions to follow, to make sure you cover all the steps.

2 In your browser, go to http://office.microsoft.com/training, and select the FrontPage entry.

Microsoft provides on-line training for all the Office applications, including FrontPage, but these do require that you have Internet access all the time that you are following the tutorials. Note that you must have the application installed on the PC that you use to access the tutorials.

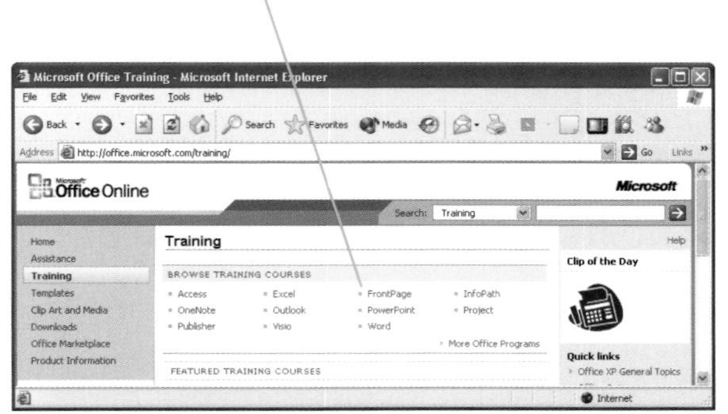

The FrontPage tutorial

As with any location or Web page reference on the Internet, this URL may change or be removed without notice. If you can't access the URL, try searching on the Microsoft Web site for "FrontPage Training" to get the latest references.

The FrontPage 2003 tutorials cover creating a Web site, features such as hyperlinks and HTML tables, and publishing the Web site. The tutorials are self-paced and interactive, and contain audio, illustrations, and practice sessions.

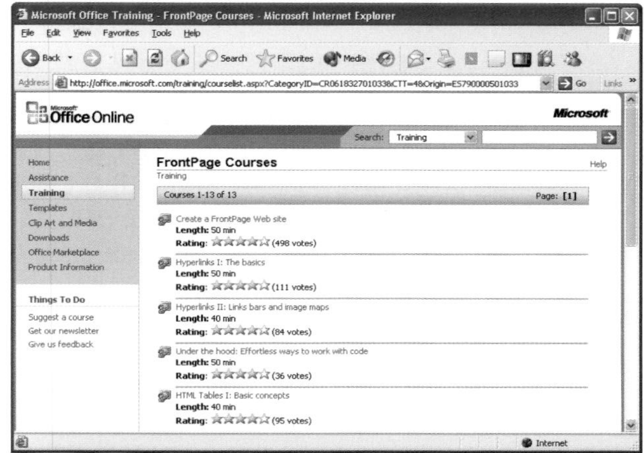

If you are using this book for self study, you can download a set of files at http://www.ineasysteps.com/books/downloads/, and use these to build and develop a Web site as described in the following sections.

Chapters two and three in this book provide an off-line alternative to the Internet based tutorials, using a similar example Web site. The files required to build and maintain the example can be downloaded from the In Easy Steps Web site. Using these files means you don't have to type in lots of text or create suitable pictures. As a result, you can concentrate on the functions of FrontPage 2003 and get familiar with the operations.

1. Click to download the self-extracting file for FrontPage 2003 in easy steps, FrontPage2003ies.exe.

2. Double click the executable file, to extract the files.

WinZip Self-Extractor - FrontPage2003ies.exe

To unzip all files in FrontPage2003ies.exe to the specified folder press the Unzip button.

Unzip to folder: A:\

Overwrite files without prompting

Unzip | Run WinZip | Close | About | Help | Browse...

3. The files are in a folder called \FrontPage2003ies. By default, this will be created in A:\, but you can specify any drive letter or folder name.

The example Web site

The scenario used here is similar to the Web site used for the on-line FrontPage training (see page 27), though the sequence of activities and the resulting Web pages are different.

The easiest way to find out about FrontPage is to go right ahead and create a Web site. This will introduce you to the style of working that it offers, and show you some of the components and procedures that it supports.

The following sections take you through the steps involved (as discussed on page 19) to define the purpose, design the Web site, create the pages, publish and maintain the Web site.

Defining the requirements

The purpose of the Web site is to tell your visitors about the sporting goods store called ChampionZone. The site will contain merchandise information, including product pictures, news and events, and links to other sites. The Web site will keep a count of the number of visitors, and will capture any comments that they care to leave.

Designing the Web site

You would normally begin by making a sketch of the structure, to illustrate the pages and components you will need.

Draw a sketch showing the main pages and files or documents to give a pictorial image of the Web site you have in mind.

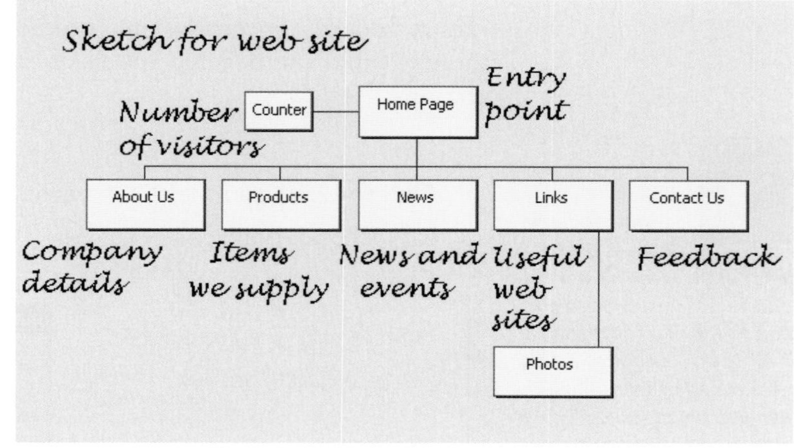

Creating or modifying the Web site off-line, on your hard disk also means that visitors to your site won't see your work in progress, until it is ready.

You'll need additional notes describing the information that should appear on each Web page. For this example, the text and graphics needed can be downloaded from the In Easy Steps Web site (see page 27).

You could start by creating the pages, but it is better to set up the outline structure first. This allows FrontPage to spell-check and validate hyperlinks across the site, and maintain dynamic navigation links.

If a Web opens when you start up FrontPage, click Close Web before starting operations on your new Web.

This creates a new Web site with a Home page which is given the default name Index.htm, so that it will be automatically displayed when visitors enter the URL for your site.

Creating the components

You should choose one of the Web site templates to start with, then add pages and links to modify or extend the structure.

To create a FrontPage Web site:

1. Select File, New. This will display the Task Pane with the New options.

2. Under New Web site, click More Web Site Templates to display the list of available templates.

3. Select the One Page Web site template, click in the Specify Location box, and enter the drive and folder for your Web site followed by the Web site name – for example: C:\Workspace\Championzone. Then click OK.

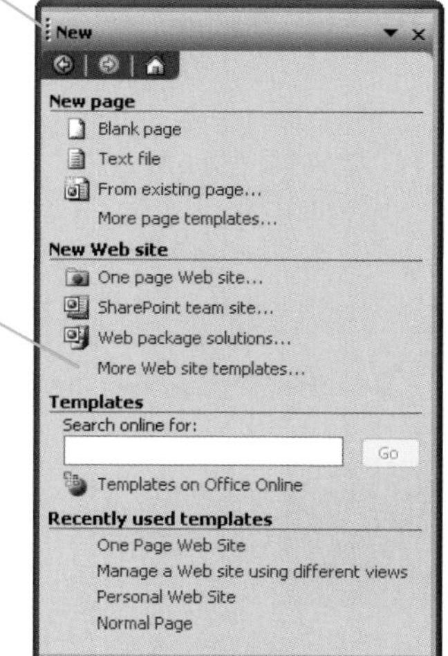

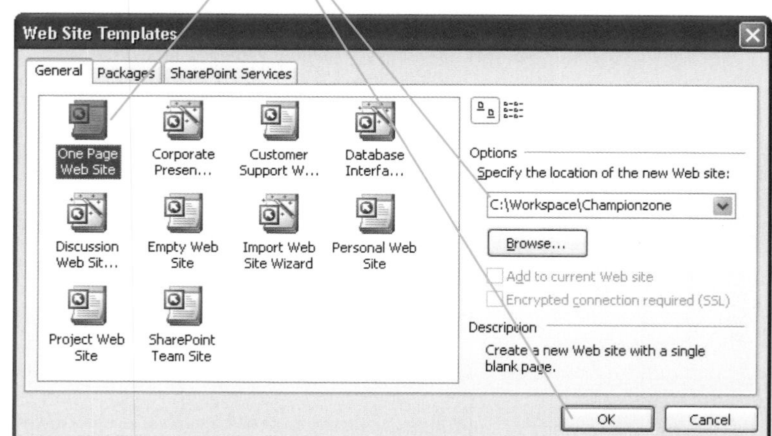

Web site structure

If the Folder list does not display, click the Toggle Pane button on the standard toolbar:

1 The Folder list shows the Home page Index.htm. Press the Navigation button on the Views bar to show the structure.

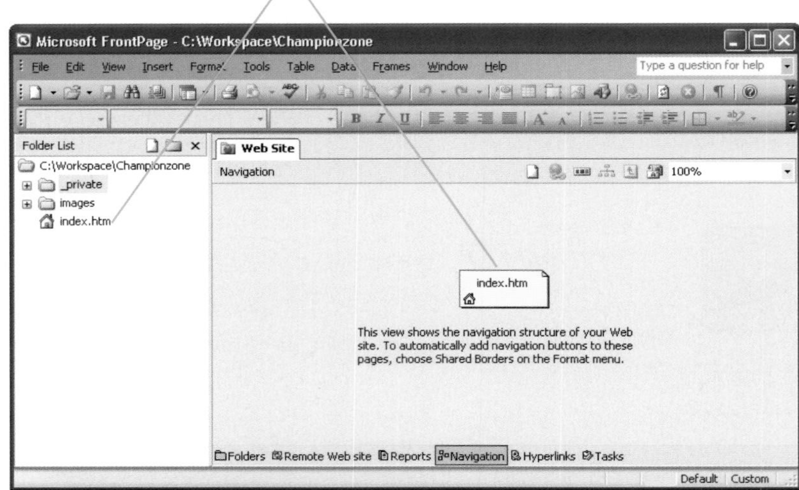

Even though you start with a single page Web, you can add more pages and change the structure as desired.

2 Select the Home page and press the New Page button, and FrontPage creates a Web page "New Page 1", linked to Index.htm.

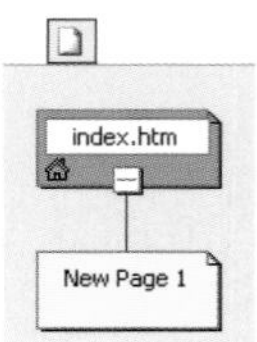

3 Press New Page four more times, then select "New Page 4" and add another page below this, to bring the total number of new pages to six.

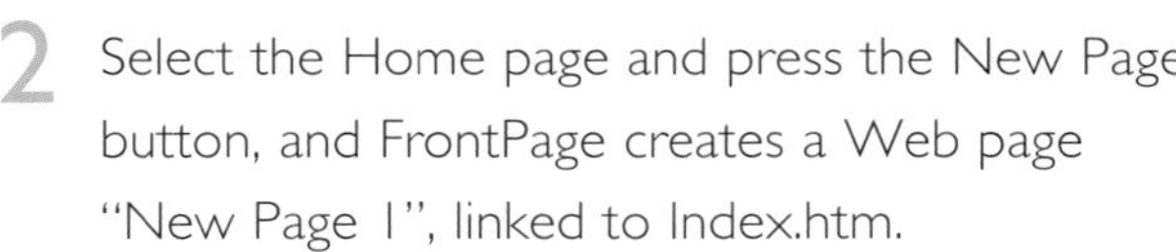

As an alternative to the New Page button, you can right-click the parent page and select New, Page. Pressing Ctrl+N will also generate a new page, but will switch to Page view. In each case, the new page is just a placeholder until you edit it or import an existing page to add content.

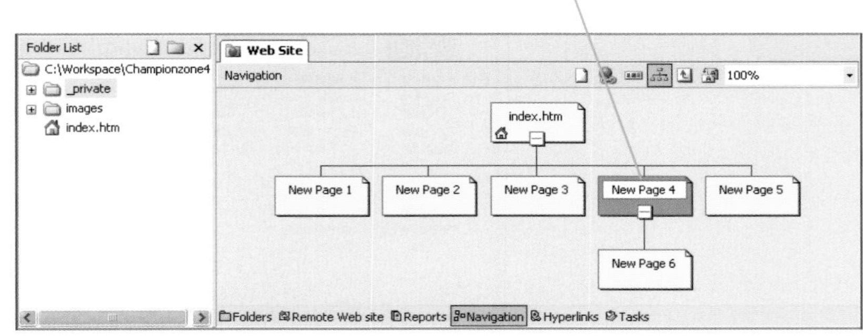

Page titles and names

Every page in the Web site will have a title and also a file name, which can be based on the title, or could be altogether different.

The new pages added below the Home page are not immediately given file names, so when you re-title the pages, associated file names are assigned, and empty page files are created.

1 With the Home page selected, press Tab to switch to the next page in the structure, with the page title ready to edit. Type *About Us* as the title and press Tab again.

You can change the title of a page by right-clicking it in Navigation view and selecting Rename.

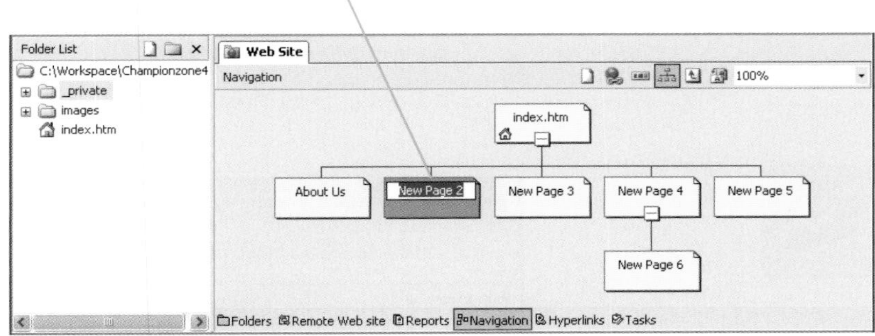

Internet standards require URLs and file names with plain ASCII characters and no blanks, so that all visitors can follow URLs, without relying on a particular type of PC, operating system or browser. When naming the pages, FrontPage changes the title to lower case and replaces blanks with underscores.

2 Type *Products*, then *News*, then *Links*, then *Contact Us*, and then *Home*, pressing Tab after each title.

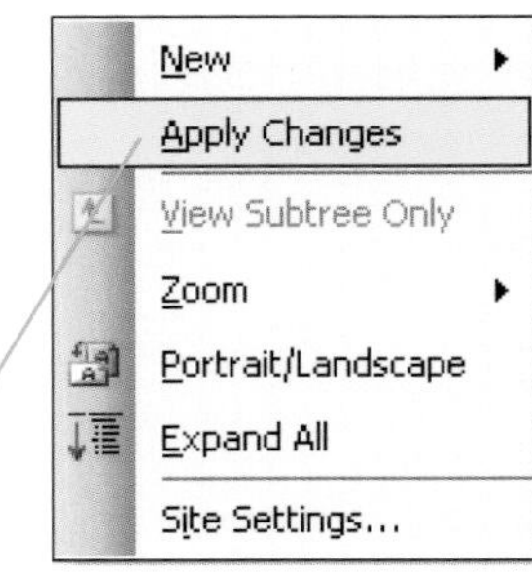

3 Right-click a clear area and select Apply Changes. The files for the new pages are created, using titles for file names.

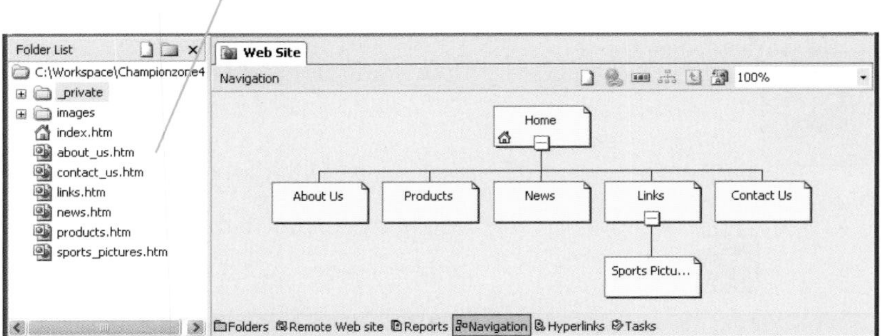

Building the Home page

Provide enough on your Home page to motivate visitors to stay to view more pages. Think also what encourages repeat visits and word of mouth recommendations.

Start with the Home page, which is the most important page on the Web site. It is the default page, the first page that your visitors will see, and it contains the links to the other pages in your Web site. To add content to the Home page:

1 Double-click the Home page in Navigation view, or double-click Index.htm in the folder list, to open the file in Page view.

2 Type the title text *Welcome To ChampionZone* for your Web site and then press Enter to start a paragraph.

The asterisk next to the file name indicates that there are changes to the file. Click the Save button, or select File, Save to write the changes to disk.

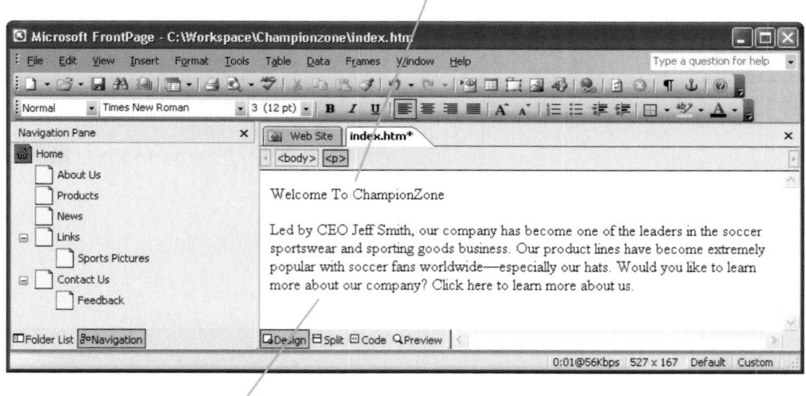

3 Type the message *Led by CEO Jeff Smith, our company has become one of the leaders in the soccer sportswear and sporting goods business. Our product lines have become extremely popular with soccer fans worldwide – especially our hats. Would you like to learn more about our company? Click here to learn more about us.*

Press the Spelling button on the toolbar to spell check the current page (see pages 82–83 for more information):

4 Right-click underlined words to correct typing or spelling errors, or to add new entries to the dictionary.

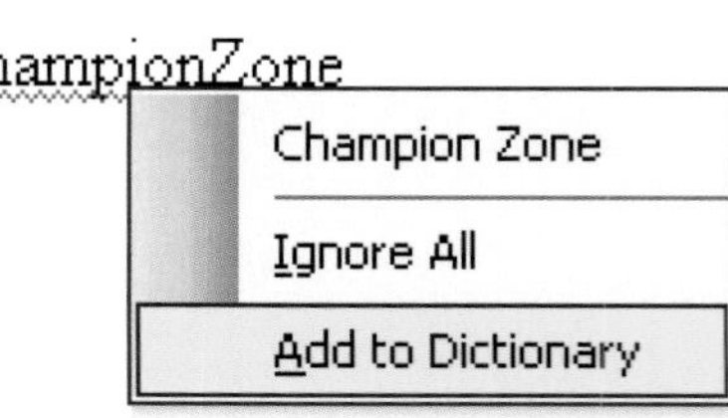

The picture that you add to your Web page could be a scanned photograph, a drawing or a PC image file or bitmap.

Now add a picture showing the ChampionZone logo. To insert the picture:

1. Press Ctrl+Home, then select Insert, Picture, and From File.

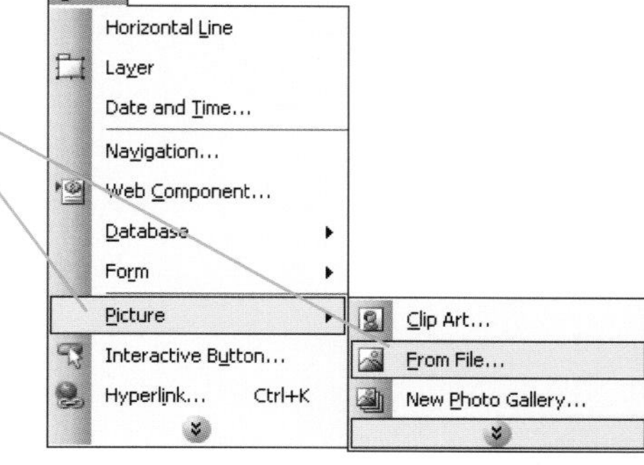

The keys Ctrl+Home put the cursor at the top left margin of the current page.

2. Locate Logo.gif in the folder *FrontPage2003ies*, click the file icon and press Insert then Enter.

The picture is added to the page at the cursor location. Press Enter to create a new line.

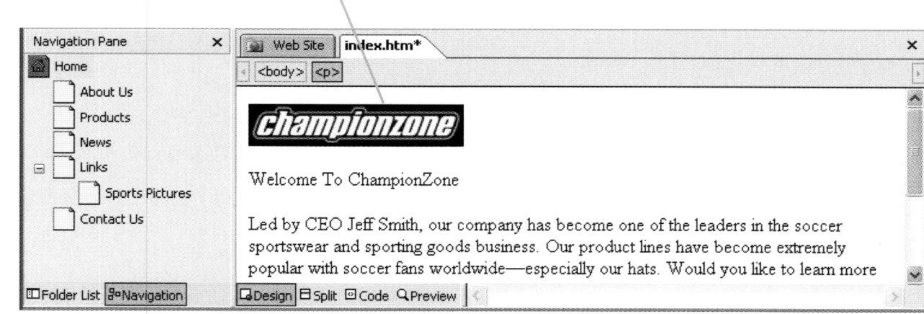

3. Save the current page. FrontPage makes sure that a copy of the image file is added to the set of files for the Web site, to ensure you can still display the picture when the Web site is published.

The graphics should be saved in the Images folder for the Web site. Click Change Folder, or drag and drop the image files later, using the Folder List.

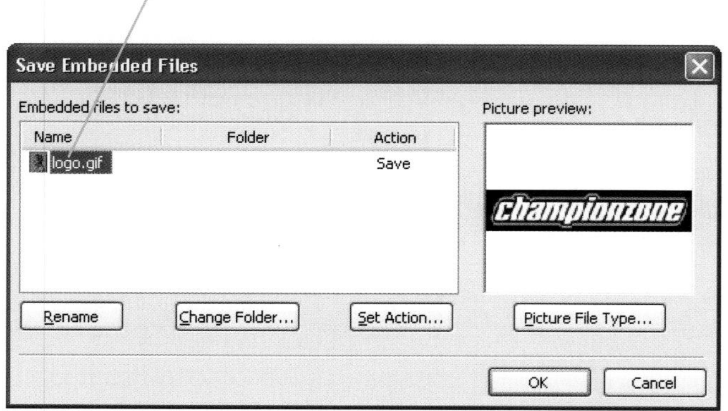

Adding a link

A hyperlink is a pointer to another page or file on the World Wide Web or on an Intranet. Here we attach a hyperlink to a graphic. See pages 55–56 for examples of text hyperlinks.

This file is a picture button to indicate that your site is based on FrontPage 2003. You can make it a hyperlink that points to the Microsoft FrontPage Web site.

For the FrontPage Logos, Microsoft recommends adding alternative text saying "Created and Managed with Microsoft FrontPage". Right click the picture, select Picture Properties, General and enter the Text as the alternative representation.

With text links, when you select a section of text and insert a hyperlink, the text is colored and underlined. With picture links, the image doesn't change. However, if you move the mouse pointer over the graphic, you'll see the URL on the status bar.

You can make a picture, word or phrase clickable, so that it switches to another Web page or a different position on the page.

1. Press Ctrl+End, then select Insert, Picture, From File. Find the file Fplogo.gif in folder FrontPage2003ies, click the icon and press Insert.

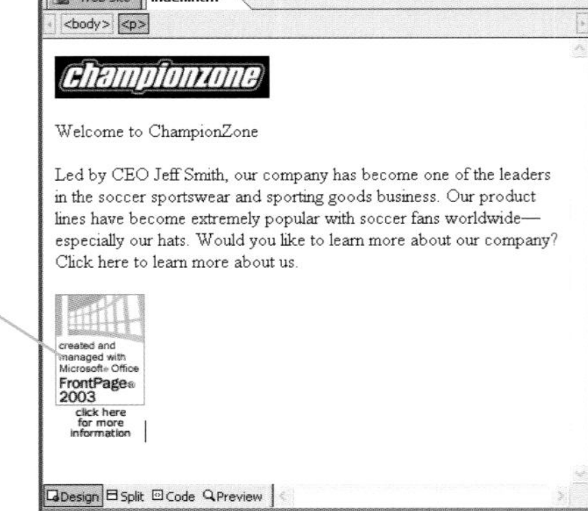

2. Click the picture, and the file handles display to show it is selected.

3. Press the Hyperlink button on the Standard toolbar, to display the Insert Hyperlink box.

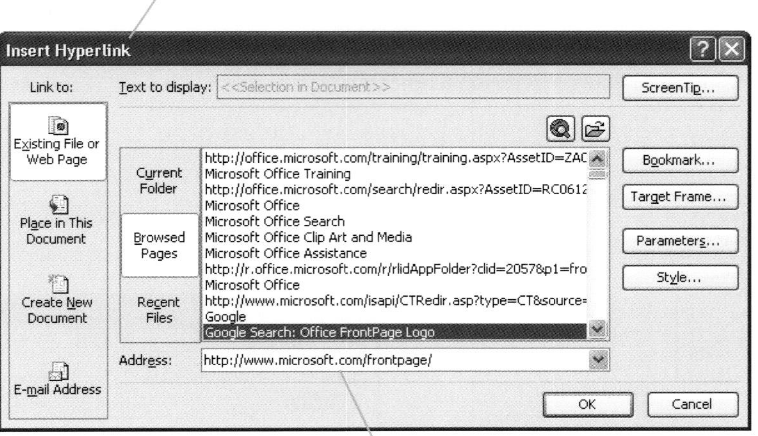

4. Find the URL from previously browsed pages or by browsing the Internet, or type in the URL for the FrontPage Web site – at www.microsoft.com/frontpage – and press OK.

Arranging the items

You can select one or more text and graphics items from the page, and apply changes to layout and orientation.

To center all the text and graphics items on the page:

1. Select Edit from the Menu bar and choose Select All. Press the Center button. Click anywhere on the page to deselect all.

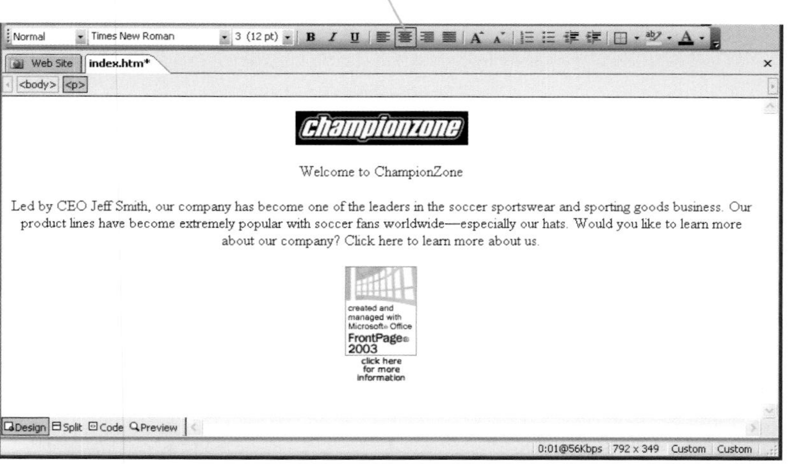

The Center button on the Formatting toolbar centers both text and image items across the width of the page.

The text and graphics will remain centered across the display, even if you change the screen resolution or the window size.

2. Resize the window and the text and graphics are realigned to maintain the centralized setup.

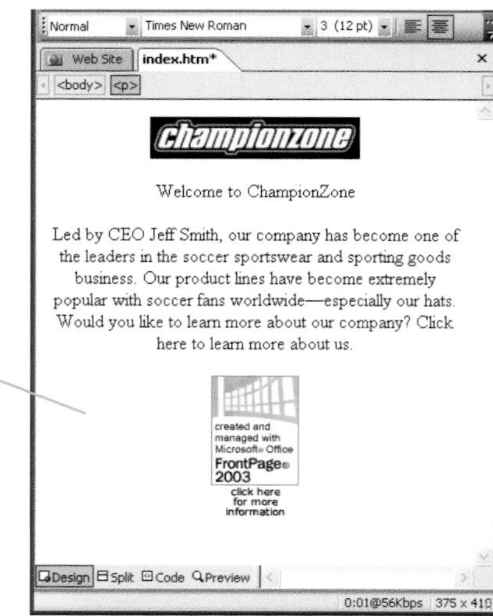

3. Click the Save button, or select File, Save to make the alignment changes permanent.

DON'T FORGET

Always try your pages at different screen resolutions, to see what your Web site visitors would get if they had a different resolution than your normal setup.

Viewing the page

You normally view the Web pages in Design mode, where they will display as they appear to visitors to your Web site. Within the text, HTML tags define the page setup and contents, but these codes are normally hidden.

You create and edit your Web pages in Page view which shows text and images as they will appear on your Web site, but without animation effects. From this view, you can also see the HTML tags that define the page contents.

1 Select View from the menu bar and click Reveal Tags.

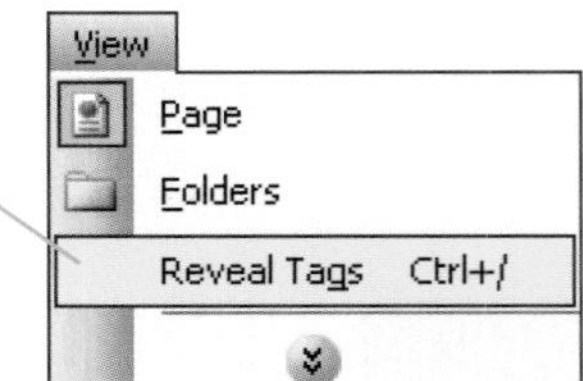

2 Graphical symbols indicate the start and end tags for HTML statements.

You can view the HTML tags in a graphical form, so you can see where the tags are placed on the page.

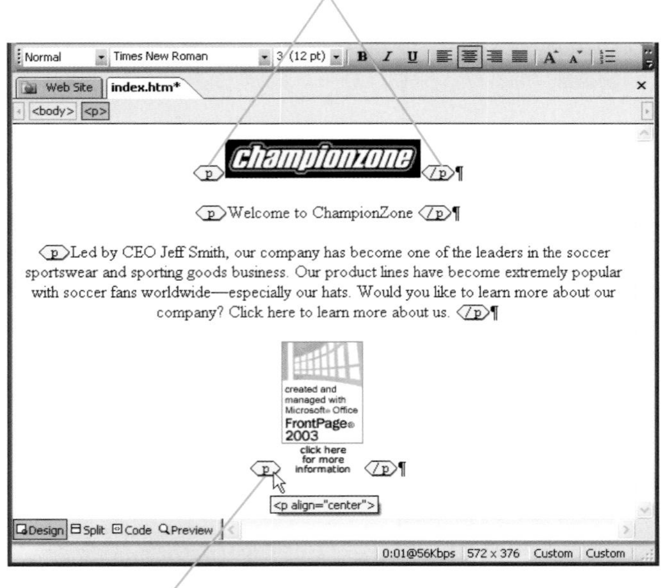

3 Move the mouse pointer over any of the tags to see the details of the tag displayed in a ScreenTip.

Reveal Tags is a toggle, with a tick to indicate when it is set. The setting reverses each time you select it. The key combination Ctrl+/ will also toggle this setting.

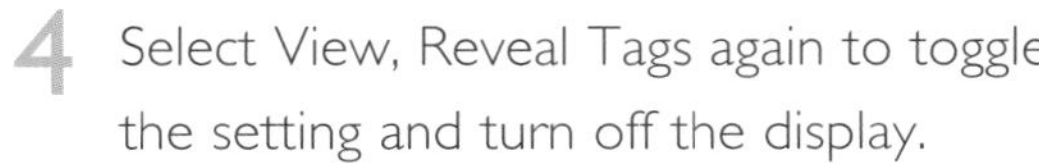

4 Select View, Reveal Tags again to toggle the setting and turn off the display.

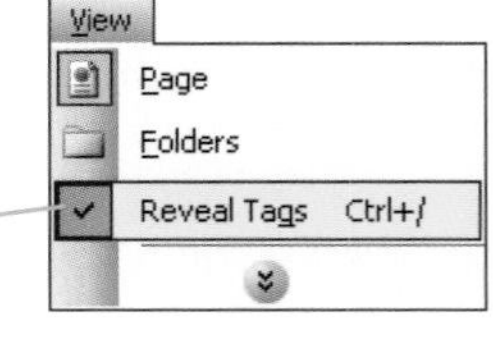

You can view the complete HTML code, in a plain text form, so you can see exactly what effects and actions have been defined.

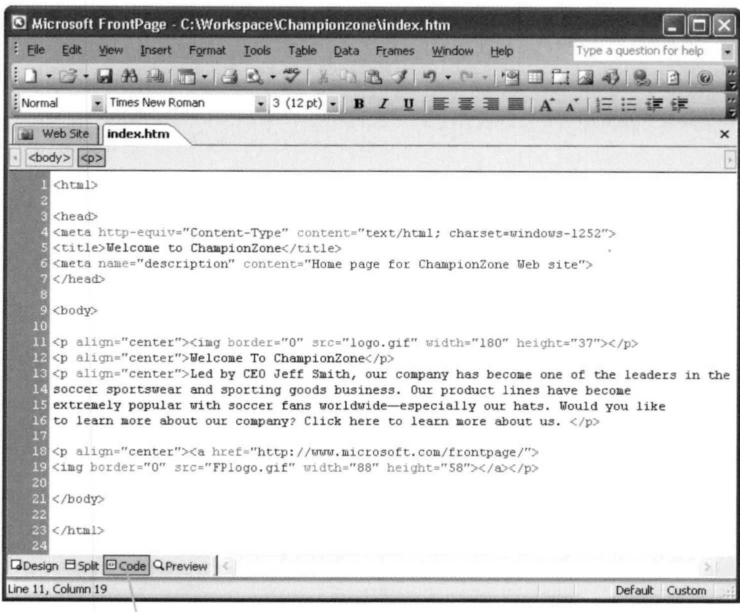

This view is meant for use by experienced Web site designers and programmers, to supplement or adapt the HTML codes that are entered into the page by FrontPage. Do not change the entries in the source code unless you are sure of the effect that will be created.

Click the Split tab to show the Design view and the Code view simultaneously, and see the effect of code or design changes (see page 17).

5 Click the Code tab at the bottom of the page to show the actual coding statements.

6 To view or change the way FrontPage generates HTML code, click Tools, Page Options, and then click Code Formatting.

Click the Design tab at the bottom of the page to return to the formatted view of the text and graphics.

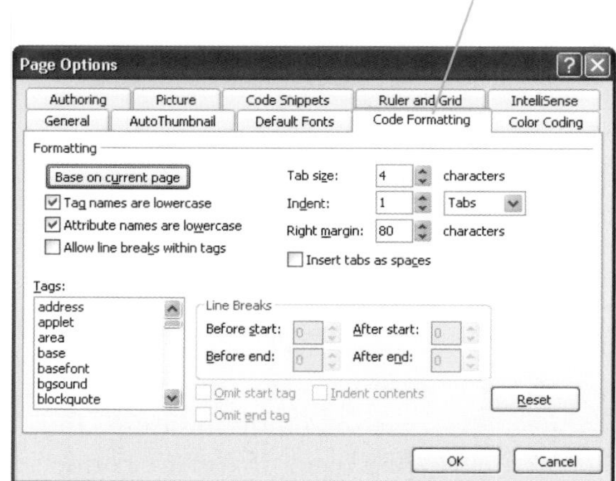

Previewing the page

Preview the page to see it as it will be displayed in the browser. You are still running FrontPage, but it utilizes code from Internet Explorer.

If you use Microsoft Internet Explorer on your PC, you can preview the page as it will appear when it has been published to the Web site.

To see the page in its final form:

1. In Page view, click the Preview tab at the foot of the display area. Animation effects for text and graphics will be enabled.

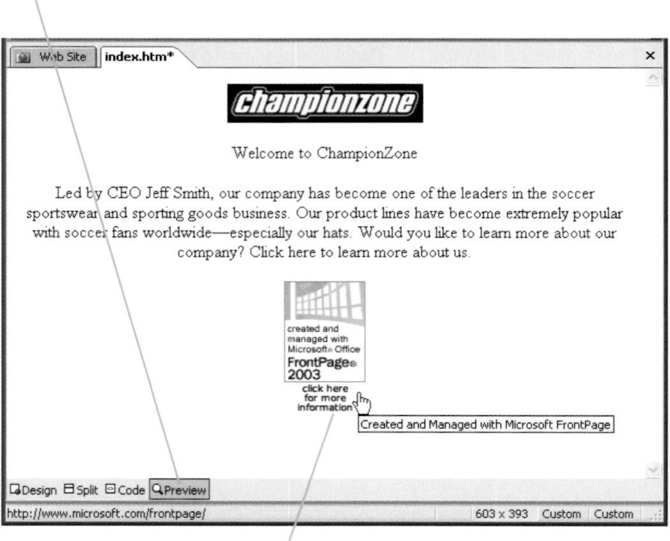

You need to be connected to the Internet or have access to the appropriate Intranet Web server, in order to follow hyperlinks.

2. Hyperlinks will become live, and will navigate appropriately (though you must be online to access Web sites).

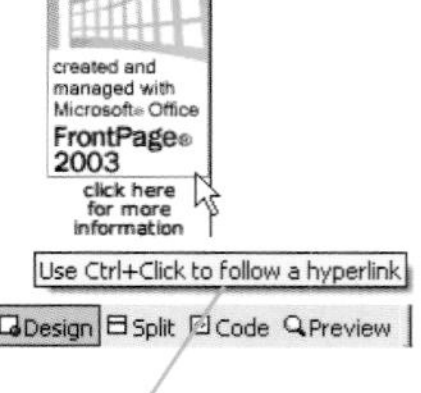

3. Press the Design tab to end this preview.

Note that you can navigate hyperlinks in your Web pages, even in Design view. Just hold down the Ctrl key as you click the link, as the screen tip indicates, and the associated Web page will be displayed. If you are connected to the Internet, you can also follow Internet hyperlinks.

You can also view the page using your browser directly. This is necessary if you are using special effects, such as graphical themes (see page 66), or if you are using a different browser than Internet Explorer. First however, you may want to check the Web page title (see page 31) since this will be on the browser title bar.

You can also change the title by right-clicking the page and selecting Page Properties.

To display the page title:

4. Select File, Save As to view the title. Press Change title to make revisions.

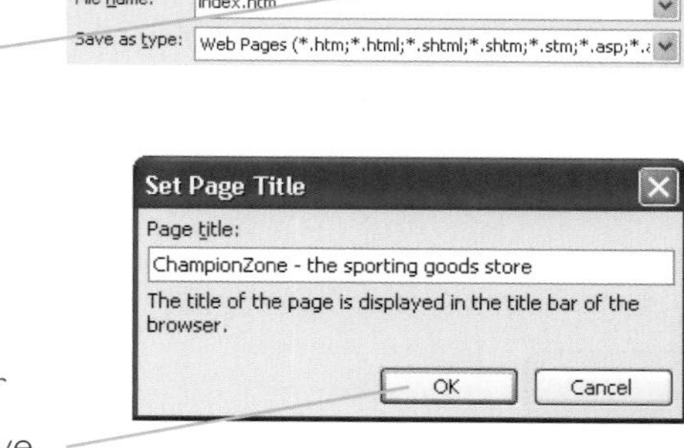

5. Enter a descriptive title for the page, click OK, and Save.

The default page title will be based on the Title that was set in Navigation view, or on the first line of text on the page, if no title was set. You may need a more meaningful, descriptive title, since it will be used by Internet search engines.

6. Select File, Preview in Browser, choose the browser and resolution, and the page is displayed in a new window.

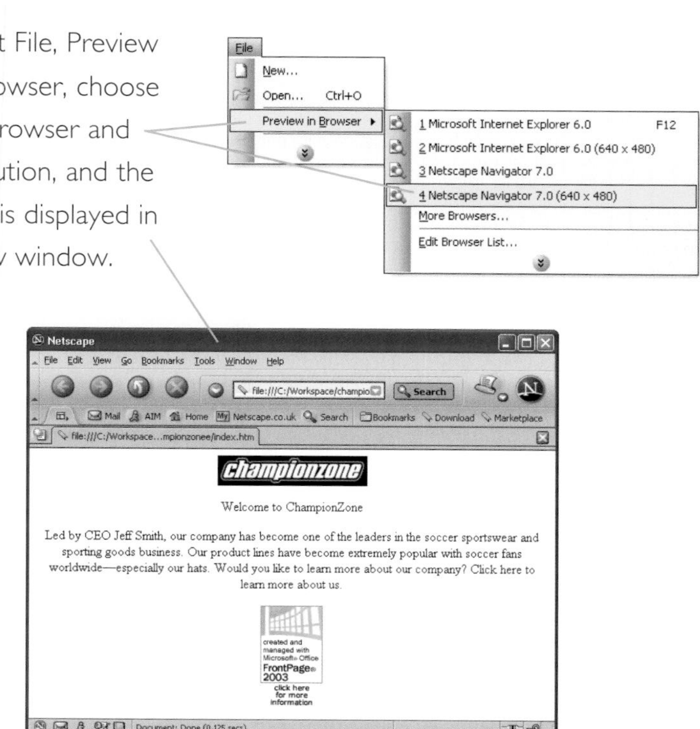

Ending and restarting

When you have finished with FrontPage for the time being, you can terminate the application without explicitly closing the Web pages that are currently open.

You'll be prompted to save any changes or new embedded files. You do not have to save the Web site as such. It is actually a folder, with the set of Web pages, files and subfolders which contain all the data for the site.

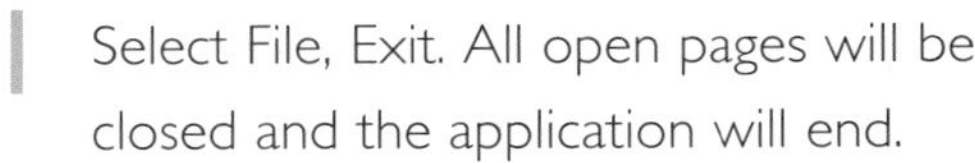

1 Select File, Exit. All open pages will be closed and the application will end.

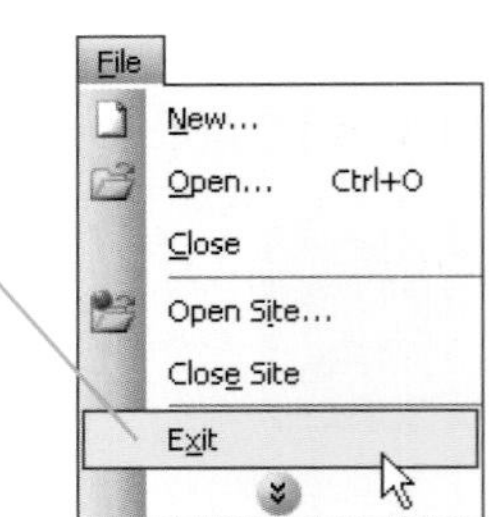

FrontPage will remember the Web name, and will reopen that Web next time you start the application

You can also open a Web site by choosing the Recent Sites item from the File menu, to select the name of the Web site you want to work on next.

2 To start working on a different Web site, select File, Close Site and then File, Open Site. A second copy of FrontPage is launched, if you don't close the current Web.

3 If you'd rather that FrontPage doesn't remember the last Web, select Tools, Options and click General. Clear the option to Open last Web site automatically when FrontPage starts.

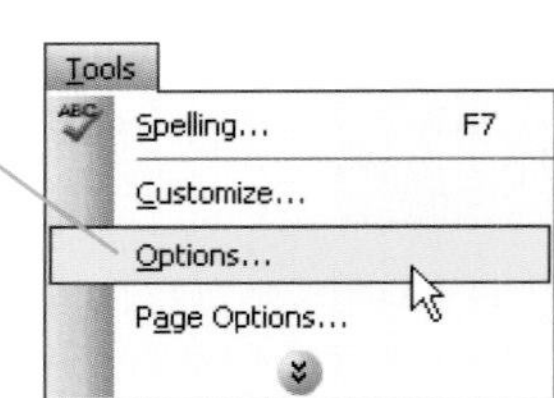

If you are working on several different Web sites, it may not be useful to have FrontPage open the last Web site every time you restart.

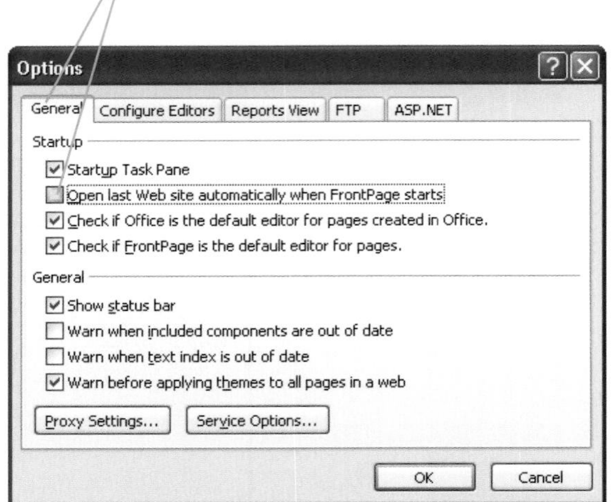

Adding to your Web site

Continue to build the sample Web site, completing the remaining pages and showing how to insert text and pictures, check that the pages will download effectively, and create and validate hyperlinks.

Covers

Chapter Three

Inserting plain text

The text that describes the ChampionZone store has already been created, so you can build your Web site without having to type in all the information.

You can also open Web pages using the File, Open command or from the Navigation view.

If there are many files in the folder, set the file type to .txt, and then only text files will display.

To add the contents of a text file to the About Us page:

1 Start FrontPage, open the ChampionZone Web site and click the Toggle Panes button to show the Folder List.

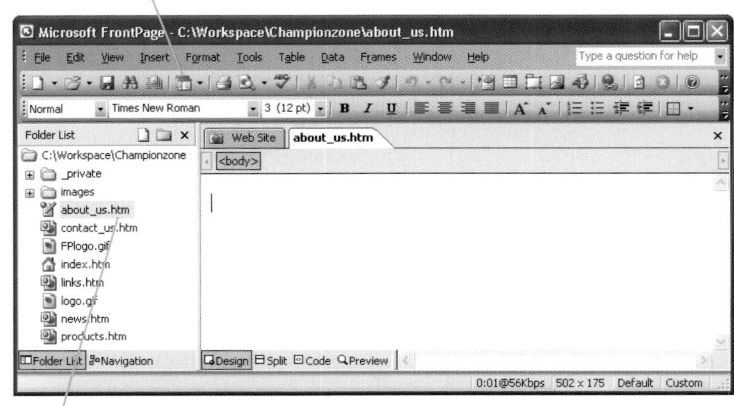

2 Double-click the About Us page to open it as a blank sheet in Page view.

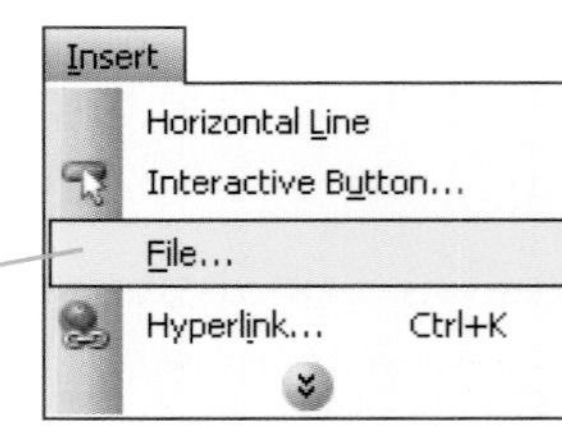

3 Select Insert, File, switch to the FrontPage2003ies folder, select the About text file, and click Open to extract the contents.

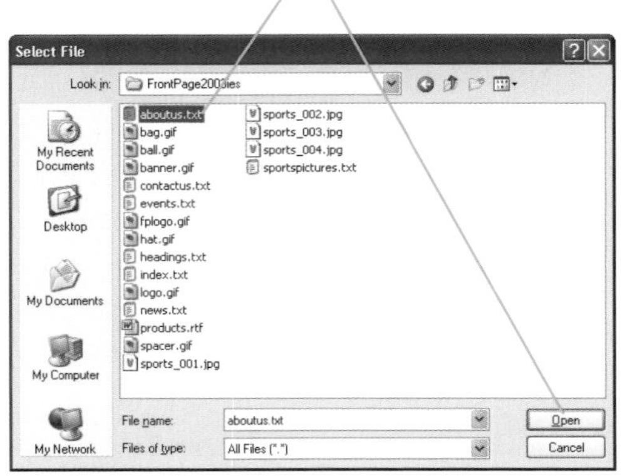

Since the file is plain text, not a Word document or HTML format, you must say how the text should be handled.

4 Choose Normal paragraphs (blank lines in the text file will be converted to paragraphs ends) and click OK.

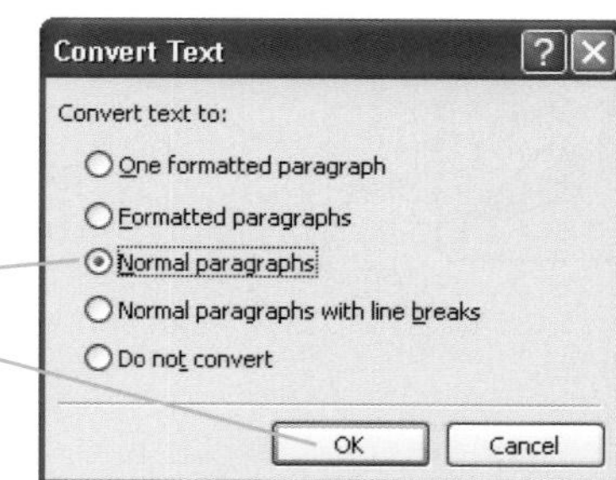

5 The contents of the text file are inserted into the page.

It looks very plain, but don't format the text at this stage. You should apply the themes and any across-the-site formatting before you consider adjusting the layout of individual pages.

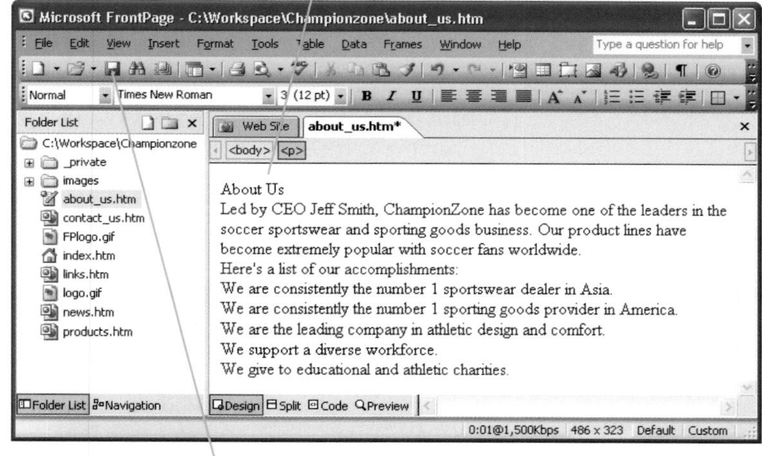

In the same way, add the text for the Contact Us, the News and the Sports Pictures pages, using the appropriate text files from the downloaded FrontPage2003ies folder. The Products page will use an RTF file (see page 44).

6 Press the Save button on the toolbar (or select File, Save) to capture the text.

As well as text files, you can insert contents from data files of various formats, including HTML, Lotus, Excel, Windows Write, Word, WordPerfect and Works. You can even select an option to recover (that is to say, to extract) text from files of any type.

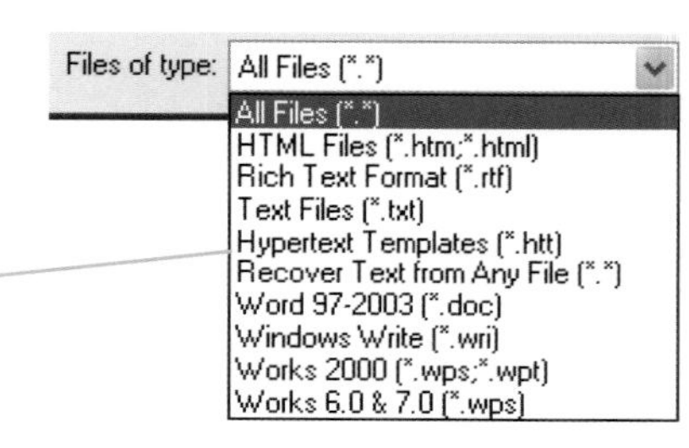

Adding formatted text

There's more text, this time in rich text format, which describes the sporting products, also available from the Tutorial folder.

The Products page will tell site visitors about the sporting goods sold by ChampionZone. On this page, you will also insert several pictures and align them so that the page layout is preserved at different screen resolutions.

1. Open the ChampionZone Web site, and then open the initially blank Products Web page.

2. Select Insert, File from the menu bar. From the FrontPage2003ies folder, select the Products.rtf file.

Since the text in this file is already formatted, FrontPage will convert it into HTML form, without requiring instructions. You'll find a page title, a paragraph of text, a list of products and some product details.

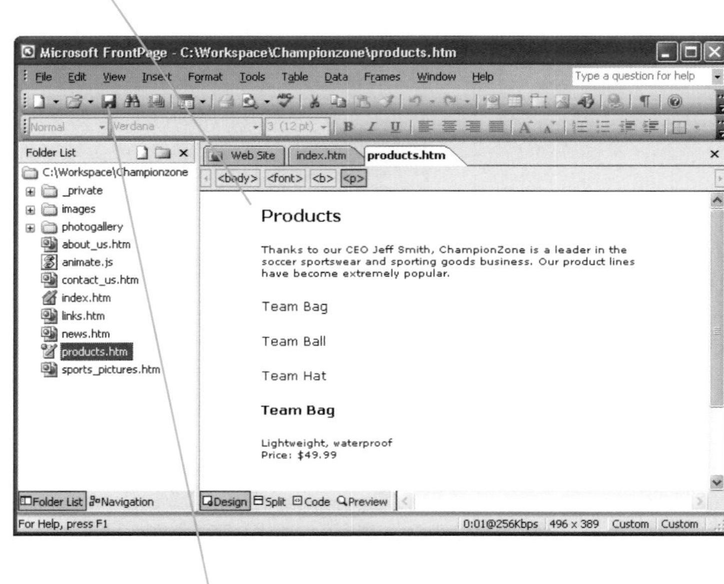

Although rtf files have some formatting they may not have the style you want, so you can make changes once the text is inserted.

3. Press the Save button, or select File and Save, to record the addition that has been made to this Web page.

To convert the simple list into a bulleted list:

4 Find the list of products on the page – the items Team Bag, Team Ball and Team Hat.

5 Highlight the list, and press the Bullets button.

The actual style of bullet will be defined when you select the theme for your Web site. See page 66.

6 The selected text is displayed with bullets.

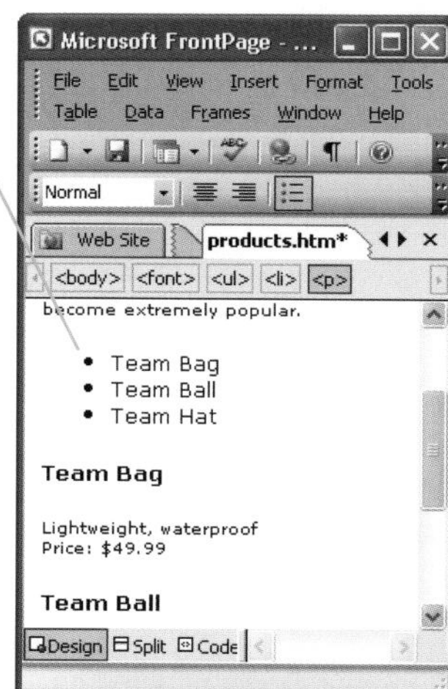

FrontPage supports all the usual word processing formats. To see a list of the functions available:

Re: step 9 – the following word processing formats are available:

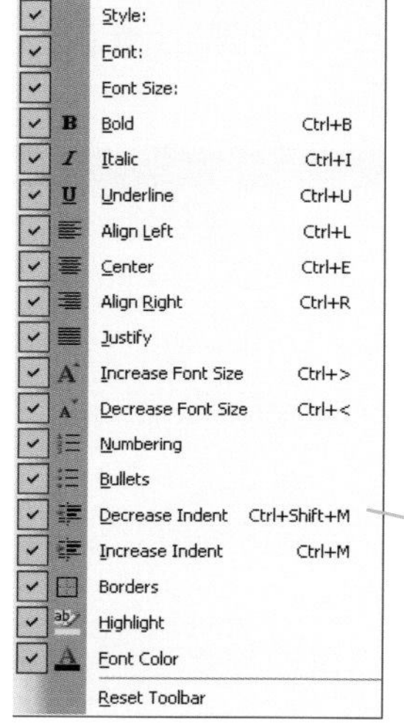

7 Click the down arrow at the end of the Formatting toolbar.

8 This displays the option to add or remove buttons.

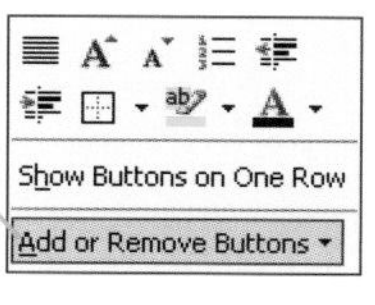

9 Pause the mouse pointer over the Add or Remove Buttons command, to display the submenu, then select Formatting. This gives you the list of the formatting buttons with their names and their keyboard shortcuts.

Adding files to your Web site

When you have a number of pictures or text files to insert into your Web site, it is quicker to add the files at one time, ahead of creating the associated Web pages.

To add files to the current Web site:

When you import a file, a copy is added to your Web site, and the original stays in the source folder.

You can import files from your hard disk, from a LAN file server, from the Internet or from a Web server.

Set the file type to GIF and JPEG, select the first name, press Shift and select the last name, to select all the files. Press Ctrl and click to de-select the files already imported (logo and fplogo). Release the Ctrl key.

1 Press the Folders button on the Views bar to switch to Folders view, and open the Images folder which is used to store graphics.

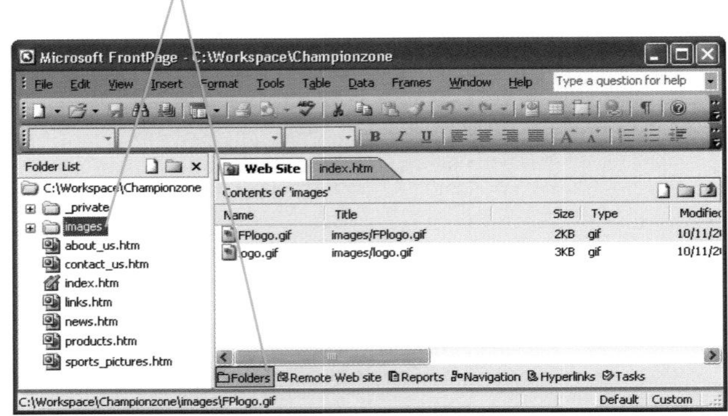

2 Select File, Import from the menu bar and press the Add File button.

3 Select the required graphics files from FrontPage2003ies.

4 Click the Open button to have the selected files added to the Import List, ready for review and revision.

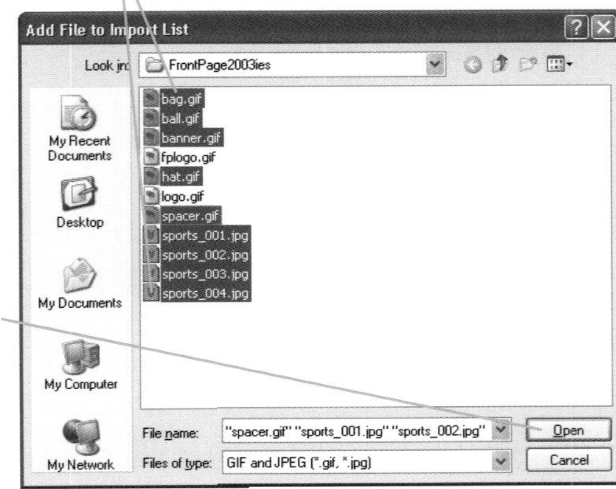

5 You can Remove items, or press Add File, Add Folder or From Site to define other items required.

To quickly import a file or a selection of files to the current Web site, drag them into the Folder List from Windows Explorer.

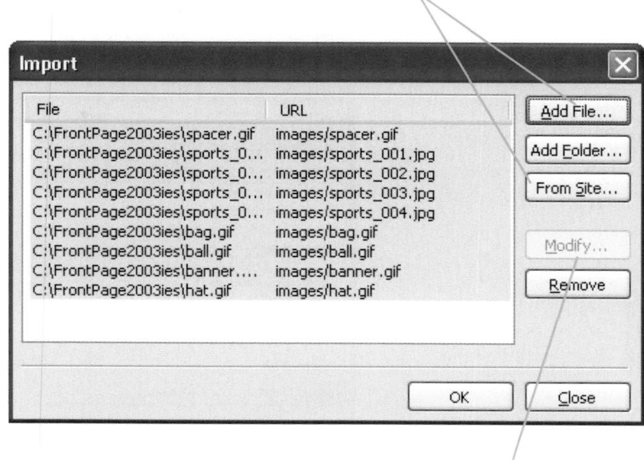

If you want to postpone adding the files, press Close. This will save the Import List. You can continue building the list and importing the files later by re-selecting File, Import.

6 Select a file and click Modify, to change the destination file name or folder, relative to the root of the current Web site.

7 Click OK to import the selected files, and store them in the target folder in the Web site.

If you reference files that are on your local hard disk or network drive, they will not be accessible to visitors to your site when you publish the Web site.

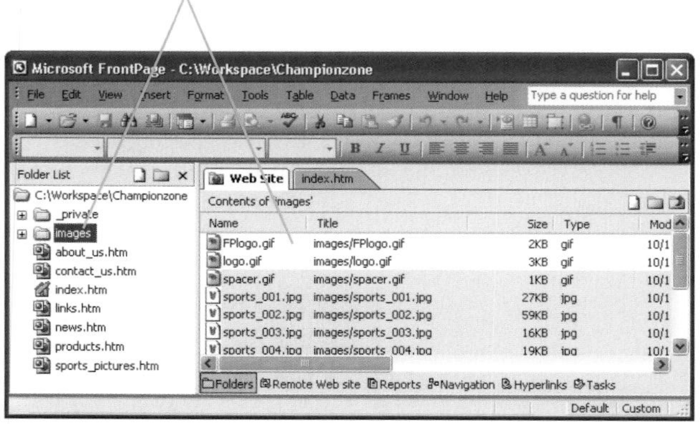

This procedure helps ensure that all the items needed for your Web site are stored in its folders ready to be published to the Internet.

Wrapping images

As well as pictures, you can insert clip art images, drawings, AutoShapes and WordArt.

Having copied the image files to the Web site folders, the pictures can now be placed in the Web page.

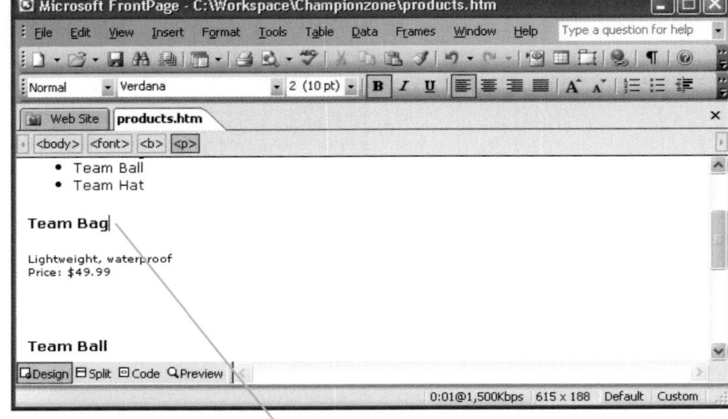

Don't insert a picture while any of the text is highlighted, or the text item will be deleted and replaced by the picture.

1. Open the Products page, click just after the Team Bag heading, to set the insertion point, then select Insert, Picture, From File.

Set file type to All Image Files. Set Views to Preview, to make it easier to identify images.

2. Open the Images folder for the Web site, select the picture file bag.gif, and click Insert to add it to the page. Then click on the picture to select it.

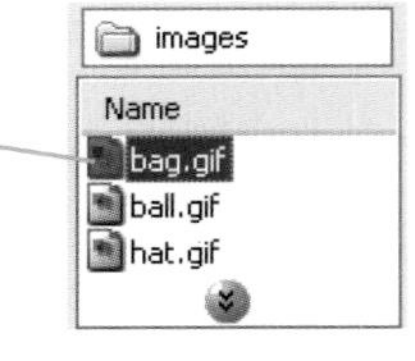

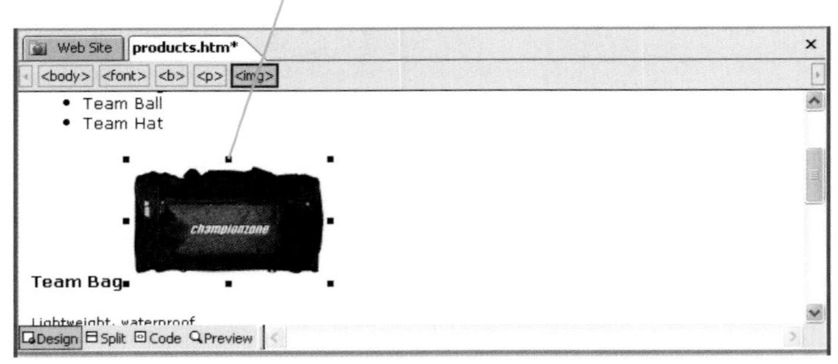

Press the Save button from time to time, to record your changes.

You can also position a picture at the right by selecting it and clicking the Align Right button on the formatting toolbar.

3 Select Format from the menu bar and click Position to display the panel.

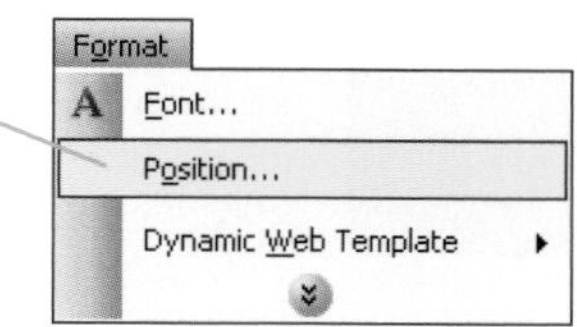

4 Choose Wrapping style Right and press OK.

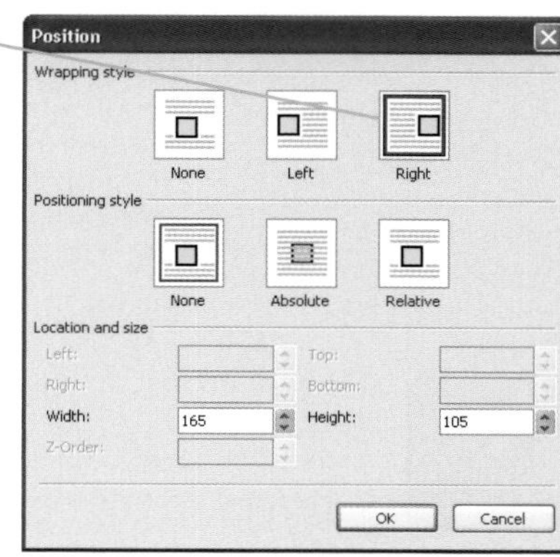

This will align the picture with the right margin of the page and the text will flow around it on the left side of the image.

5 Repeat steps 1–4 two more times, to insert and position Ball.gif after Team Ball, and Hat.gif after Team Hat.

By positioning pictures in the margins, your page layout will be preserved when the page is viewed at a different resolution and size than the default that you use for creating the Web site.

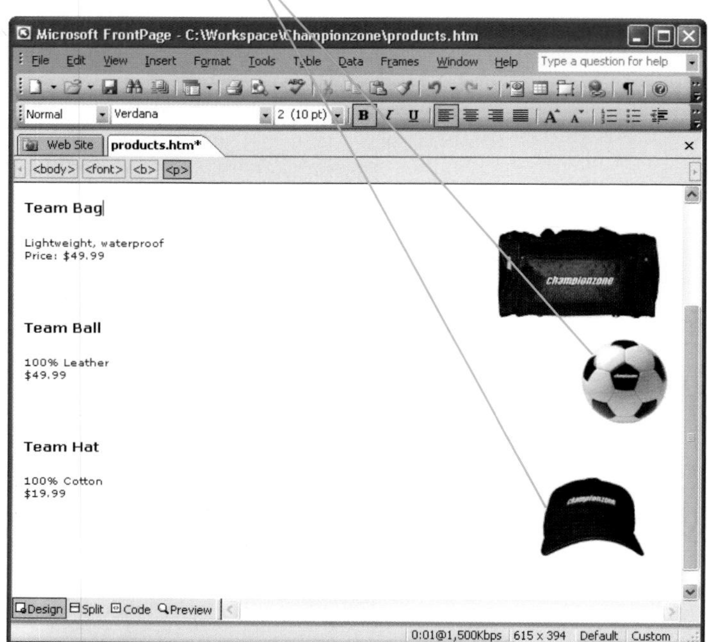

A page of photographs

It is easy to obtain digital images, with a scanner or digital camera. You can also have your photographs developed and transferred to a CD-ROM.

One type of Web page that is very popular with Web builders is the page of photographs. However, you need to understand the impact of photo images on your Web site performance.

1 Open the Sports_pictures.htm Web page, and insert the text from Sportspictures.txt file, in the FrontPage2003ies folder (if not already added - see page 46). Save the page to capture the text.

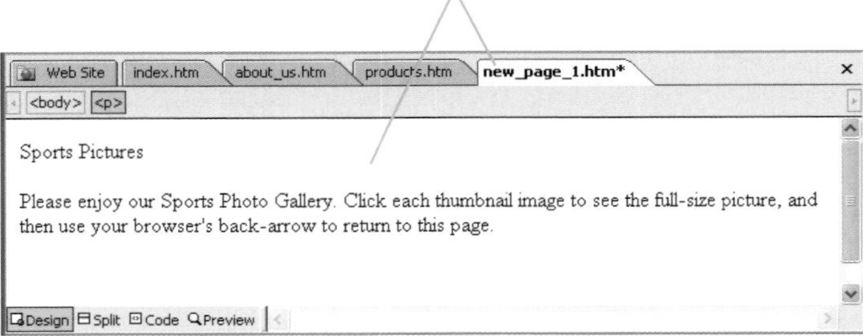

The page will be using thumbnail images that point to the full size pictures. First however, we'll see what happens when we add the full pictures.

2 At the bottom of the text, select Insert, Picture, From File and select the four pictures Sports_001-004 from the Images folder. Press Insert to add them to the Web page.

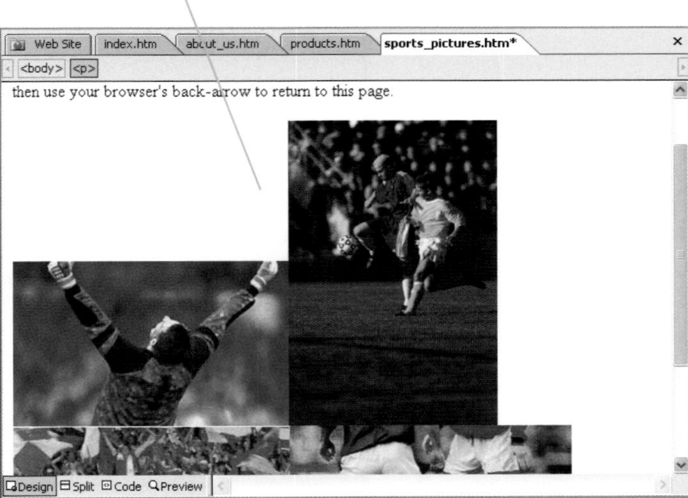

You would usually need to adjust the size and position of the images seen on the page. In this case however, we are just checking the transfer times, so layout doesn't matter.

Unless your visitor has a very high speed connection, the download times with full pictures will be far too long.

The status bar displays an estimated time for the page to download over the Internet, assuming optimum performance.

To check the timing at particular speeds:

1:03@28.8Kbps	times
28.8	1:03
56	0:34
128	0:14
256	0:07
384	0:04
512	0:03
1,000	0:01
1,500	0:01

3. Click the Estimated Time on the status bar, select a line speed, and note the time. The times for the small images in the example range from 63 secs at 28.8Kbps to 1 sec at 1.5Mbps.

With these times, some visitors may lose interest and press Stop on their browsers before seeing what's on the page. To avoid this, you should make sure that delays are minimized and let your visitors know when they will be transferring larger amounts of data.

These are best case estimates assuming that there are no delays anywhere over the links between your PC and the Web site server.

One option is to replace the pictures with smaller thumbnail versions. Then the page will appear quickly, with enough of a preview to encourage a closer look. By selecting an individual thumbnail, the visitor explicitly requests the full picture, and only one picture at a time need be downloaded.

FrontPage can automatically generate the smaller version for each picture.

4. Right-click the picture in Design view and select Auto Thumbnail, to create a thumbnail graphic and a hyperlink to the original.

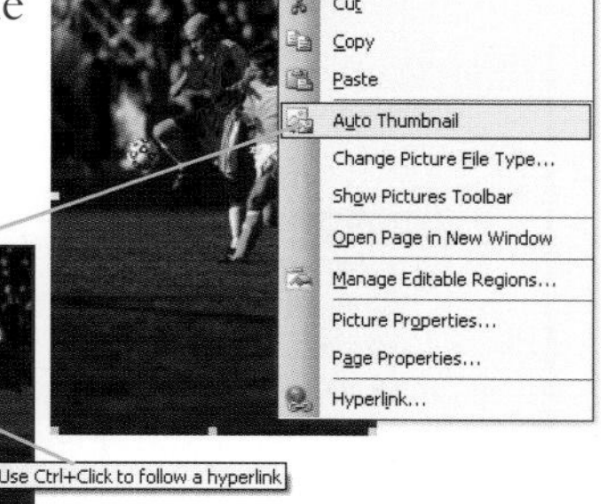

However, it is usually easier to use the Photo Gallery to do the layout. See pages 52–53 to create a Photo Gallery feature. To use this, remove the pictures added so far.

5. If you want to cancel the picture inserts, click the arrow next to the Undo button and reverse the actions.

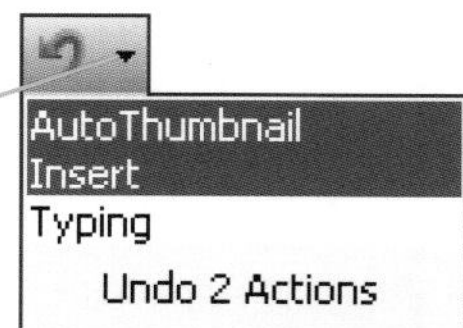

Photo Gallery

You can add a Photo Gallery component to the Web page, to manage collection of photographs or other image files. You can also add captions and descriptions to the images, reorder the images, change the image sizes, and switch layouts.

FrontPage includes the Photo Gallery with predefined layouts for photographs and other images.

1 Click below the text, and select Insert, Web Component.

2 Select Photo Gallery from the left, and Horizontal Layout from the right.

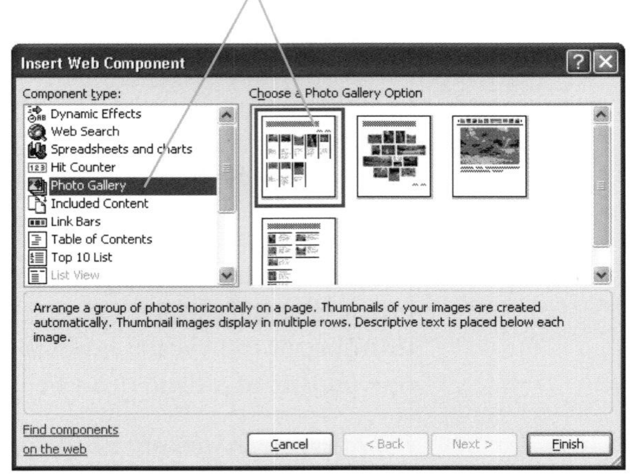

FrontPage doesn't alter the original picture files. It makes a copy of each picture, resizes and resamples it to reduce the display resolution, and associates a hyperlink to the original picture file.

The thumbnail images are stored in a Photo Gallery folder added to the Web site.

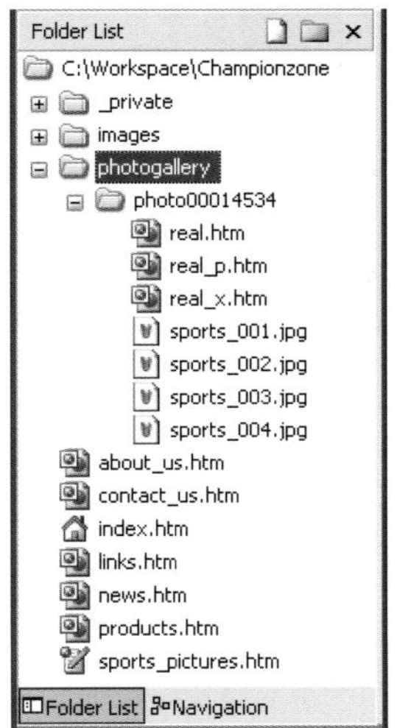

3 From the Properties panel, click Add, Pictures from Files.

4 Select the four pictures Sports_001-004 from the Images folder, as before. This time they will be displayed separately from the Web page.

The Photo Gallery Properties panel will be re-displayed, listing the selected image files.

To make changes and adjustments to an existing Photo Gallery, right-click the pictures and select Photo Gallery Properties from the quick menu.

You can use the same font as the rest of the page, or set up custom font definitions for the Photo Gallery text.

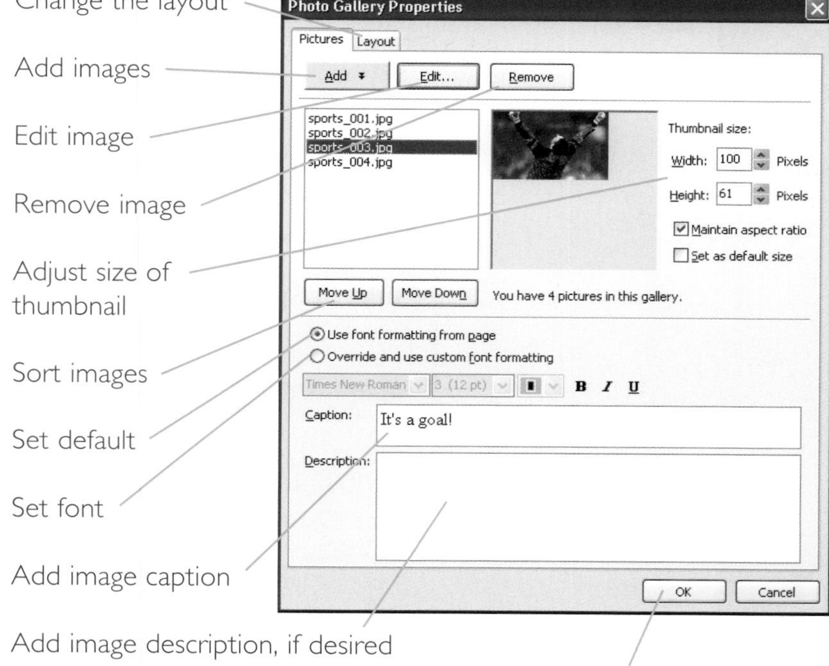

5 Press OK to record the changes to the page and save the embedded thumbnail pictures:

In Design view, press Ctrl and click the thumbnail image, to see the full image. In Preview you just click the thumbnail – no need to press Ctrl.

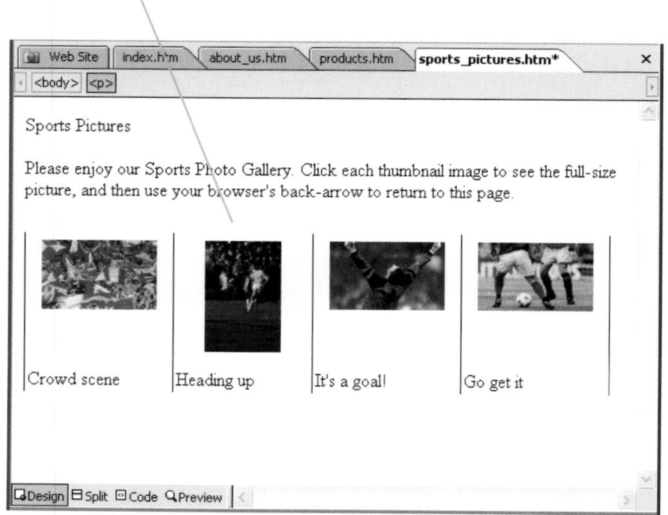

Links page

One sign of a good Web site is that it will direct visitors on to other places of interest, so they don't have to retrace their footsteps, and they get the benefit of searches that have already been performed.

To set up the Links page for ChampionZone:

1 Open the Web page Links.htm, type *Links to Sports Sites* as the first line, select Style Heading 1, and press Enter.

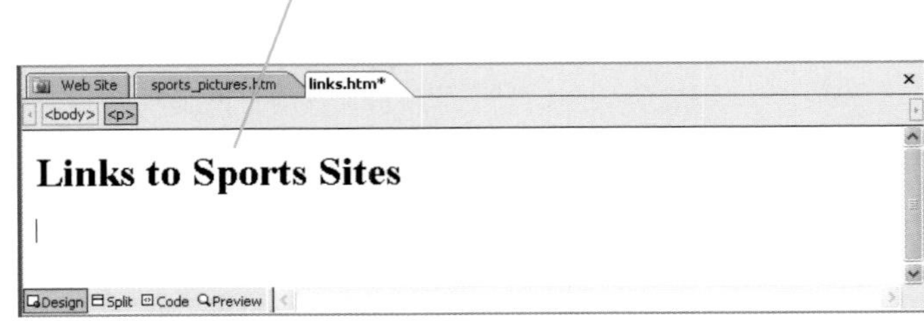

Dynamic HTML is an extension of the HTML language for presentation effects for text and objects, without the need for programming.

2 Click in the text and select View, Toolbars, Dynamic HTML Effects.

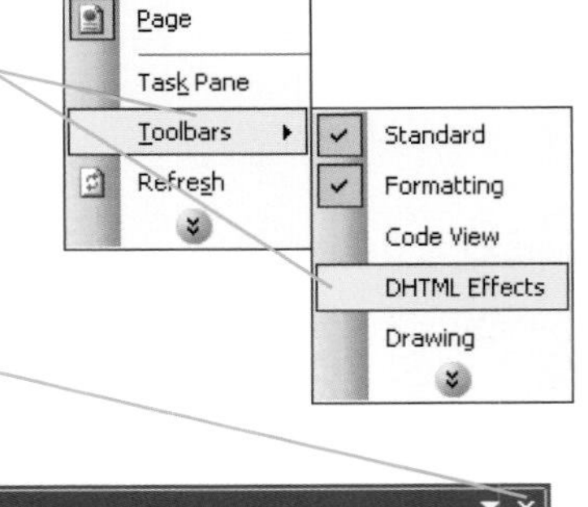

3 On the DHTML Effects toolbar, Choose On: Page load and Apply: Hop, then click the Close button.

4 Press the Preview tab, or select Preview in Browser from the Standard toolbar, to see the Dynamic HTML effect in action.

To change the effect, click the text in Page Design view, select Format, Dynamic HTML Effects and choose Elastic, Drop in by word, or Hop, etc.

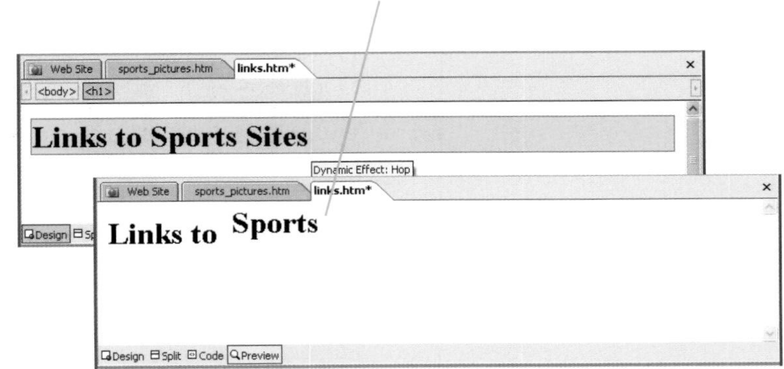

Creating text hyperlinks

You can turn a selected item of text into an active link to a page or a file in your Web site, on your local file system, on a Web server, or on another site on the Internet.

1 Press the Down arrow, type *MSN@ Sports*, highlight the text and click the Insert Hyperlink button.

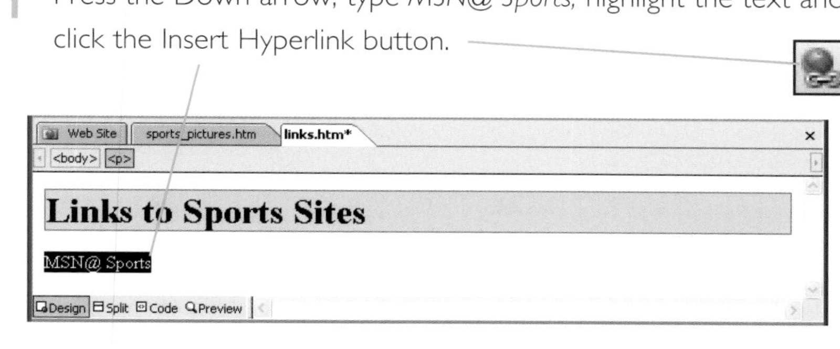

To enter special symbols in your text, select Insert, Symbol, click the desired character, then press Insert and Close.

2 In the address box, type <u>www.msn.espn.go.com</u> for the MSN sports page, then click OK (FrontPage adds the <u>http://</u> prefix).

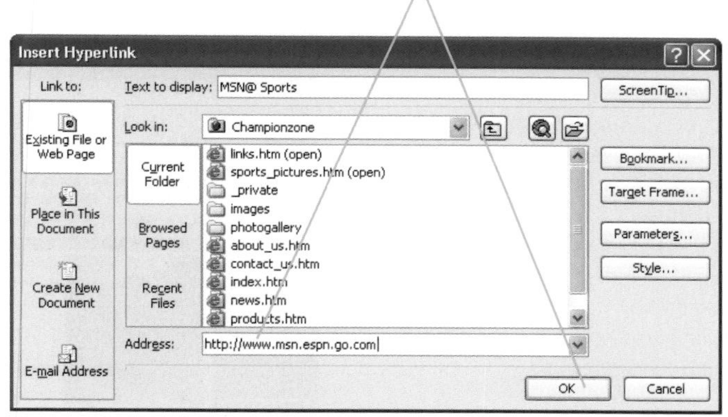

You can associate a URL with a graphic to create a picture button (for an example, see page 34).

3 Press the Down-arrow to de-select the text. Note that the text is underlined and colored blue to denote a hyperlink.

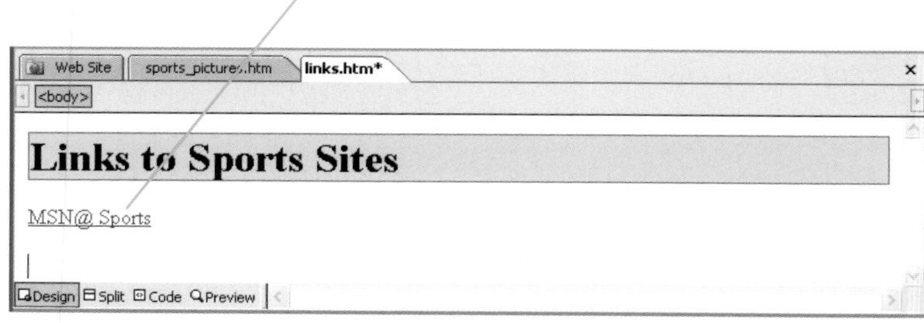

When you press Ctrl and click this link, or just click if the page is displayed in a browser, you will display the MSN sports page.

Automatic and verified hyperlinks

To become an automatic hyperlink, your text must start with www. The actual URL in this case is: <u>http://sports.yahoo.com</u> but your browser will locate the correct page if you type: <u>www.sports.yahoo.com</u>.

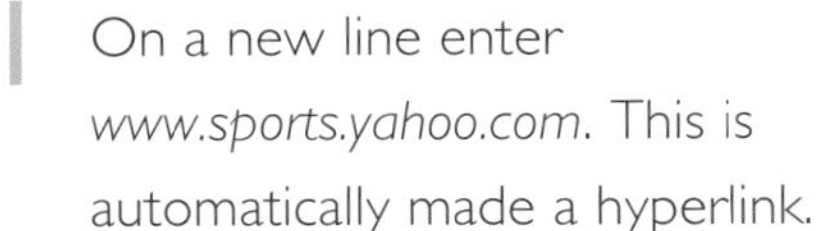

1 On a new line enter *www.sports.yahoo.com*. This is automatically made a hyperlink.

2 Highlight the text and type replacement text *Yahoo! Sports*. The associated URL is unchanged.

3 On a new line, type *The National Football League*, highlight the text and press Hyperlink, then Browse the Web. In your Browser type the URL <u>*www.nfl.com*</u>.

The best approach is to use your Web browser to validate the URLs, though you must be connected to the Internet in order to check out Web site addresses.

You can also copy URL shortcuts from your Favorites list, or from an existing hyperlink on a Web page, by right-clicking and selecting Copy Shortcut, then pasting into the URL box or straight onto the Web page.

Add the links that you find helpful and want to tell your visitors about. When you have finished entering links, press the Save button on the toolbar to record the changes to your Web page.

4 Press Alt+Tab to switch back to FrontPage Insert Hyperlink and click OK to associate the now verified URL with the text you placed on the Web page.

Enhancing the Web site

Continue working with the ChampionZone Web site, adding formatting and navigation bars and graphical themes. Preview and test the Web site and prepare it for publication on the World Wide Web.

Covers

Chapter Four

Formatting headings

Choose fonts and formats that make your Web site look interesting, but try to be consistent.

When you have created the pages for your Web site, you can apply font and text style changes to the contents. It is helpful to tackle the pages as a group, so you can easily compare the pages and provide similar effects.

To open all the pages in the Web site and apply styles to the paragraph headings:

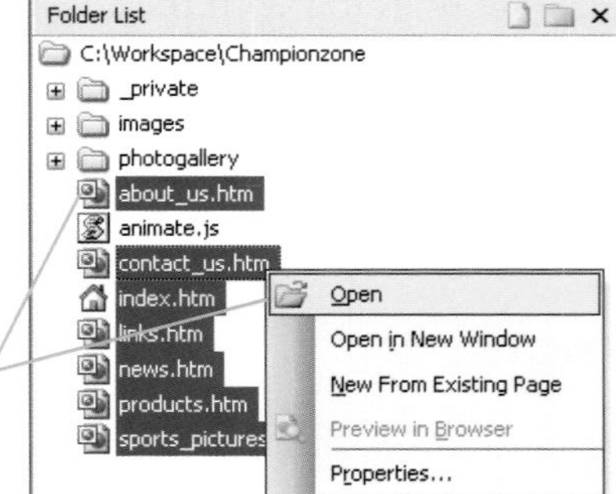

1 Select Folder List, highlight all of the Web pages, right-click the selection and click Open.

FrontPage always opens a Web site with a new, empty page ready for use. You can ignore this since it goes away when you open one of your existing pages.

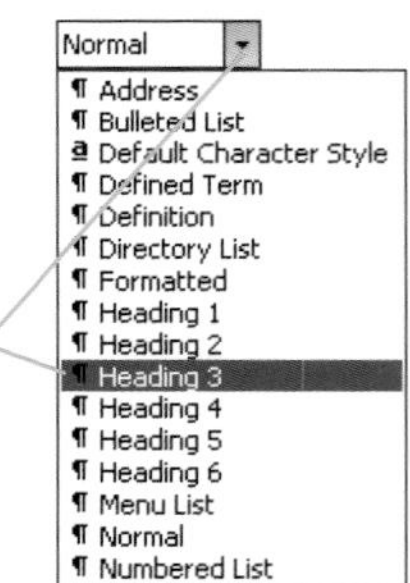

2 Click the Page tab for the home page Index.htm

3 Click in the heading text, and select Heading 3 from the Style list. The text is made bold, and the size is increased.

Heading styles are universal HTML standards, and range from level 1 (the largest size) to level 6 (the smallest).

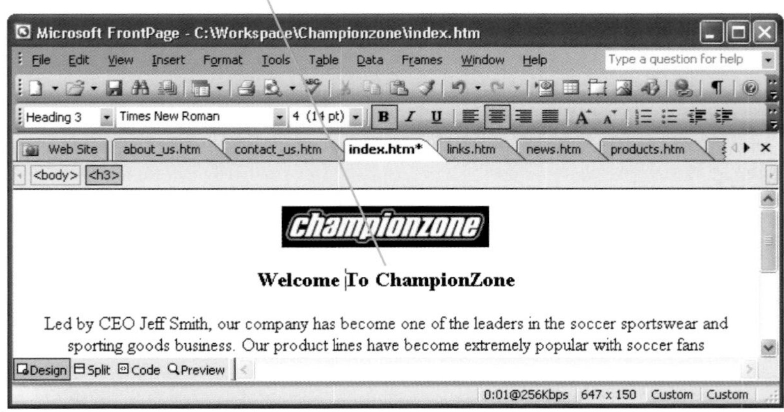

4 Click the Page tab for the About Us Web page, click in the heading text and apply the Heading 4 style.

To be more accurate (and make it less tedious) you can use the Format Painter to copy an existing format to other pieces of text.

5 Re-select the About Us heading and double-click the Format Painter button on the toolbar. The cursor changes to match.

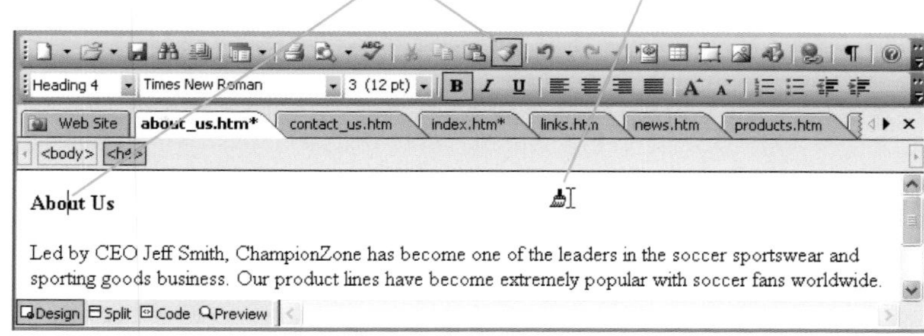

If you double-click the Format Painter, it remains selected until you click the button again. If you single-click, the Format Painter is de-selected after first use.

6 Select the Products page and heading to apply the format, then repeat the process for the Sports Pictures and News headings.

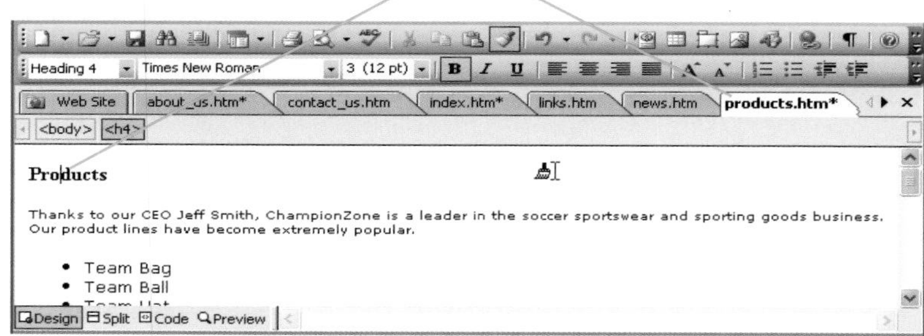

You should not use Format Painter for text that has other formats such as DHTML effects, since it would replace all the formatting and therefore switch off the extra formatting.

7 Click the Format Painter to clear the selection, open the Links page, click the heading and apply the Heading 4 format.

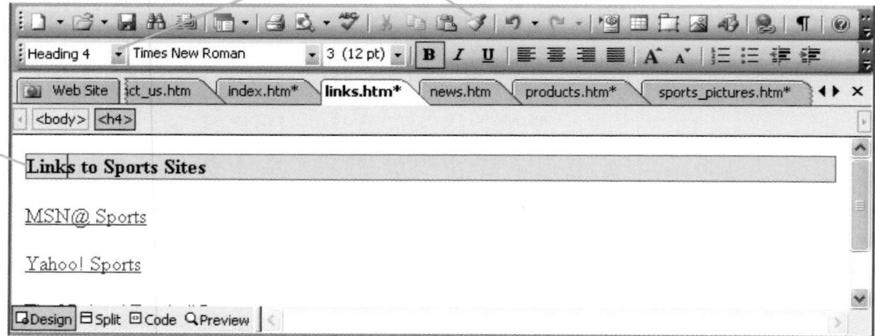

Connecting pages

Creating pages is only the first stage. You must link your Web pages together to make them into a true Web site.

1. Start FrontPage and open the ChampionZone Web site, and select View, Navigation to show the Web pages created so far:

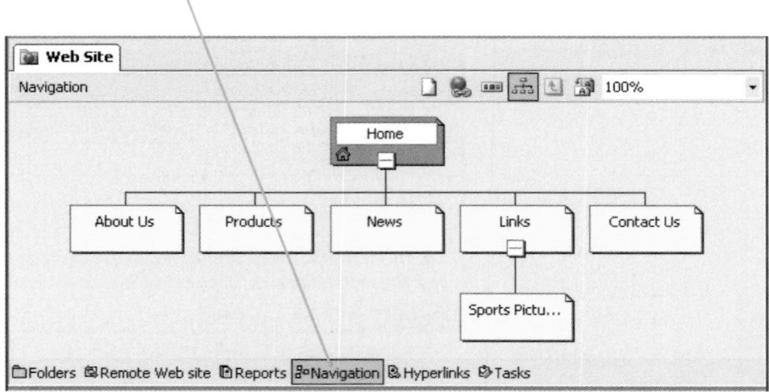

These pages have hyperlinks to image files and to other Web sites, but as yet there are no links between the pages within the site.

There are several ways you could add links between the pages:

Manual links

You can manually create hyperlinks on the home page to the other Web pages, and also put links on those pages back to the home page. These links will allow your visitors to navigate around your Web site. This method gives you the most control over the connections between the pages, but is the most effort also.

You can define shared borders for your Web pages, to provide a consistent method of storing the link bars and other components (see pages 62–63).

Shared borders

FrontPage can create, manage, and automatically update link bars that connect the pages in your Web site. You can make changes and additions to the Web site without having to explicitly update links.

Frames

Frames divide the browser window into different areas, each of which can display a different page. These are known as Frames pages. One of the frames can be used to contain a list of hyperlinks to the pages in the Web site. This requires more manual intervention when pages change, but the same Contents frame can be used on all the pages, so the amount of updating is minimized.

The FrontPage Banner and Contents template provides a layout that includes a Contents frames page. See page 140 for details.

Manual links

This manual approach lets you see what is involved in connecting pages, but you may have to revise the links whenever you add, remove or rename any pages.

1 Mark text on the Web page, click Insert Hyperlink, and select the target Web page and click OK.

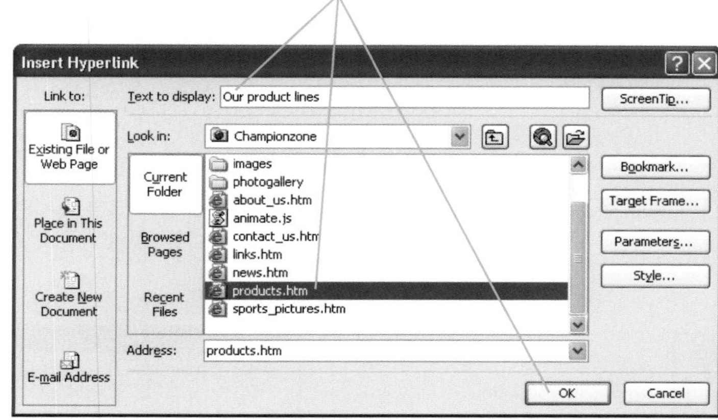

You would add hyperlinks in this way when you want a link for a graphic or within a text section of the Web page.

2 Drag and drop a Web page from the Folder list onto another Web page to create a link. The file name becomes the screen tip.

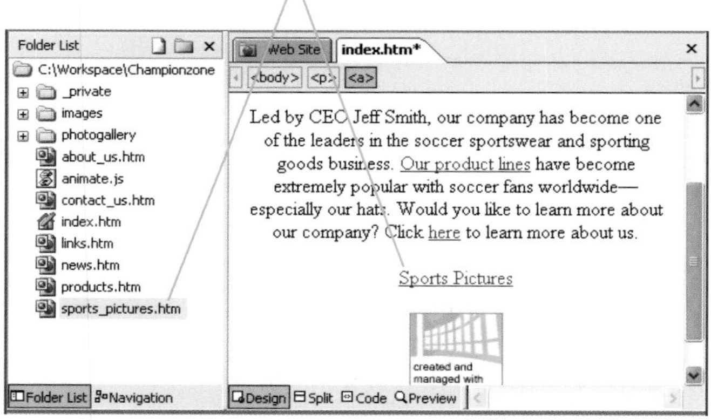

There are other ways to add links manually to your Web pages, but it is better to let FrontPage create and manage the links for you, so that your Web site is automatically updated when you add or remove pages.

3 Click the Web Site tab and then click the Hyperlinks tab, to see the links that have been defined on a Web page.

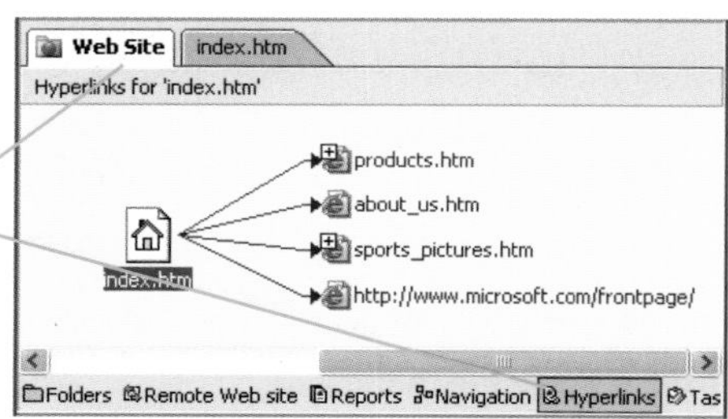

Shared borders

You use shared borders to position the same content (for example logo, copyright notice or contact details) on multiple pages, to save changing each page individually. It also means that you only have to modify content in one place to update all pages.

You can set the defaults for shared borders for the Web site as a whole, and apply individual changes to the settings for particular pages, for example turning off a shared border on certain pages.

You can enable the authoring option Navigation, which will let you create link bars manually without having to enable shared borders.

A shared border is a region that is common to some or all of the pages in your Web site. It may be along any edge of the page (top, bottom or either side). Shared borders can be used to hold page banners, which display the page title or other text. You also use shared borders to hold FrontPage link bars.

To enable shared borders in FrontPage:

1. Select Tools, Page Options, click the Authoring tab and choose Author-time Web Components and Shared Borders.

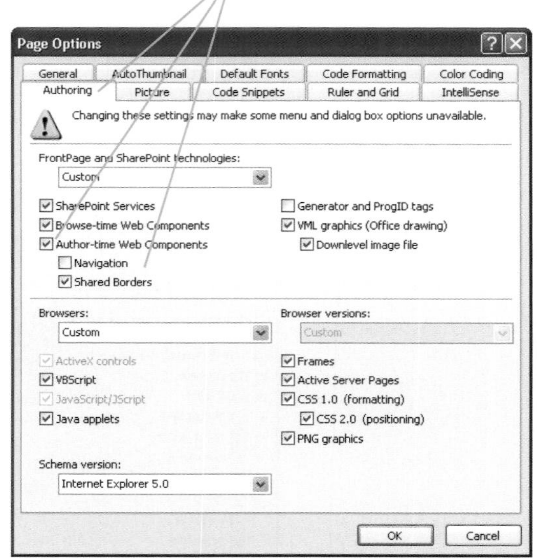

2. Select Format, Shared Borders, choose All Pages, select Top and Left, and include Navigation buttons for each. Do not select the Right or Bottom fields. Click OK to save.

Shared Borders
Apply to:
All pages
Selected page(s)
Top
Include navigation buttons
Left
Include navigation buttons
Right
Include navigation buttons
Bottom
Reset borders for current page to web default
Border Properties...
OK
Cancel

By default, the top border shows pages at the same level and the left border shows pages below the current pages. No bar appears when there are no qualifying pages.

3 Open the Index.htm home page to view the shared borders with page banner and links bar.

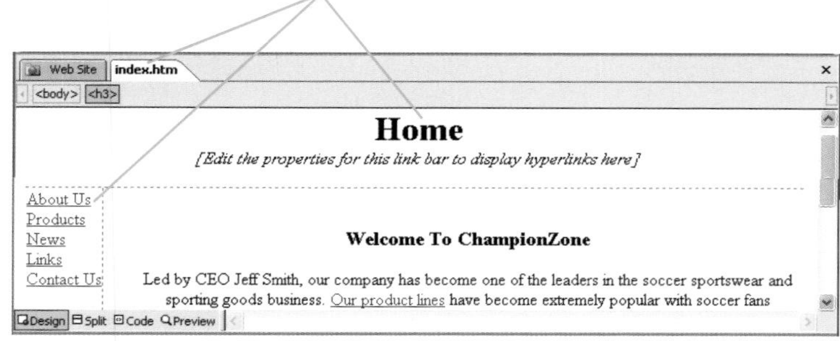

The top level Home page has just a page banner at the top border, and links to lower level pages on the left border.

4 Double-click the page banner to change the text. Note that this will also change the page title shown in the Navigation view.

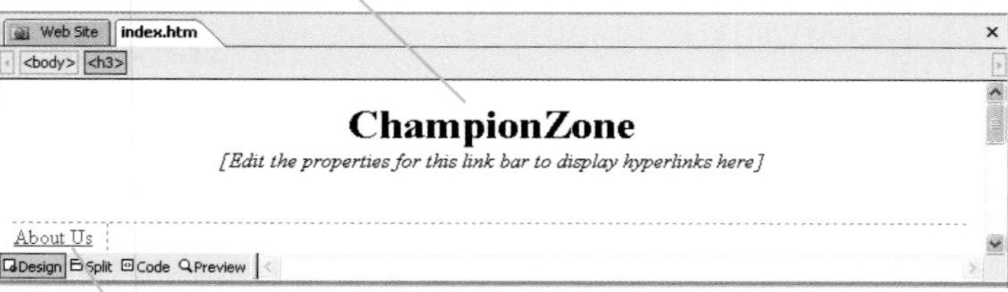

5 Hold down Ctrl and click About Us in the link bar, to open and display that page.

The About Us page (like the other second level pages) has the links bar on the top border, but no links in the left border.

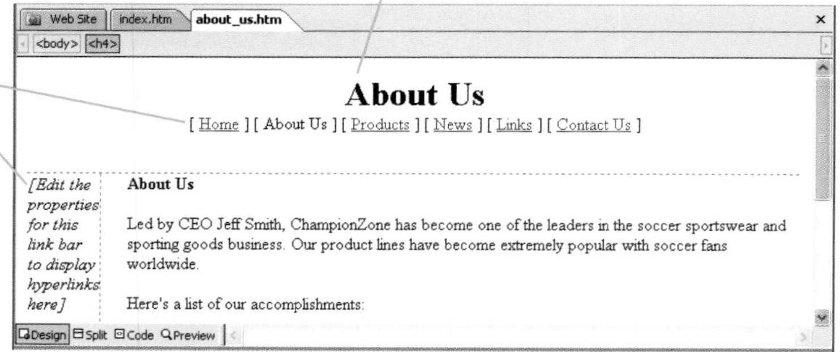

Customizing link bars

Since the changes apply to all pages, you can adjust the properties from any of the Web pages.

1 Double-click the links bar on the top border for the About Us page, to open the Properties for the Top bar.

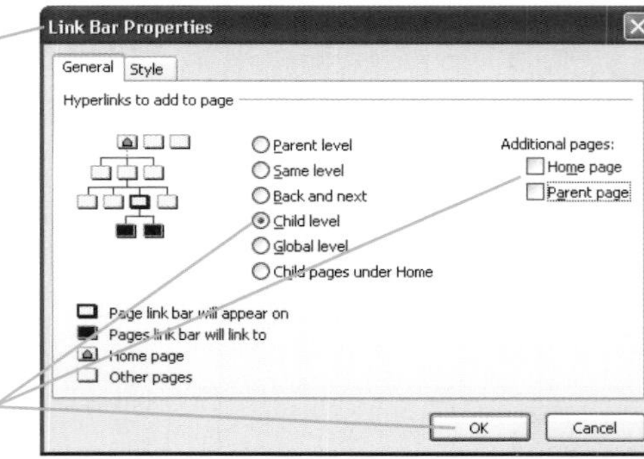

2 Click Child level, clear the check marks for Home page and Parent page, and click OK.

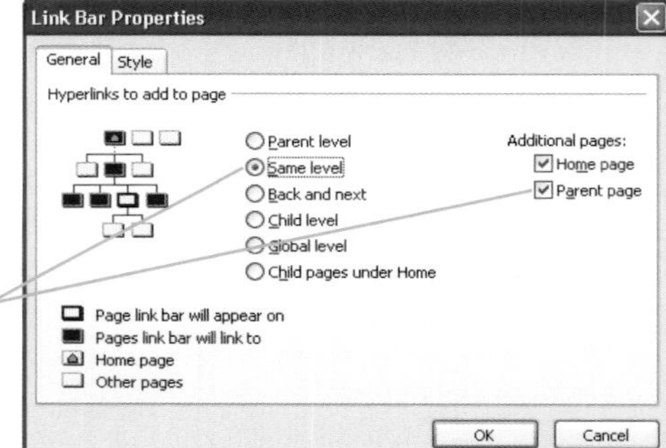

Use Preview in Browser rather than the basic Preview tab, to see the bars in their final form.

3 Double-click the vertical Links bar area, click Same level, Home page and Parent page.

4 Click OK, then select File, Preview in Browser to see the page as visitors see it.

The Top border shows the page banner only, since there are no lower level pages. The left navigation bar shows all five site pages and will include any new pages that may be added at one level below Home.

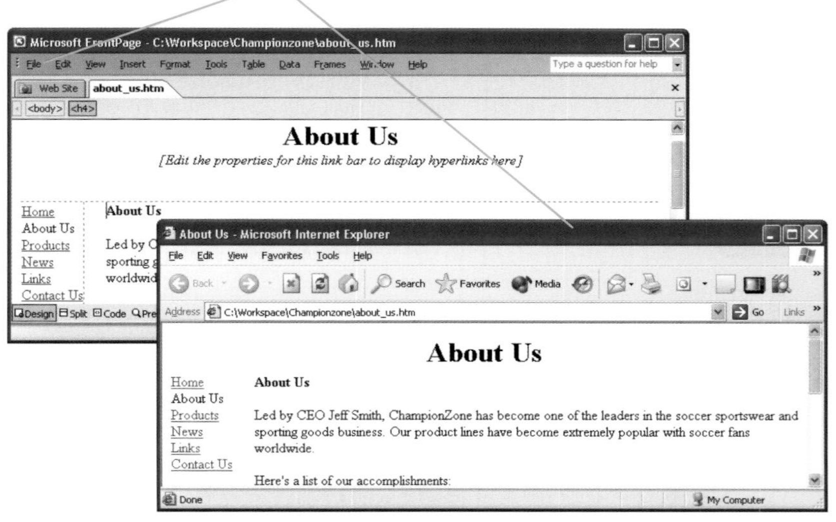

Bookmarks

Sometimes, especially with long or complex Web pages, you may want a link that points to a specific place, not just the top of the page. You use bookmarks for this.

1 Open the Products page, highlight the heading Team Bag and select Insert, Bookmark (or press Ctrl+G). Click OK to define the bookmark. Repeat for the headings Team Ball and Team Bag.

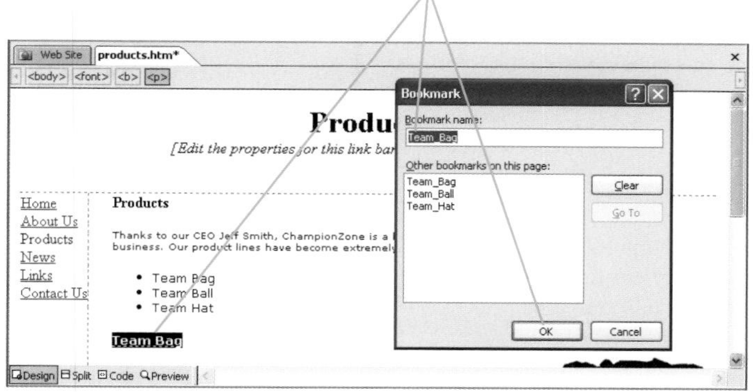

You can highlight a graphic and define a bookmark for it, or even just click a position on the page and define a bookmark. Since there's no text, you'll have to provide a bookmark name.

2 Select the bulleted text Team Bag and click Insert Hyperlink. Click Place in This Document, and choose the Team Bag bookmark, then click OK. Repeat for Team Ball and Team Bag.

You can reference bookmarks from within the same Web page, or as part of a hyperlink from a different Web page.

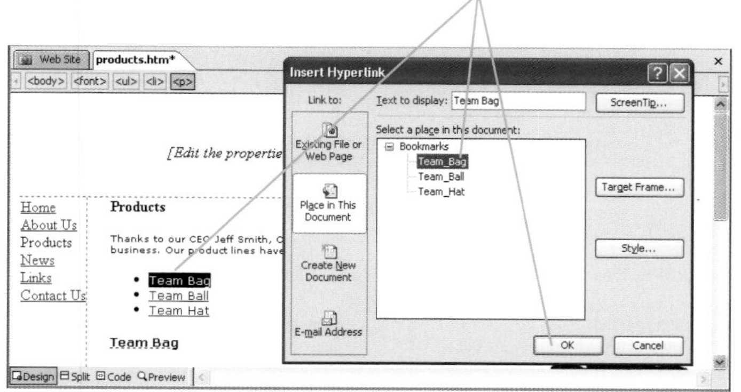

3 In Design view, text with a bookmark defined will be underlined with dashes. A bookmarked position is indicated by a flag. There's no indicator for graphics with bookmarks. The dashes and flags do not show in Preview or in the Browser.

Graphical themes

Despite all the effort so far, the Web pages are still quite plain. It takes color and graphics to liven them up and make them into a real Web site.

You are saved the detailed design job, since FrontPage has more than 50 professionally designed themes to apply to your Web site. These specify bullets, fonts, pictures and buttons, and are applied to pages, page banners and navigation bars, to produce an attractive and consistent appearance.

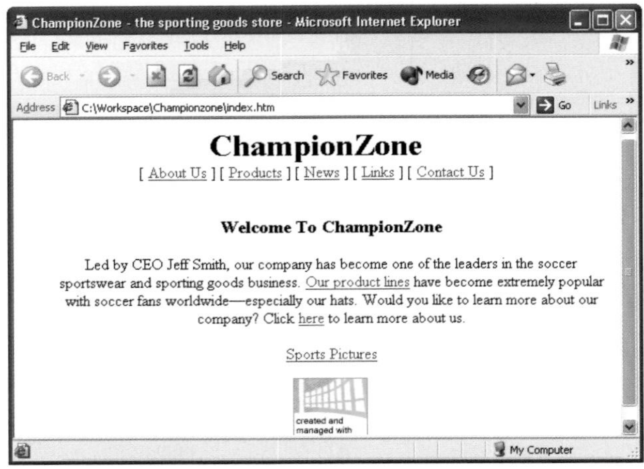

1 Select Format, Theme, and click on any name to explore the options.

Format
Font...
Paragraph...
Theme...
Dynamic Web Template

2 The chosen theme will be applied to the current page so that you can see its appearance and style.

Click the arrow that appears when you hover over a theme icon, to apply the theme as the default, to apply it to the selected pages, or to customize it.

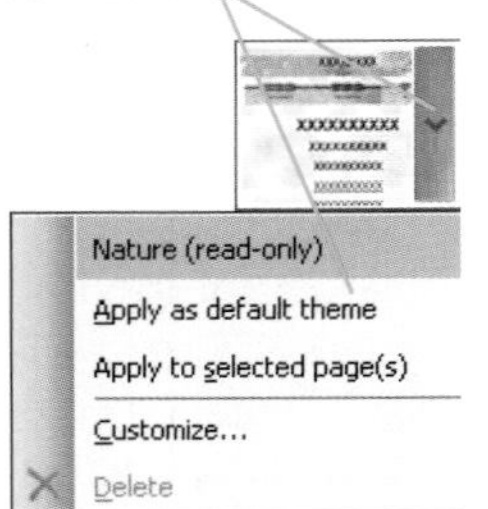

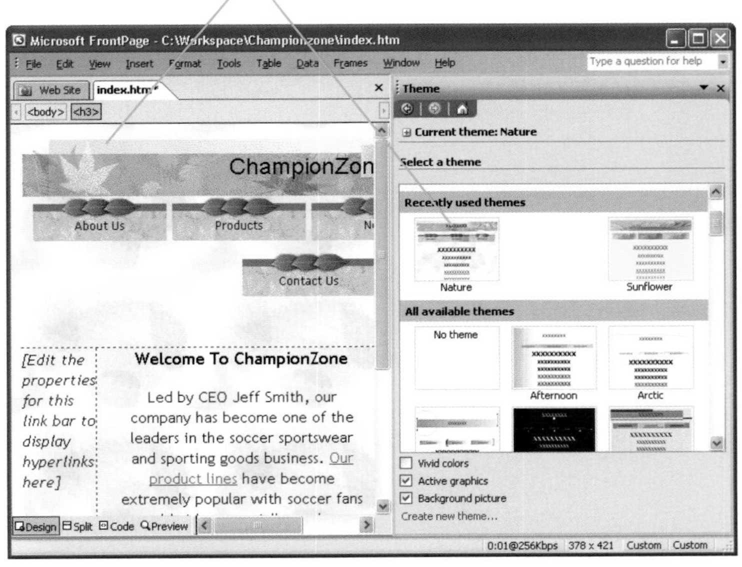

If you apply a theme having selected all the pages in your Web site, it becomes the default theme for that Web site. New pages will automatically make use of that theme when they are created.

Graphical navigation

When you apply a theme that contains animations, and you select Active graphics, you enable page banner animations and navigation bar rollover effects. To see a theme's active graphics effects, apply the theme and then Preview in Browser.

1 Open the Home page, and Preview in Browser. Note how the links change as you move the cursor over them.

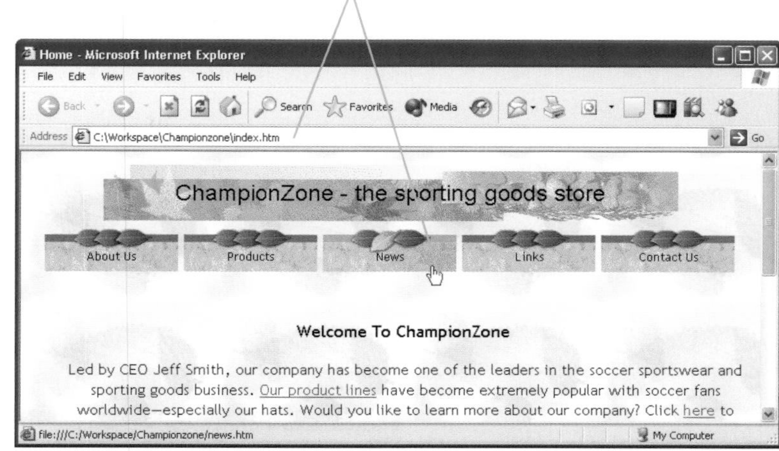

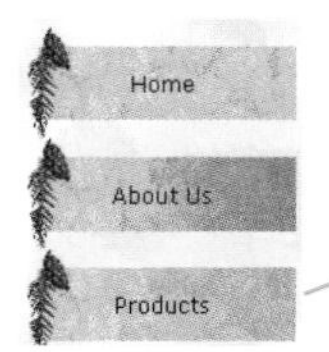

You can double-click the vertical links bar area on any page, even the Home page, since changes apply to all the Web pages. Scroll to the top of the list of styles to find the entry that says Use Page's Theme. The plain text entry is right at the bottom of the list.

2 The vertical links bar by default uses plain text links. To change to graphical links, double-click the links bar and click the Style tab.

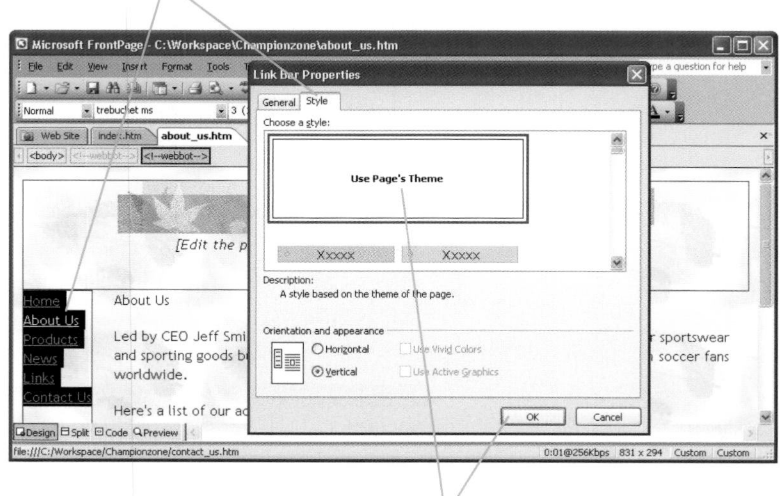

3 Choose Use Page's Theme, and click OK. FrontPage changes the format for the left link bar to use the graphical buttons.

Customizing the theme

You can edit the colors used in any portion of the theme, replace any of the graphics, and modify the styles for text items.

You can create your own theme or modify the settings for the themes supplied with FrontPage. To modify the Nature theme:

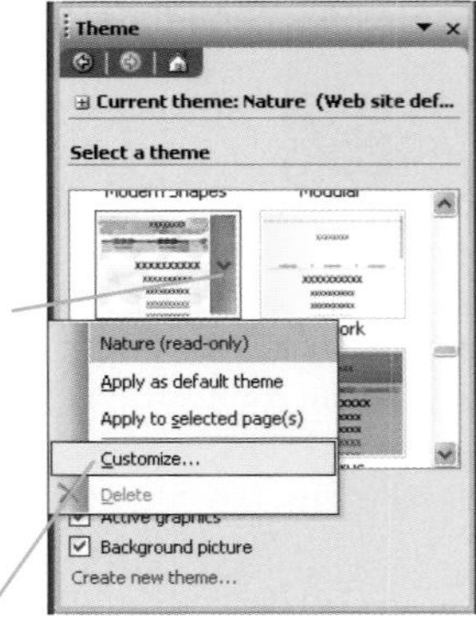

1 Open the Web site and the Home page, select Format, Theme to display the Theme task pane. Hover over the Nature theme icon and click the arrow.

Select Create New Theme at the bottom of the task pane, to build a new theme from scratch.

2 Click Customize, and then click Graphics. You could also modify Colors and Text settings.

3 Select Banner from the Item list. Select banner.gif and press OK and then Save.

You will find the banner in the Images folder for the Web site, if you imported it with the other image files (see pages 46-47) or look in the FrontPage2003ies folder.

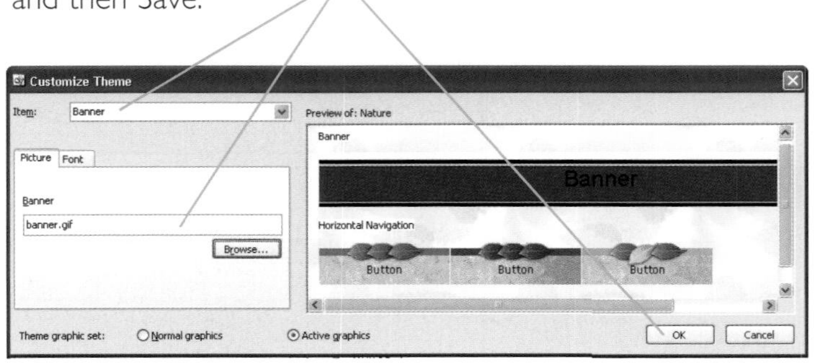

The supplied themes are marked as read-only, so you must save an existing theme under a new name.

4 The Nature theme (like all the themes) is read-only, so you must accept the Copy of Nature name supplied, or provide a new name such as ChampionZone for the modified theme.

5 Click OK to save the new theme, then click the down arrow and select Apply as default theme.

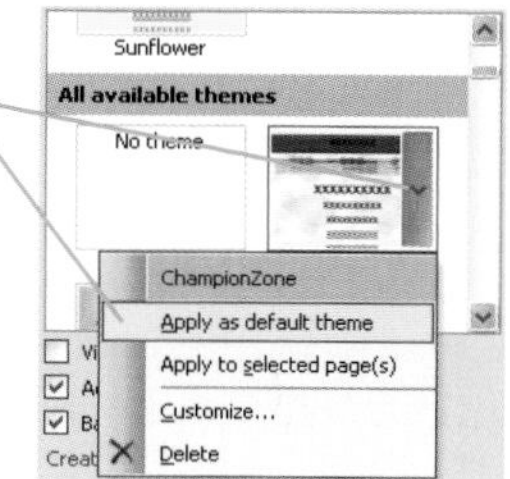

The new theme is applied to all the pages in the Web site. The effects show up immediately, in the Design view.

6 To see the Web with the modified theme, without placeholder text or formatting marks, press the Preview in Browser button, or select File, Preview in Browser.

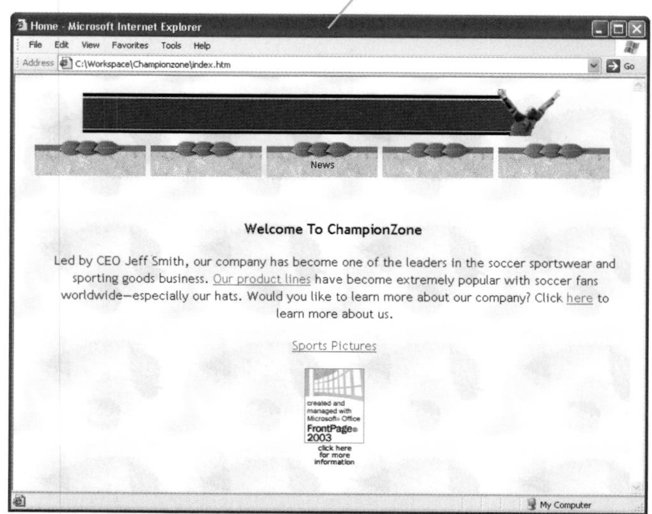

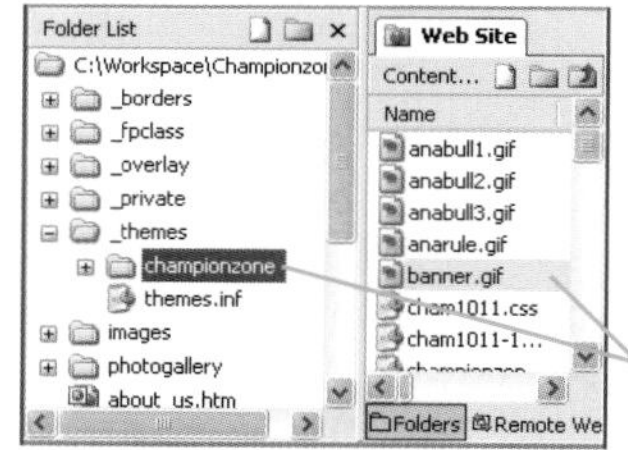

The elements of the new default theme, including the banner image, are stored within the Web, in the _themes folder. This is a hidden folder, so it won't show up in Windows Explorer unless you set the folder options to show hidden files and folders.

Arranging files and folders

It is useful to display the Folder list at the same time, to get a Windows Explorer style overview of the files and folders. You can then click [+] to expand folders, or [–] to collapse.

You arrange the files and folders in your Web site using the Folders view. With this you can change the locations of files without worrying about invalidating hyperlinks or losing access to banners, buttons or navigation bars.

To view the contents of the Web site:

1. Click the Toggle Pane button to show the folder list, or click the Folders tab. Double-click a folder to display its contents.

Click a heading such as Size or Type once to sort in ascending order, and click again to sort in descending order.

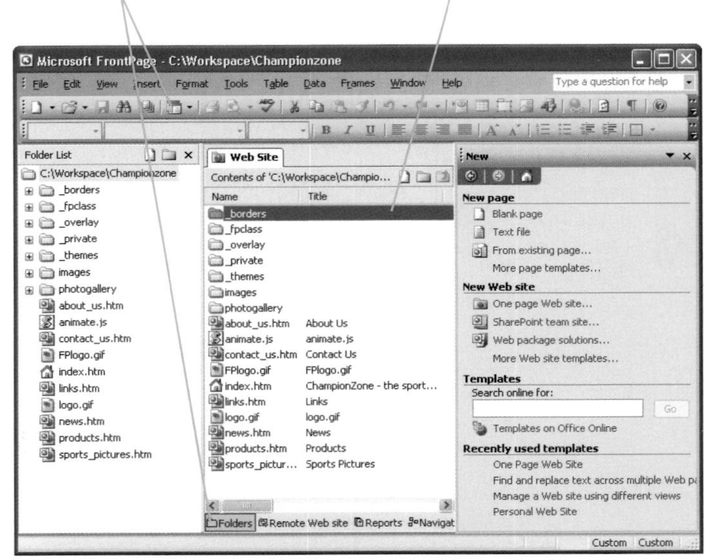

By default, FrontPage provides a folder for “images”. If you create a Photo Gallery, FrontPage also generates a folder structure to hold the thumbnail images.

Don't use Windows Explorer or other file managers to rearrange the contents of your Web site – it would break the hyperlinks.

The main folder should normally contain the HTML (.htm or .html) files for Web pages. You might have saved embedded images files there also, and DHTML may have added some JavaScript (.js) applet files there. So you could have a mixture of file types.

It is much easier to maintain the Web site if you group files together. For example, you should put all picture files into the Images folder. You should also have folders to contain special

Hold down the Ctrl key to select sets of files that are not listed in consecutive order.

purpose files such as audio clips, video clips or applets. You should use the Folders view to rearrange the locations of the files, and create the additional folders you may require.

2 Select the first picture file, hold down the Shift key and select the last picture file.

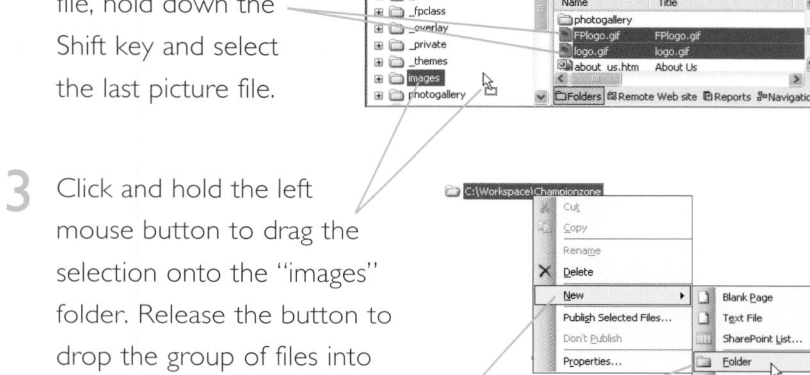

FrontPage displays Rename while it moves files since it is updating all the hyperlinks to those files.

3 Click and hold the left mouse button to drag the selection onto the "images" folder. Release the button to drop the group of files into the "images" folder.

4 Right-click the folder within which you want to create the new subfolder. Select New, Folder from the context menu displayed, or open the folder and click the New Folder button.

Whenever you move files in Folder view, FrontPage will automatically adjust all references to the files in all Web pages concerned.

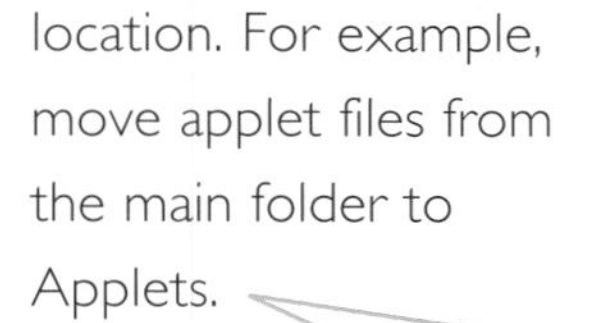

5 Drag and drop files from their current location to the new location. For example, move applet files from the main folder to Applets.

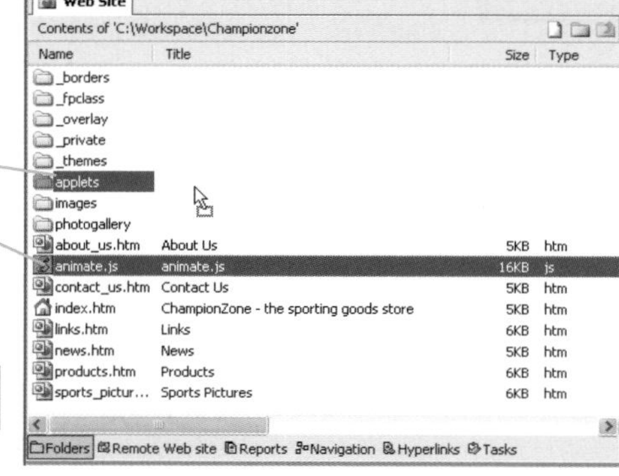

You can create a new page in Folders view or in Page view, but it won't participate in the link bars until you add it to the Navigation view *(see page 72).*

6 Open the main folder and click the New Page button to create another Web page.

Adding a new page

When you use themes and shared borders for all pages in the Web site, new pages that you create will inherit the attributes that you have specified. However, you also have to show FrontPage where the page fits in the overall Web structure.

Depending on its level in the structure, the new page may be added to the navigation bars in the shared borders and appear on the other pages.

This page will be completed with the addition of a feedback form, as described in the next chapter (see page 74).

1 When you create a new page in Page view, or open a page created in Folder view, it reminds you it has not been added to the navigation structure.

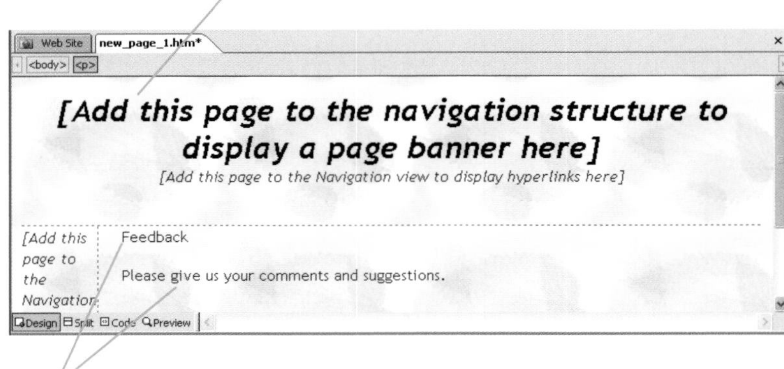

2 Add the text *Feedback*. Press Enter then add *Please give us your comments and suggestions.* Then select Save. If the page is not already named, the default name is the first line of text *feedback*.

3 Switch to Navigation view, and drag the new file from the folder list to the appropriate position on the Web structure.

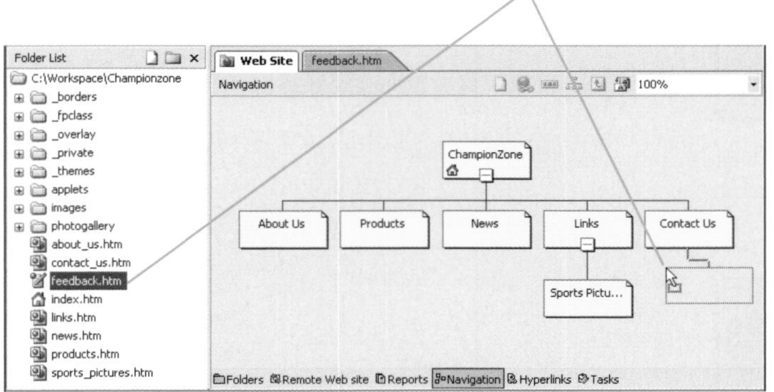

The page will now display the page banner and the appropriate links for its position in the navigation structure will be added to the link bars on the Contact Us and the Feedback pages.

Finalize the Web site

Complete the final items, such as the feedback page. Display reports to check that the Web site has everything needed, and confirm that the Web site is ready for publication on the Internet or the Intranet.

Covers

Chapter Five

Request feedback

With a feedback option on your Web site, you can gain information as well as distribute it.

The last page added to the Web site was Feedback. The purpose of this page is to provide a means for visitors to the Web site to contribute their comments and suggestions.

To create a form for responses:

1 Open the ChampionZone Web site and the Feedback page, and press Ctrl+End.

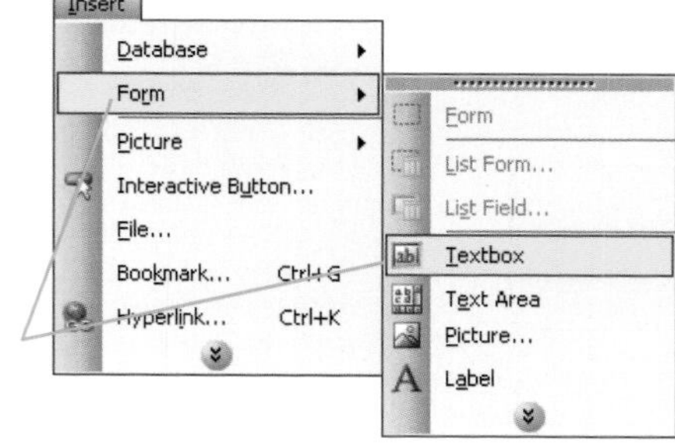

2 Press Enter to create a new line, and select Insert, Form, Textbox.

FrontPage inserts a new form on the current page. The dashed lines indicate the form's boundary. By default, a new form contains Submit and Reset push buttons.

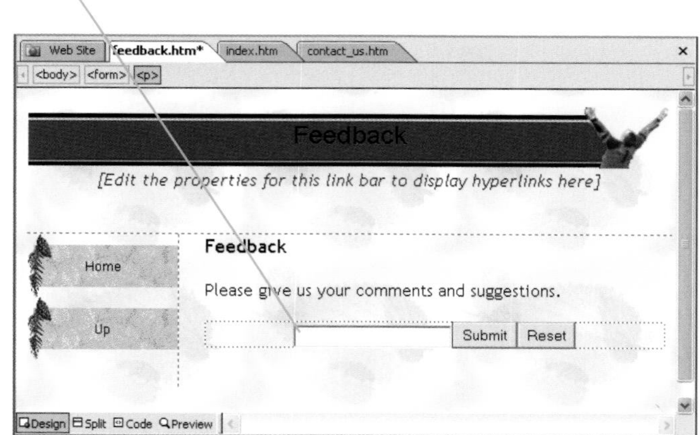

3 With the cursor left of the Submit button, click the Center button on the toolbar and then press Enter to add an extra line. Press the back-arrow to go to the start of the form.

The form makes it easier to collate and interpret feedback, especially if you want the analysis to be automated.

You can add text boxes, check boxes, menus, radio buttons, pictures and push buttons to your forms, to make it easy for the visitor to enter useful details.

Holding down Shift while pressing Enter creates a line break. Line breaks are useful for spacing lines of text more closely together than standard paragraph spacing.

HOT TIP

The default size of scrolling text box is very small but can easily be enlarged to show more lines and longer lines of text (see page 76).

To illustrate how to customize forms, you will add several input fields that help visitors supply useful details with the comments.

4 Type *Your Name:* and then press Shift+Enter to create a line break, move the cursor after the text box and press Enter to add a line.

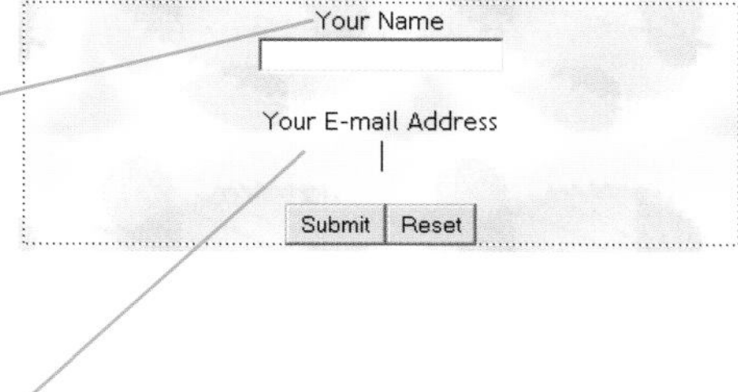

5 Type *Your E-mail Address:* and press Shift+Enter. Select Insert, Form, Textbox as in step 2, to add a data entry box.

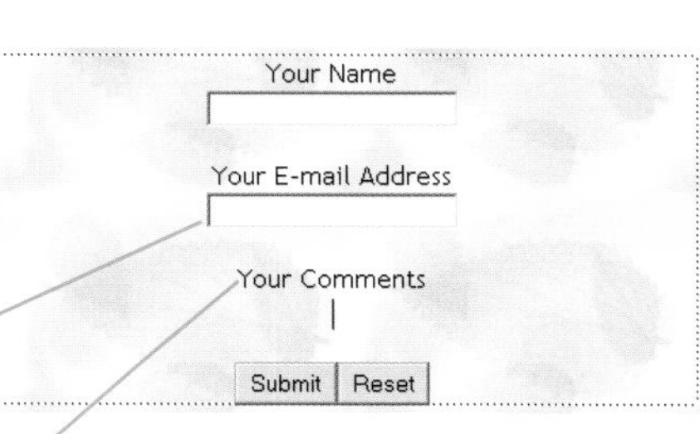

6 Press Enter to add a line. Type *Your Comments:* then press Shift+Enter.

7 Select Insert, Form, Text Area to insert a scrolling text input field.

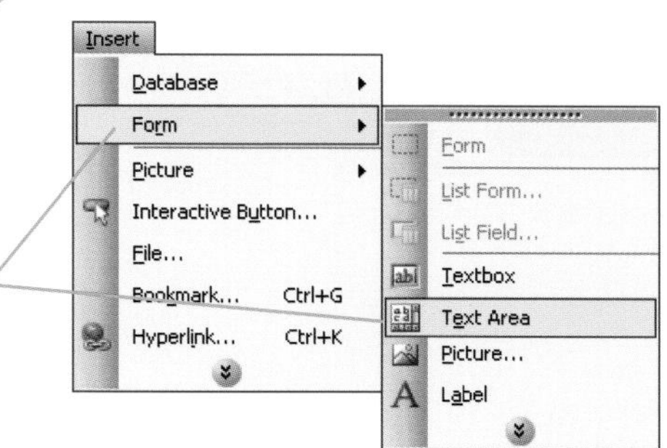

This provides a scrollable text box which can accept large amounts of text, but has a default width of 20 characters, and displays just two consecutive lines of the text at a time.

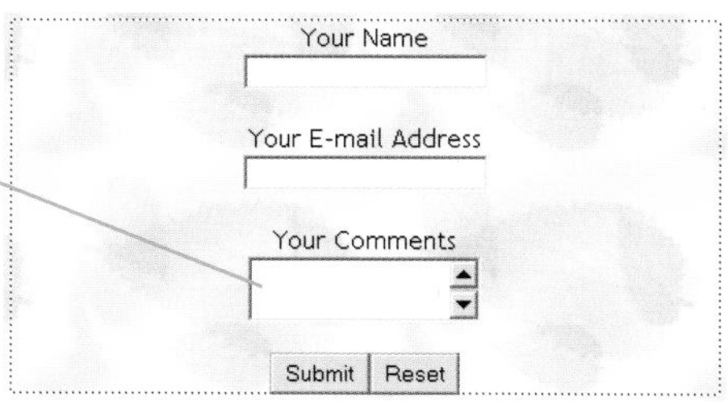

Adjust the form

When you display the properties for text boxes or scroll boxes, you can also change the default names.

Provide an adequate input field to encourage visitors to make comments at reasonable length.

You'll be prompted to save the changes to your Web page, before the browser loads the page from the Web site folder.

You can view the form in the browser, and practice adding text, but you can't test data collection with your form until you publish your Web site (see Chapter 6).

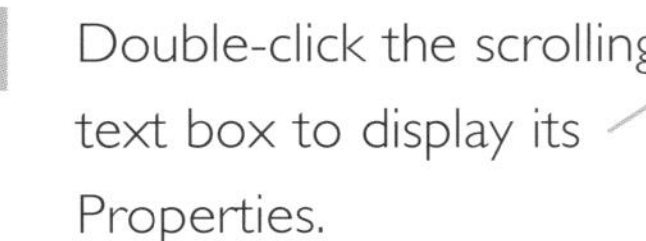

1. Double-click the scrolling text box to display its Properties.

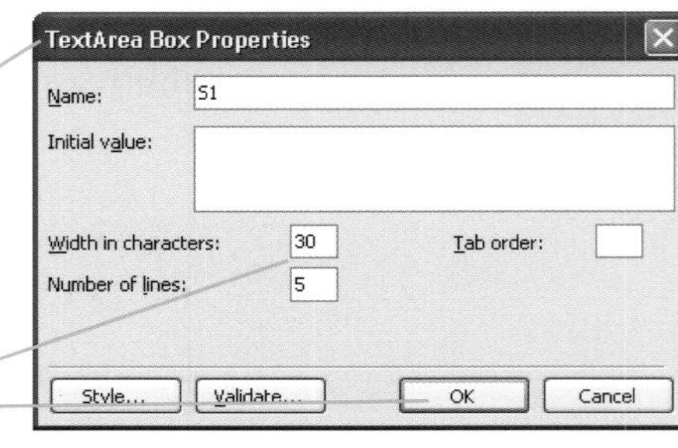

2. Change the width to 30 characters and the number of lines to 5, and press OK.

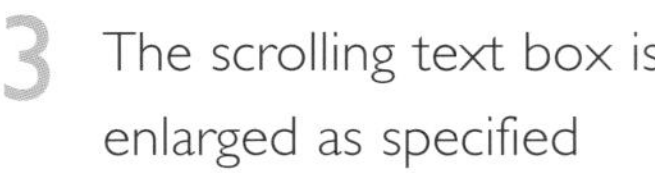

3. The scrolling text box is enlarged as specified

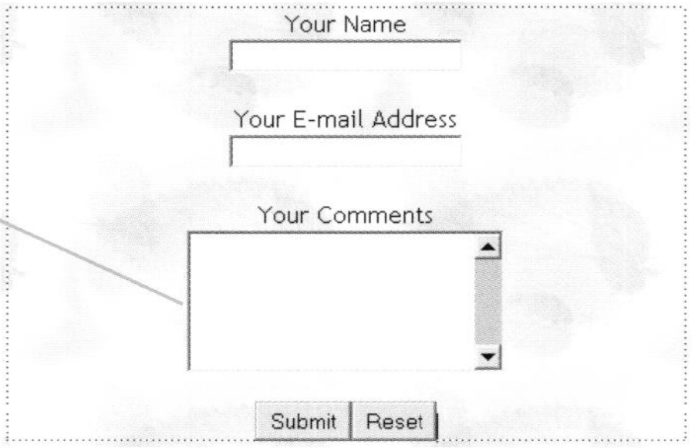

4. Press the Preview in Browser button to view the page in its final form, and save all the changes.

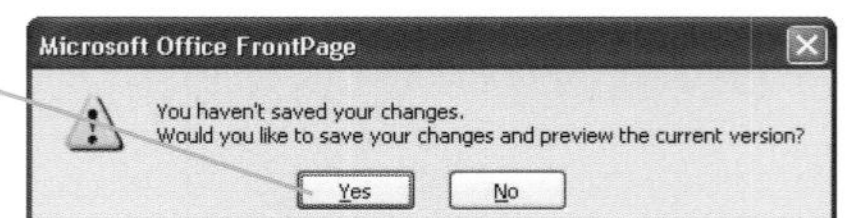

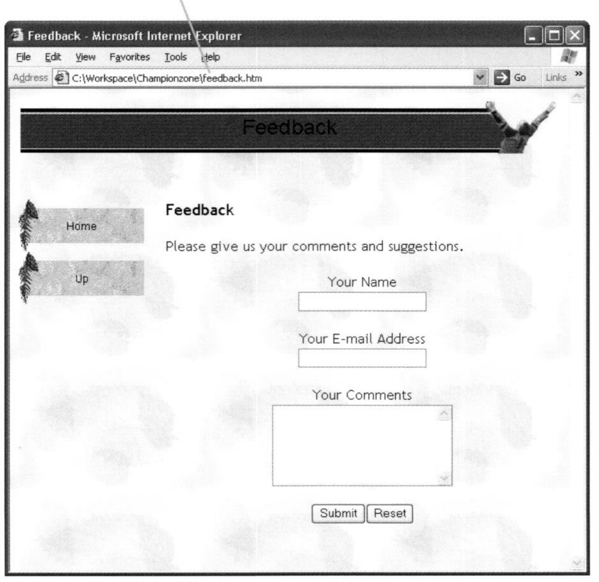

Which browser?

The browser is a key element in your Web site, since that is how your visitors will access the pages, when you have published the Web site. It is essential to understand what browsers they may be using.

When you view your Web pages with your browser, you will see what your visitors will see, as long as they have the same browser as you, or one with support for all the functions that you use. This may be more difficult to achieve than you might think. Your visitors may use a completely different PC and operating system, and they have the choice of over a hundred different browser products, each with multiple versions. Of course, the majority can be expected to use the common products, which the Browser News (see http://www.upsdell.com/browsernews/stat.htm) identifies as Internet Explorer, Netscape and Opera.

You don't have to cater to all browsers but you should be aware of the implications of using different browsers, and decide to what extent you can make allowances.

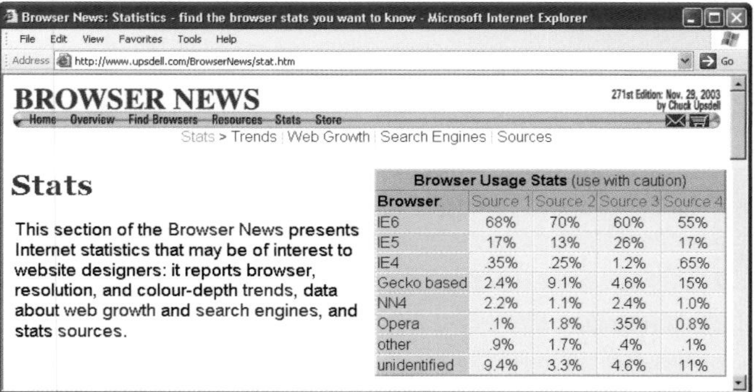

Browser Usage Stats (use with caution)

Browser	Source 1	Source 2	Source 3	Source 4
IE6	68%	70%	60%	55%
IE5	17%	13%	26%	17%
IE4	.35%	.25%	1.2%	.65%
Gecko based	2.4%	9.1%	4.6%	15%
NN4	2.2%	1.1%	2.4%	1.0%
Opera	.1%	1.8%	.35%	0.8%
other	.9%	1.7%	.4%	.1%
unidentified	9.4%	3.3%	4.6%	11%

Of course, visitors to your site are not restricted to Windows, so there may be other browsers not available on a Windows platform.

From this Web site you can connect to Web sites for the individual browser products and download the ones that you want to use to check out your Web site.

95% of visitors may be expected to use Internet Explorer or Netscape Navigator. Even then, you need to allow for the range from versions 3–6 currently available for each of these products.

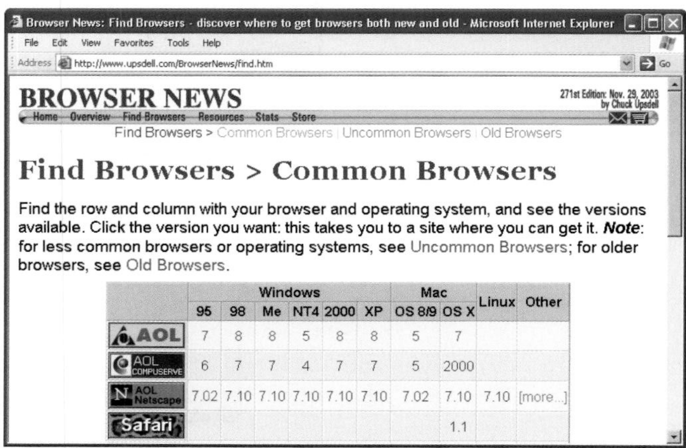

	Windows						Mac		Linux	Other
	95	98	Me	NT4	2000	XP	OS 8/9	OS X		
AOL	7	8	8	5	8	8	5	7		
AOL CompuServe	6	7	7	4	7	7	5	2000		
AOL Netscape	7.02	7.10	7.10	7.10	7.10	7.10	7.02	7.10	7.10	[more...]
Safari								1.1		

Use extra browsers

You can't dictate the resources that your visitors will have available, but you can avoid conflicts or at least warn visitors of potential mismatches.

You can obtain copies of most browsers from the Internet. For details of the three main browsers, visit the following Web sites:

- http://channels.netscape.com/ns/browsers/
- http://www.opera.com/pressreleases/
- http://www.microsoft.com/windows/ie/default.htm

To use an extra browser:

1. Open a page in your Web site, and select File, Preview in Browser.

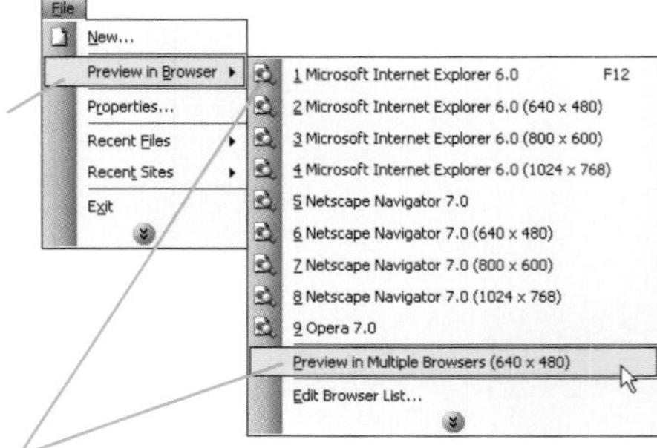

Your choice of screen size and browser will become the defaults (as used by the Preview in Browser button) until you select different settings.

2. Select the browser and screen size combination, or click Preview in Multiple Browsers.

There's a preview in multiple browsers for each screen size and, as with the single preview, the last size used becomes the default.

Review the Web site

View all the pages in your Web site. Note any items that fail to operate as expected. Repeat the checks with other browsers. If there are browser-based limitations, you can modify the items, or add a suitable caution to the page.

1 Open the Home Page, select File, Preview in Browser and pick the window size you use as your preferred size e.g. 800 x 600.

2 Click on the Navigation bar to change Web pages. For example, select Links, then Sports Pictures.

You would switch back to FrontPage to center the Photo Gallery and delete the blank line above the thumbnail images.

3 Observe the layout and note problems. For example, you may decide that photo thumbnails should be centered on the page.

When you make any changes in FrontPage, Save the page, and press Reload or Refresh to see the effect in your browser.

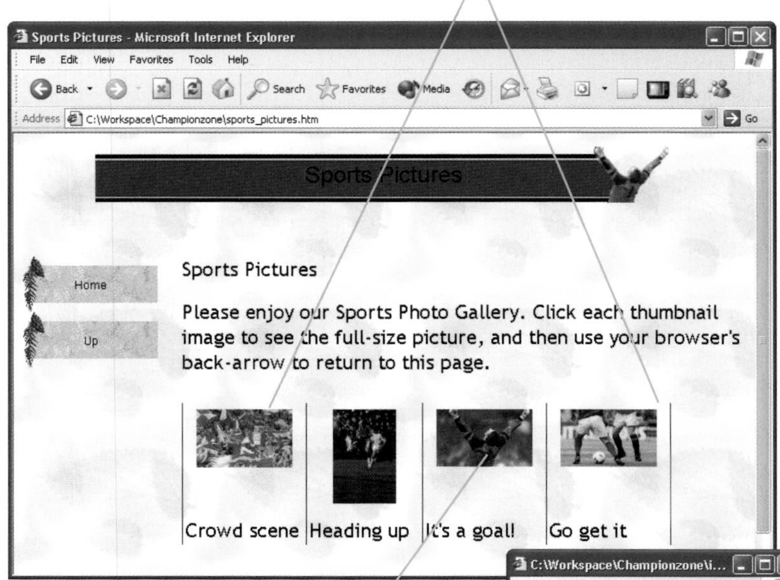

4 Click on a Thumbnail to display a photograph full size. Click the Back button to return to the main Sports Pictures Web page.

Modify text

You can make global changes to the Web site if there are terms that you use on several Web pages, and you decide they need adjusting.

You can make a change to selected pages or all pages in the Web site, but you can only replace text in parts of the page that can be edited directly. Text in page titles must be modified individually.

To modify a section of text:

1. From any view, select Edit, Replace. Choose All pages, and enter the current and new text values.

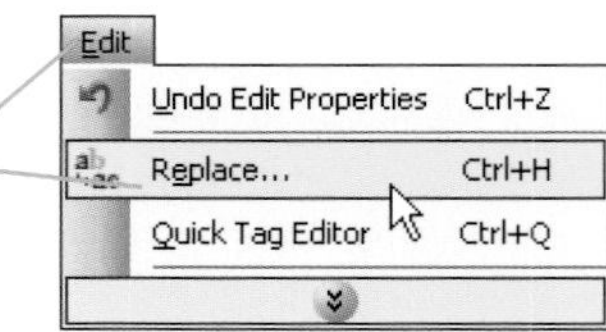

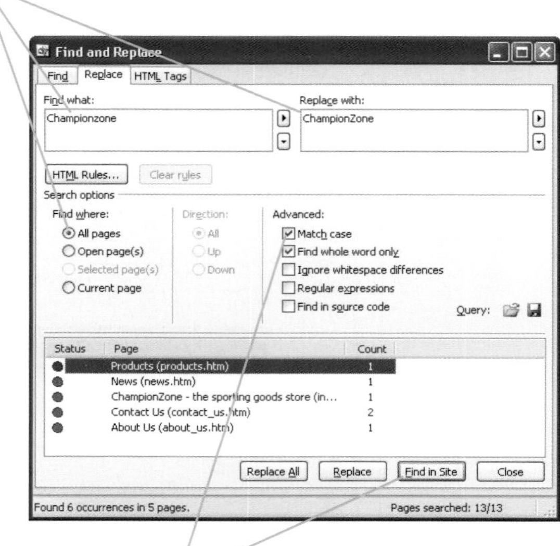

You can skip individual pages where you are sure that changes to the text would not be appropriate.

2. Set Match case or Find whole word only if needed and press Find In Site. Double-click the first entry to open the relevant page.

If the changes definitely apply to all the entries on the page, you can complete all the replacement operations in one step by pressing Replace All.

3. Apply changes to the current page. Click Find Next to skip a change, or Replace to change and find next.

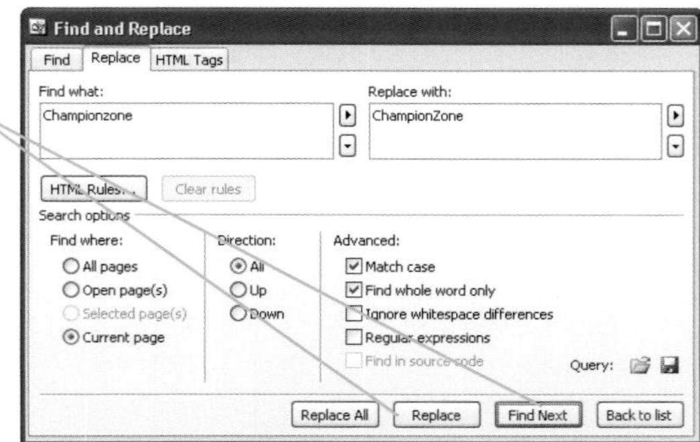

4 When each page is finished, you are prompted to save and close the current document and move on to apply the changes to the next page.

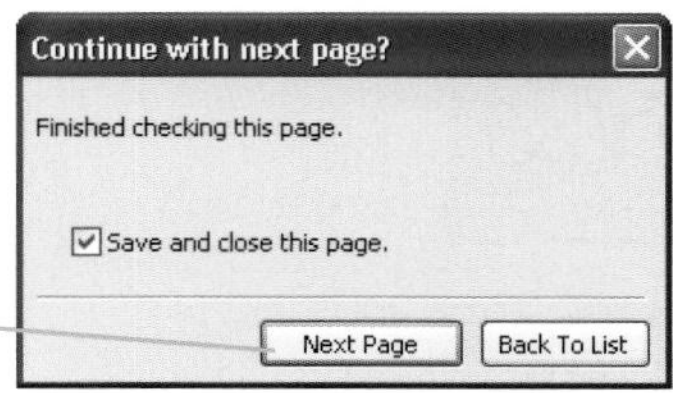

5 If you press Replace All to change all the occurrences on the page, you are told how many matches were found and replaced.

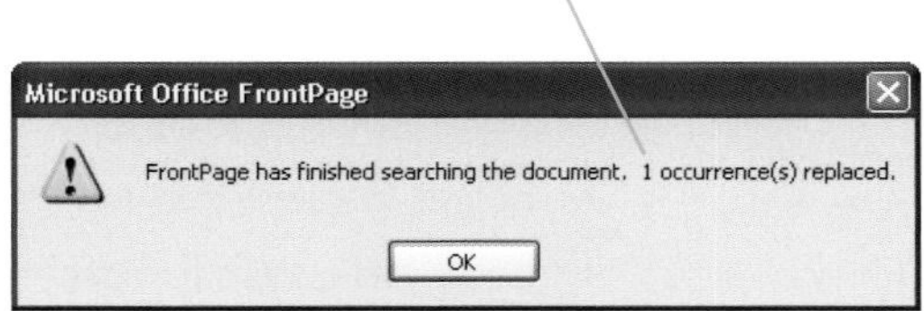

FrontPage 2000 featured an Add Task button which allowed you to add the Replace operations to the Task list. This option is not available in FrontPage 2003.

6 When the final page is completed, you are prompted to save and close the last document.

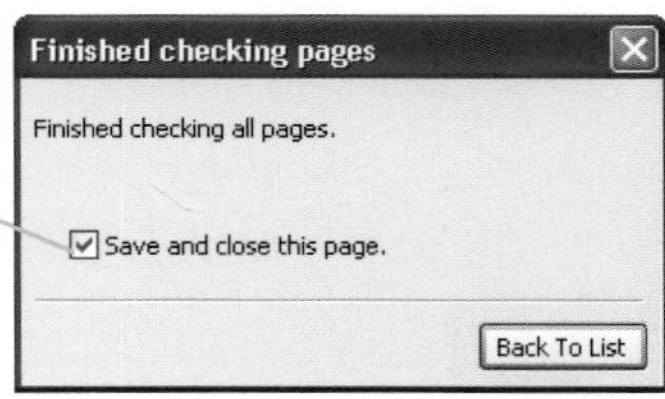

When you have finished the Replace operation, the report shows which pages have been edited and the count of changes.

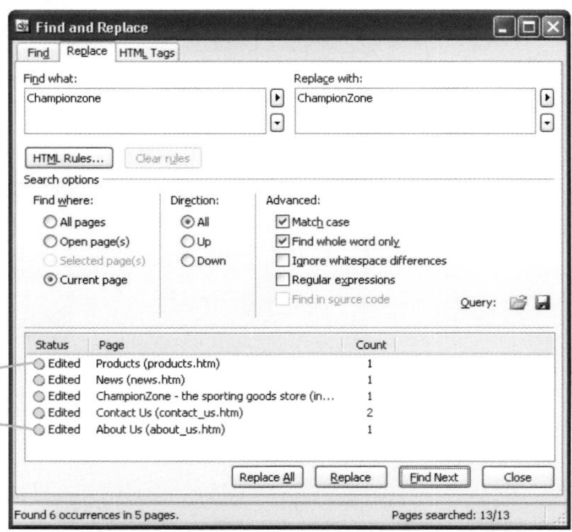

Check spelling

Before you can consider your Web site complete, you need to check the spelling (and typing) on the Web pages and related text elements.

Background spell-checking will identify possible spelling errors with underlines. You can retype the words or use the spell checker to correct them, as you build the individual pages. However, you should also make it a practice to carry out a full spell check of all the Web pages, just before you are ready to publish the Web site.

To check the spelling for the entire site:

1. From any view except Page press the Spell Check button or click Tools, Spelling.

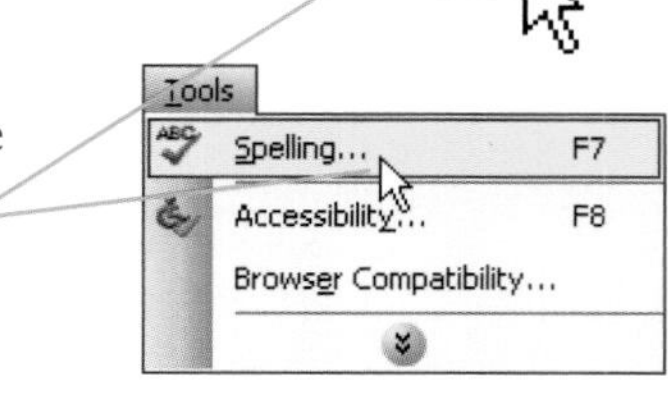

In Page view, you can check only the current open page. Global checking is not offered.

2. Select Entire Web site and Add a task for each page with misspellings, and click Start.

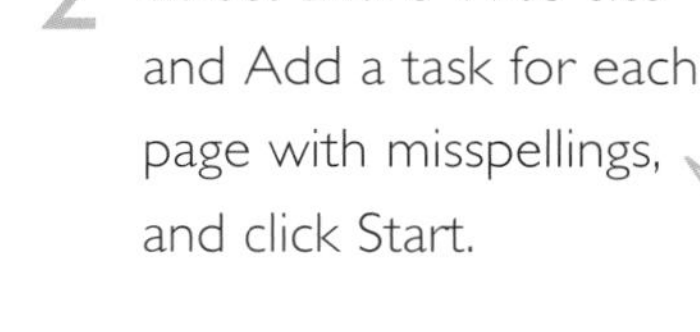

FrontPage will analyze the text and will display a list of tasks for all the problems identified.

Text on items such as page titles in page banners will not be included in the check and must be checked in the Page edit view.

3. Click Start, and the spelling tasks will be initiated.

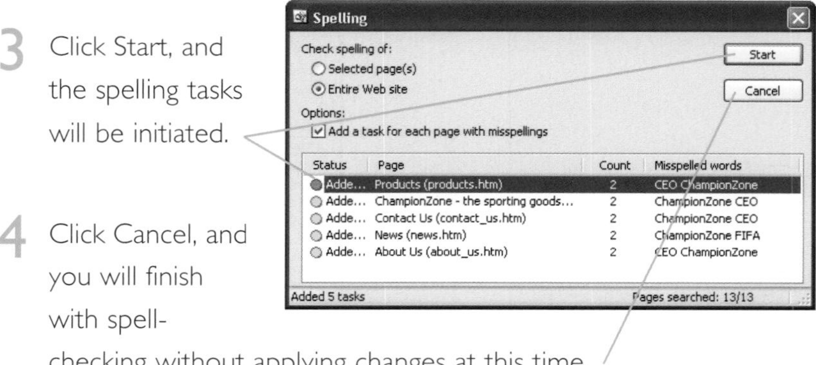

4. Click Cancel, and you will finish with spell-checking without applying changes at this time.

When you Cancel the spelling activity, the change instructions will already be added to the task list, so they can be processed later.

The Tasks mechanism makes it possible for several people to check a large Web site, and then have all the tasks completed at one time. This reduces the possibility of multiple concurrent changes that could cause some changes to be lost or overridden.

5 To display the list of Tasks, select View, Tasks from the taskbar, or click the Tasks tab on the Web Site view.

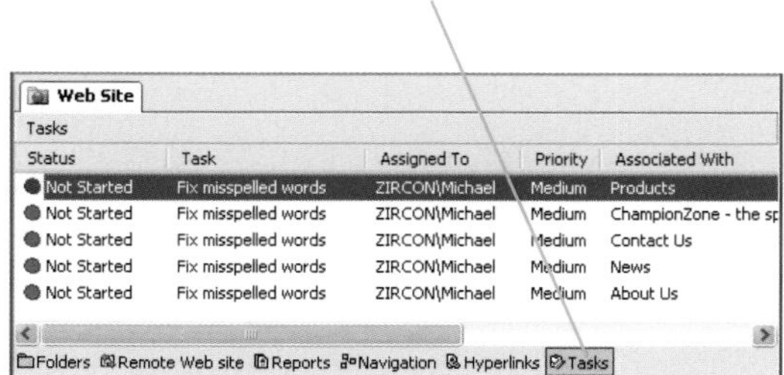

The details of the selected task are shown. You can change the task name, set the priority or assign it to someone else in your group. Click OK to save changes.

6 Double-click a task on the list, or right-click the task and select Edit Task in the menu to show details..

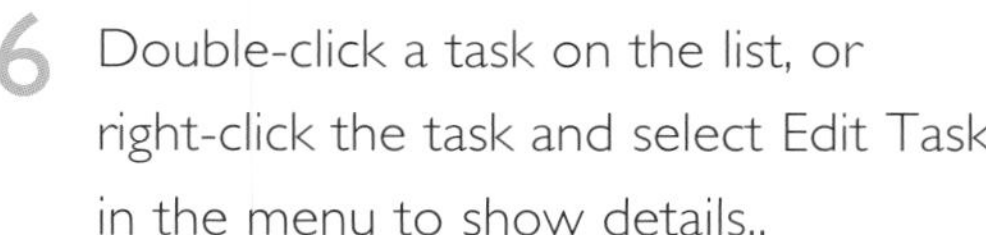

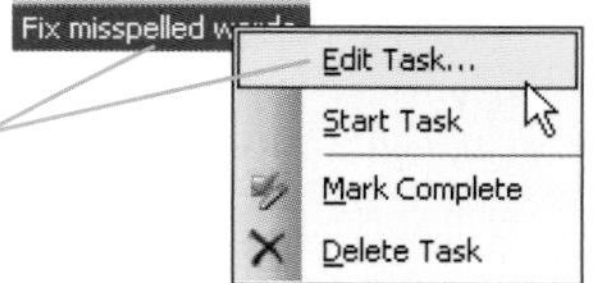

7 Click Start Task to open the page. You could also have selected Start Task from the menu.

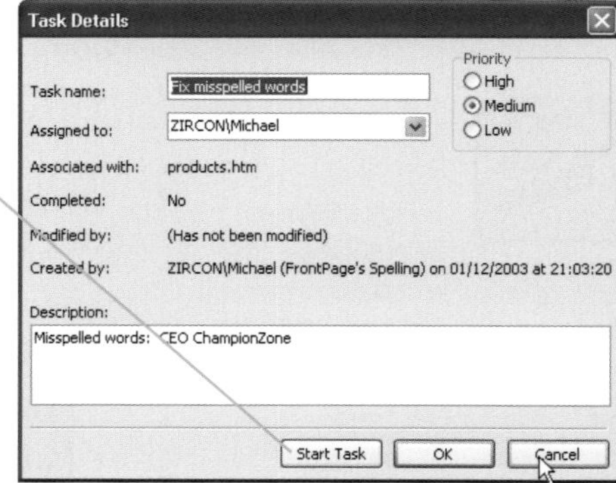

8 Select the correct spelling, and click Change or Change All, or Add a new word to the dictionary.

Additions are made to the custom dictionary used by the other Office applications, so you won't have to add special terms for every application separately.

You can Ignore special terms that are rarely used, to save adding them to the dictionary. Type the replacement word in the Change To box, if the correct spelling doesn't appear in the suggestions.

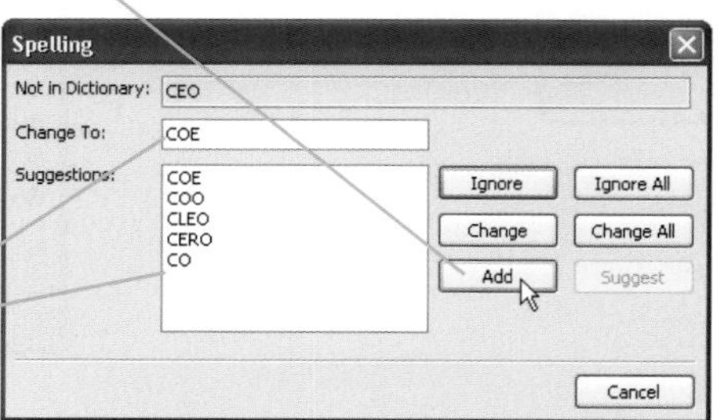

Mark tasks complete

It is best to mark tasks as completed, since they are then removed from the list of outstanding tasks.

1 Click OK when the spelling corrections for a page are completed.

2 Select Save for the page, and you will be prompted to mark that task as completed.

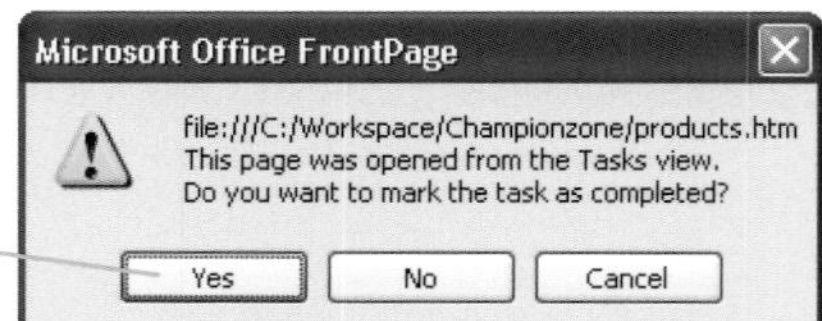

FrontPage recognizes that the Web page was opened from Tasks view and therefore offers to mark the associated task as completed.

3 If you don't update the status of the task when the associated file is saved (or if no Save was needed), you can right-click the task and select Mark Complete, at a later time.

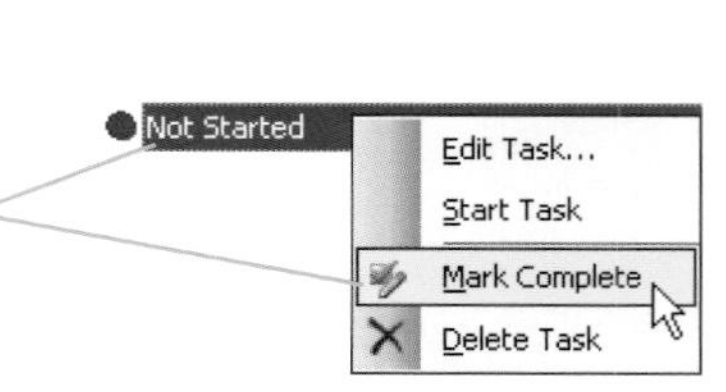

If words are added during one task, there's no need to take action if they were selected in succeeding tasks, since the revised spelling will be accepted automatically.

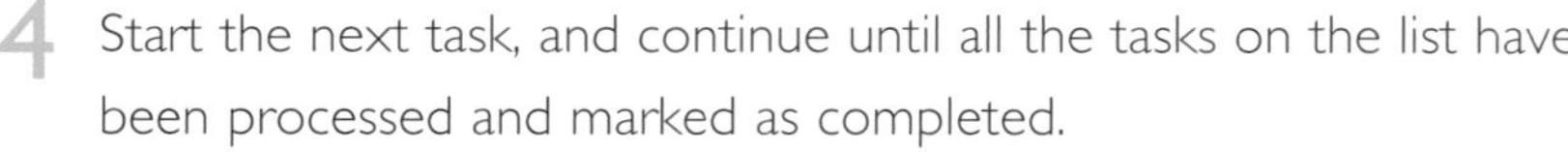

4 Start the next task, and continue until all the tasks on the list have been processed and marked as completed.

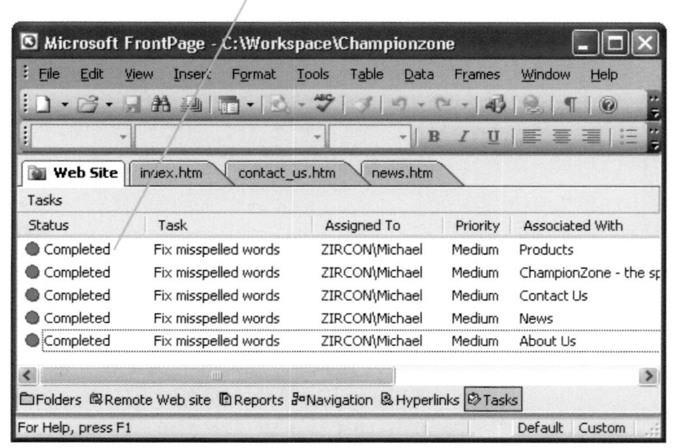

The next time you open the Web site, you'll find that the completed entries will no longer appear. FrontPage by default hides completed tasks (see page 85).

Create new tasks

You can use the Tasks list to record the need for any type of activity. For example, you could assign a research task to an individual in your group, and log the task in the list. When the research report has been produced, mark the task as completed.

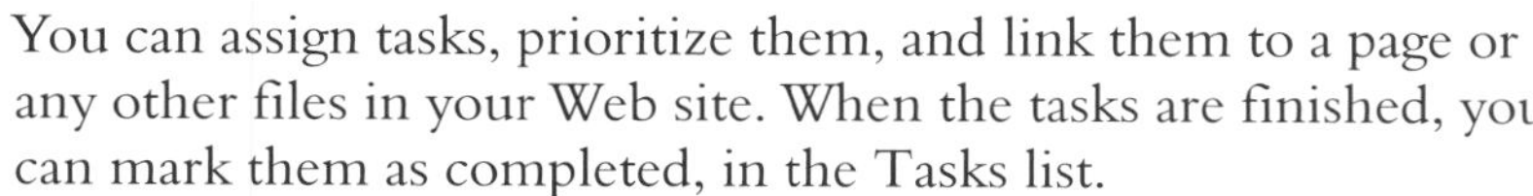

You can assign tasks, prioritize them, and link them to a page or any other files in your Web site. When the tasks are finished, you can mark them as completed, in the Tasks list.

To create a task:

1. Open the Web site, press the down arrow next to the New button, and select Task.

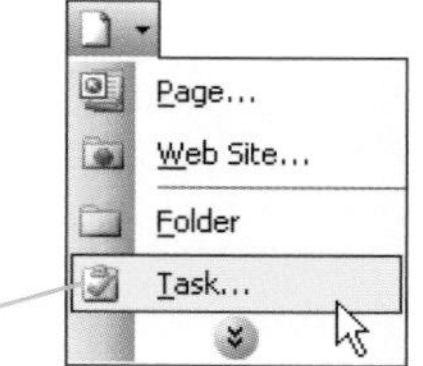

2. Enter the details for the task, including the name, the person it is assigned to, the priority and the description, and then press OK.

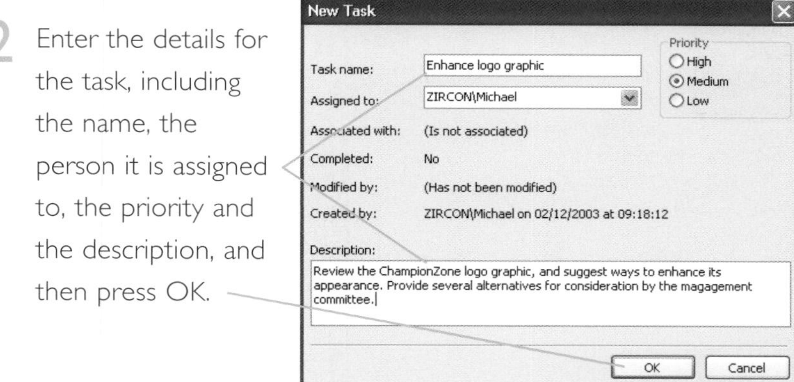

The Assigned To name is pre-filled with the system and user name from the PC. This can be changed to any name – it does not have to show the machine name. FrontPage remembers the names you enter, so next time, you can click the down arrow and select from the list.

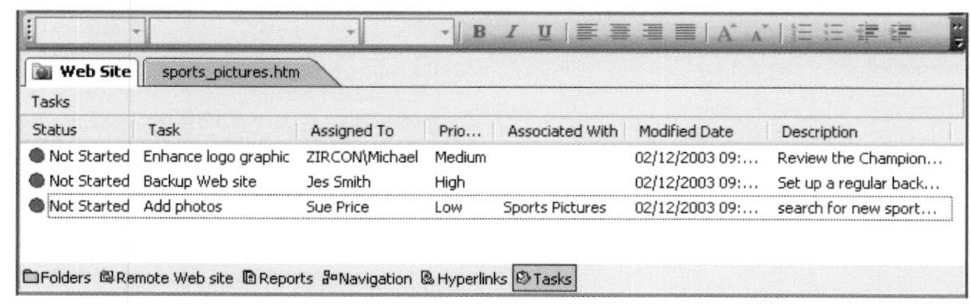

If you create a task in Page view while editing a page, the task is automatically associated with that page. To associate a task with a page or file in another view, select the file, and then create the task. If no pages are open, the task will carry no file association.

When completed, tasks are normally hidden, but you can choose to display them if you wish.

3. Right-click the background in Tasks view and click Show History to toggle the display on or off.

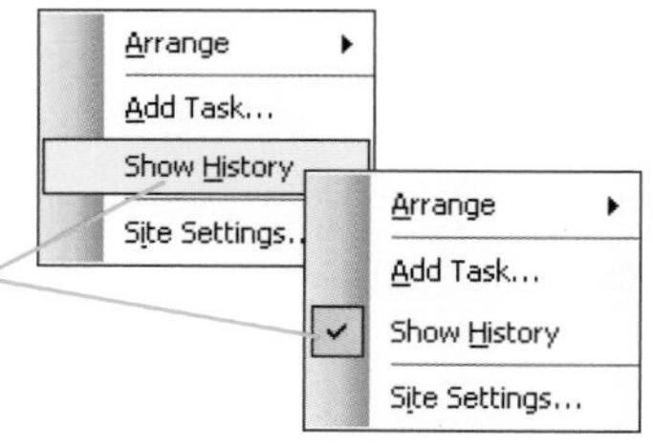

Web reports

FrontPage provides reports to help you identify any problems with your Web site, before you send the files or the updates to the Web server.

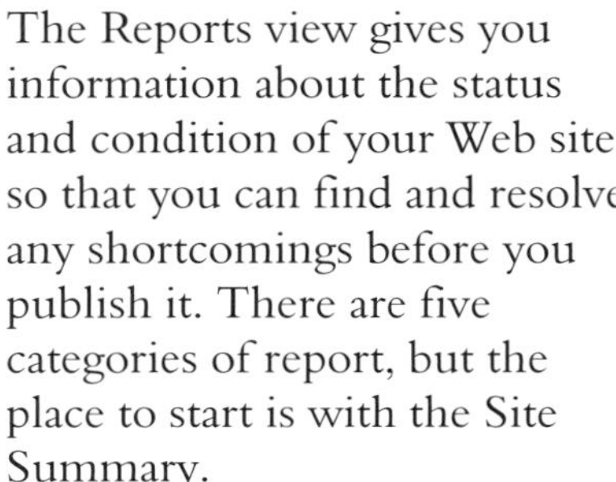

The Reports view gives you information about the status and condition of your Web site, so that you can find and resolve any shortcomings before you publish it. There are five categories of report, but the place to start is with the Site Summary.

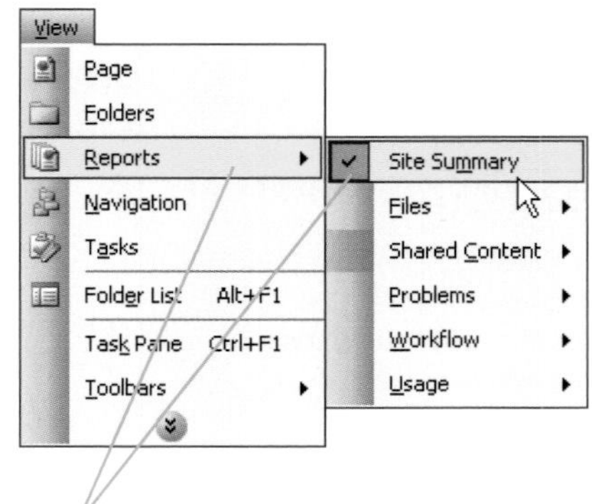

If you'd like to see a different report displayed when you click the Reports view, select Views, Reports and choose the category and the report you want.

1 Open the Web site, and select View, Reports, Site Summary. This becomes the default report.

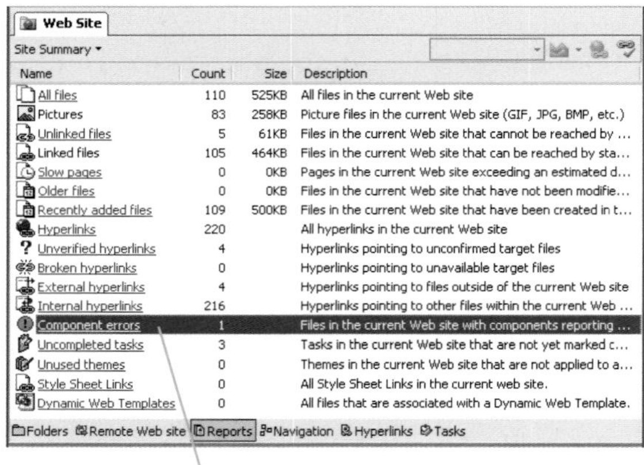

The "Site Summary" gives you an overview of the Web site. "All files" tells you the disk space you will require at the Web server. "Slow pages" warns of any pages that may be a problem during download, and the various hyperlink reports tell you if there are any issues with links.

2 Click the link on a report line to see more details. For example, click Component errors to show the list of files reporting errors.

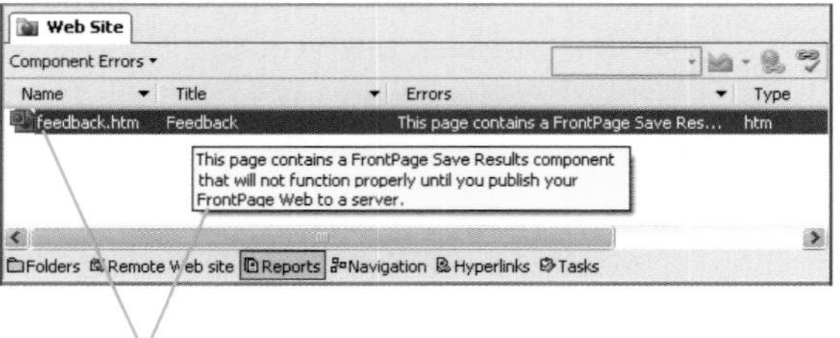

This is a warning message, to remind you about server extensions.

If you rename or relocate files using the Folders view, the integrity of URLs will be maintained. Using normal Windows commands will invalidate the URL references.

The Broken Hyperlinks report will alert you to any errors in hyperlinks. These could be due to mistyping of URLs, or to changes in file names or locations made after the URL was set up.

For the detailed list of the broken hyperlinks in the Web site:

3 Click any one of the hyperlink summary lines, to display the Hyperlink report.

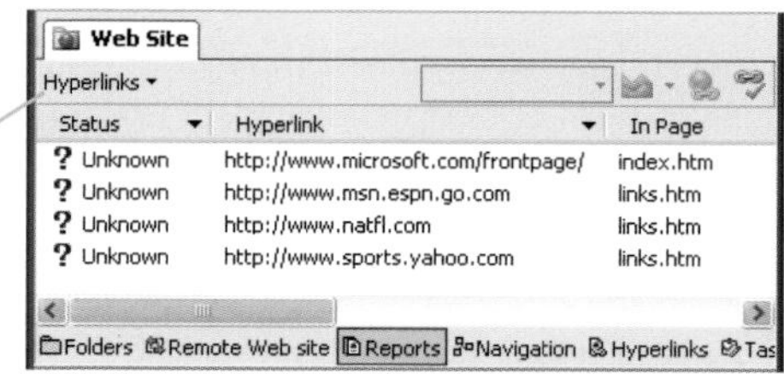

Any invalid hyperlinks are displayed. FrontPage will also list the unverified external hyperlinks, and will verify them for you.

4 Click Yes to verify the hyperlinks, if you are connected, or click the Verify Hyperlink button on the Reports toolbar later.

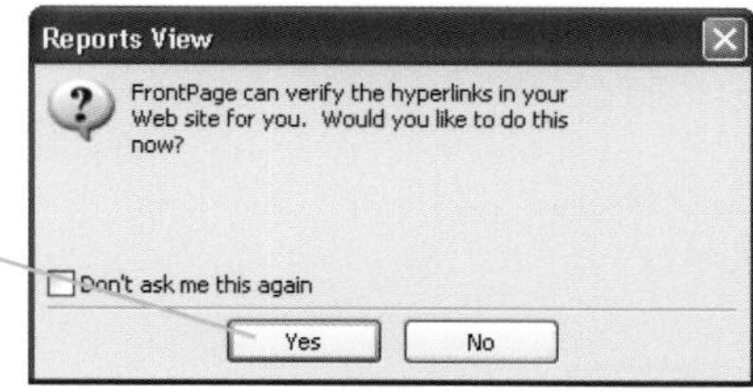

If there are many external hyperlinks in the Web site, it may take some time to carry out this command, since FrontPage must connect to each external Web site to verify the hyperlink.

5 FrontPage connects to the Internet to check out the links.

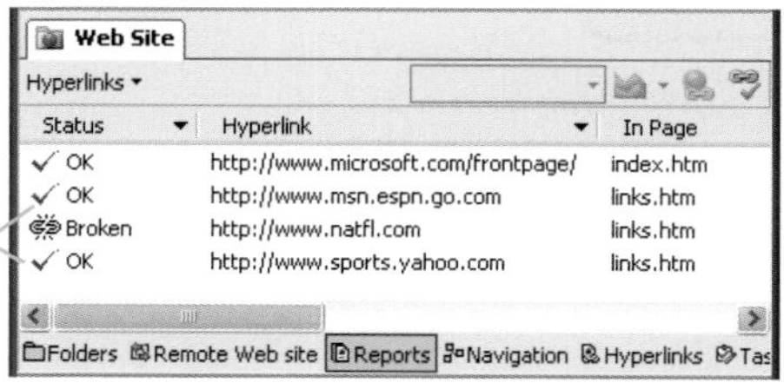

6 Right-click a hyperlink and choose Edit Hyperlink or Edit Page, to correct any errors in the hyperlink addresses specified.

7 Click the toggle Show Internal Hyperlinks to see the full list of hyperlinks, internal and external. Click again to hide the Internal links.

Backup the Web site

When you have checked your Web site and corrected any errors, you should make a backup copy before publishing.

You can make a backup copy of all the files and folders in the Web site. However, the preferred way is to publish the Web site to a folder on your hard disk. This ensures that all necessary files are saved, in the correct structure.

To publish the Web site for backup:

1. Open the Web site, select the Web Site tab and then the Remote Web site tab. Click Remote Web Site Properties.

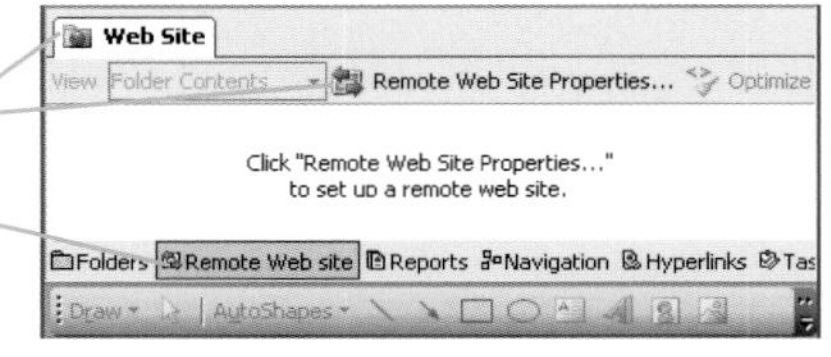

FrontPage refers to the original Web site as Local and the destination Web site as Remote, even if they are both on the same hard disk.

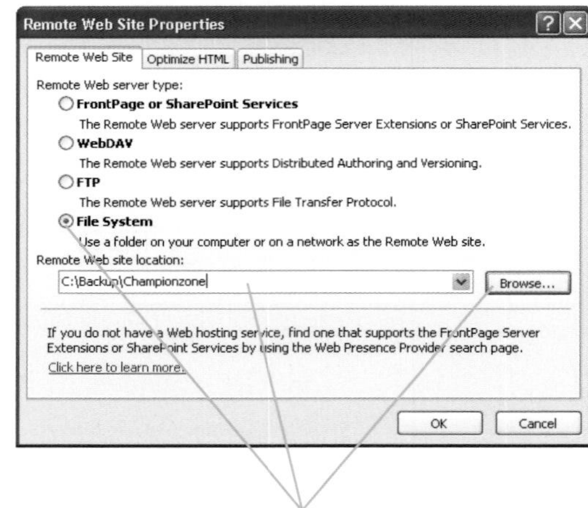

2. Click File System to use a folder as the remote Web site, then Browse to locate the backup folder on your hard disk (or on a networked drive). Select the folder to hold the Web site copy.

You must create a new empty folder in the backup location, ready to receive the Web site, the first time you make a backup.

3. Click OK to publish. If this is a new folder, FrontPage will create a Web site structure within it, ready for publishing.

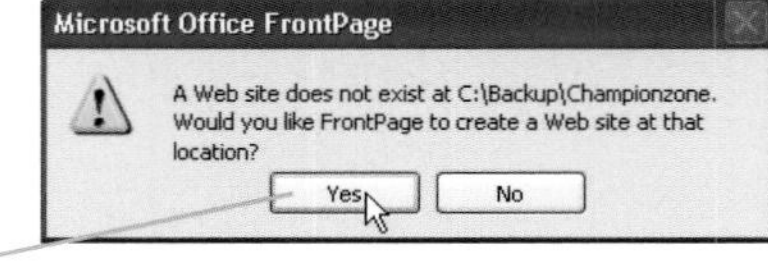

On the first backup, all files and folders will be copied, unless you mark some as not for publication.

4 Right click any files that you do not want transferred, and click Don't Publish. Select Local to remote.

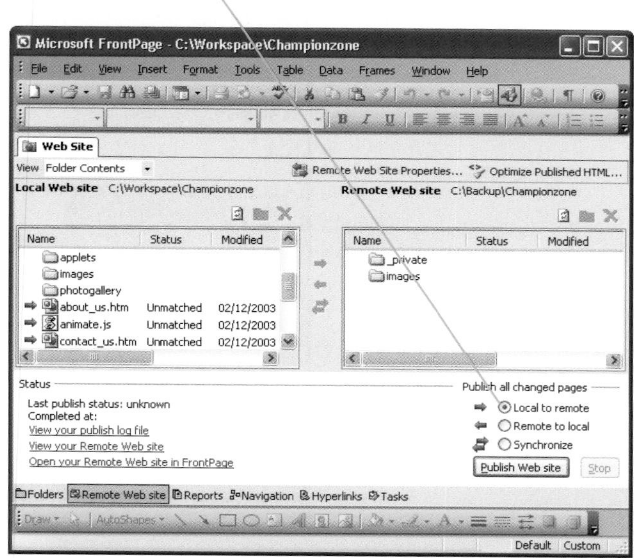

5 Click Publish Web site, and FrontPage transfers the files and folders of your Web site to the specified destination.

If you press Stop to cancel publishing in the middle of the operation, files that have already been published remain at the destination.

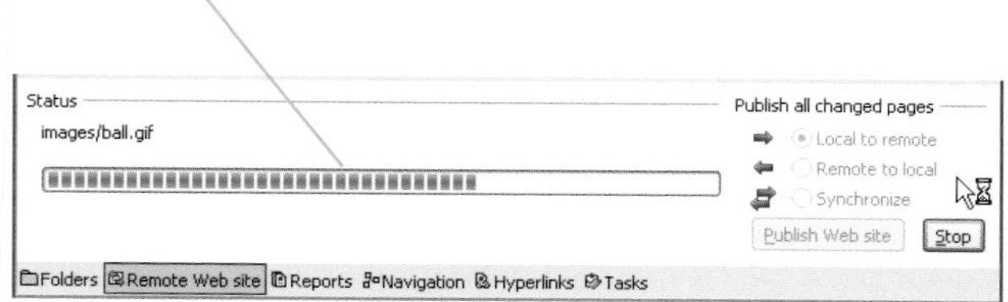

6 FrontPage identifies files that have special requirements such as SharePoint Services, or Server Extensions.

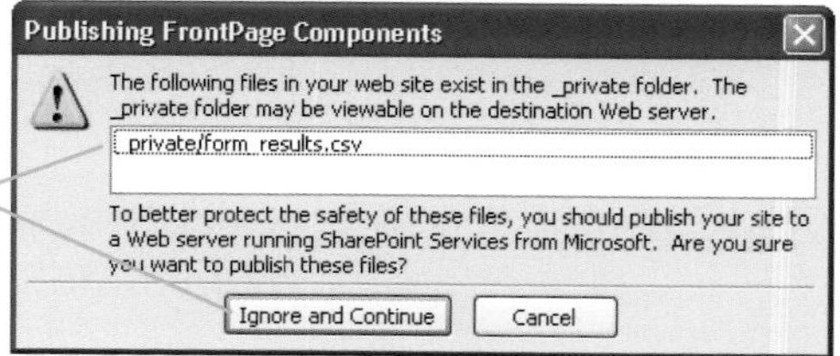

FrontPage identifies which files have been updated since the last backup and marks them for publication. The first time, all the files will be selected.

When the transfer completes, the Remote Web Site Properties are re-displayed, and show that the two sites are now completely in sync with one another.

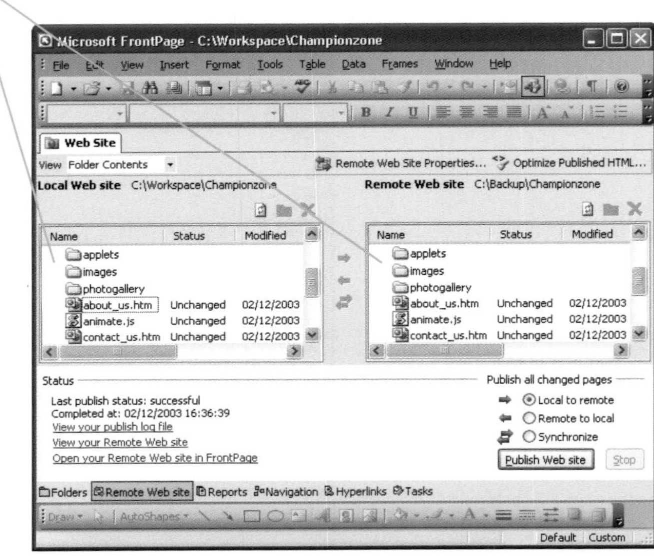

You can restore the backup version from here, by selecting Remote to Local then clicking Publish Web site.

If you make changes to the local copy of the Web site, and then re-display the Remote Web Site Properties, the files that have changed are identified. Click Publish Web Site to transfer just the changed files to the backup location.

Click View your Remote Web site to work with the files and folders in Windows Explorer, or click Open your Remote Web Site in FrontPage.

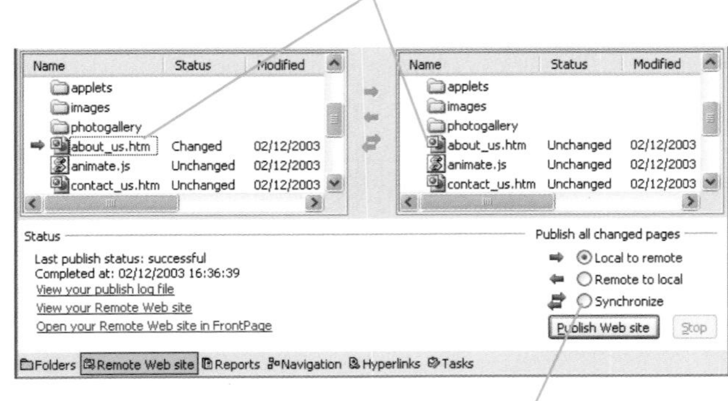

Click Synchronize to bring the two copies into line, if changes have been made at the two locations.

Publishing the Web site

When you have all the components, and you have checked all the links, you can finally transfer the Web site to the Internet. The process depends on the type of ISP or WPP you are planning to use.

Covers

Chapter Six

Ways to publish

Your ISP provides the connection to the Internet and usually provides your email accounts also. Your WPP (Web Presence Provider) provides the Web site space and the tools you require to build and maintain your Web site.

When you are ready to display your Web site on the Internet or on your company Intranet, you must publish your Web site, which means copying all the files and folders in your Web site to a Web server, where visitors can browse. You should already have checked for broken hyperlinks (see page 87), and verified that the pages look the way you expect.

To publish to the Internet, you need a WPP, preferably one offering a Web server with FrontPage Server Extensions or Microsoft SharePoint Team Services installed. You also need the Web server location, and your user name and password.

SharePoint Team Services from Microsoft is a team Web site solution included with FrontPage 2003. You use it to create workspaces to manage group activities.

FrontPage Server Extensions

The server extensions are not essential, but they give your Web site the full FrontPage functionality, such as form handlers, search forms, hit counters, and component features. FrontPage will maintain your files and hyperlinks. Each time you publish the Web site, FrontPage compares the files on your local computer to the files on the Web server. If you move a file in your Web site on the hard disk, FrontPage will update and correct any hyperlinks to it, and then make the same corrections to the Web server files, the next time you publish the Web site.

You can also edit the Web site directly on the Web server, although in that case the hard disk version will not stay in sync.

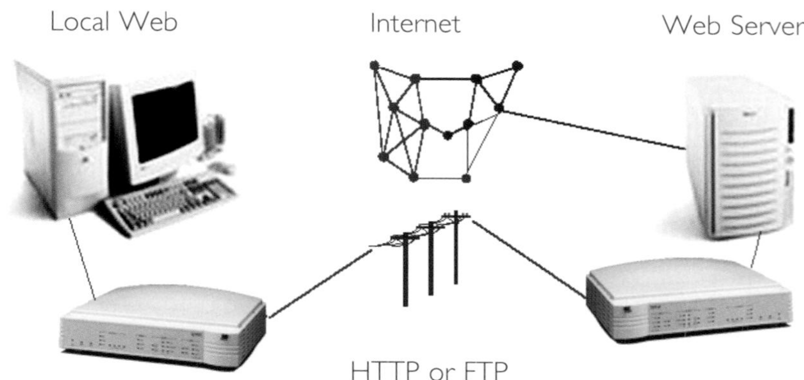

HTTP or FTP

The server extensions also influence the way you publish the Web site. If your Web server has the extensions, then FrontPage can publish using HTTP (Hypertext Transfer Protocol). Otherwise, it publishes your Web site using FTP (File Transfer Protocol).

Domain names

Sometimes the account name is combined with the server name, to create the URL. For example, account Maprice at Hypermart.net would have the address: http://maprice.hypermart.net/

It may be less expensive to use a service that specializes in domain name registration. For example, the domain FPineasysteps.com was registered at GoDaddy.com, and later transferred to the WPP InterKey.net.

You will find that many of the usual names are already taken, and you may have to try a number of options before finding a name that is not yet in use. Not all endings need be free for you to use a name, as long as the ending you want is still available.

The process may take two or three days to complete and make the URLs addressable.

The WPP will provide you with an account name that you can use as a subdomain name to specify the address for your Web site. For example, with FreeWebs.com and the account Maprice, you'd address your Web site as: http://www.freewebs.com/maprice/.

If you want a full domain name such as maprice.com, so that you can address your Web site as: http://www.maprice.com/, you need to register the domain name and pay an annual fee. You can use your WPP or ISP to register the name.

To register a domain at FreeWebs.com

1. Open the domain registration part of the site, http://domains.freewebs.com to check your desired domain name.

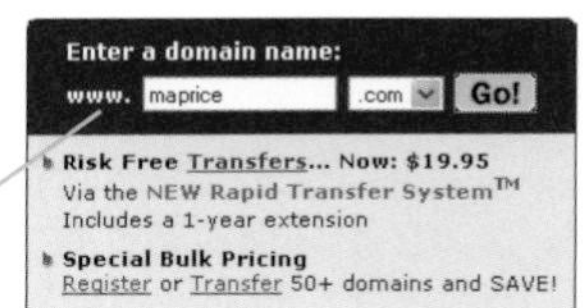

2. When you've found an available name, select the domain types you want, for example .COM or .US.

3. Click the Smart Registration button, provide your details and complete the purchase of your domain.

Select a WPP

If your ISP does not provide the required Web site services, use Thelist.com (see page 11) to search for a suitable WPP.

1 Click Personal Hosts, specify the type of service you want (e.g. a free service with domain name registration and FrontPage support), and click Find Hosts.

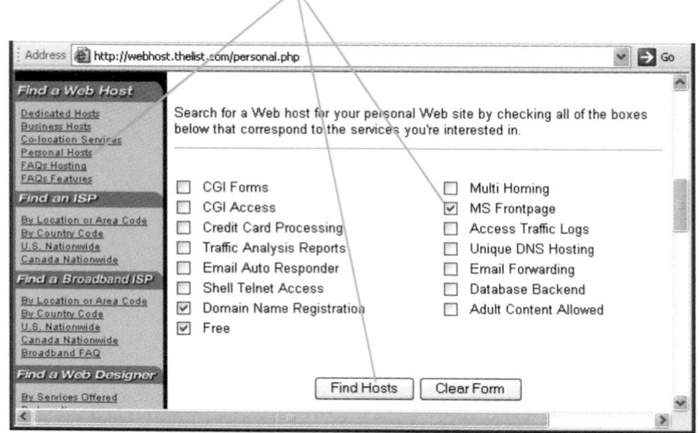

FreeWebs.com for example offer design services, CGI forms, message boards, credit card processing, traffic analysis reports, email forwarding and daily site backups, in addition to the services specified in the search. The basic service is free, but you need to subscribe to the premium services for extra facilities.

2 Select one of the entries, such as Freewebs.com, to find details of the other services that are offered.

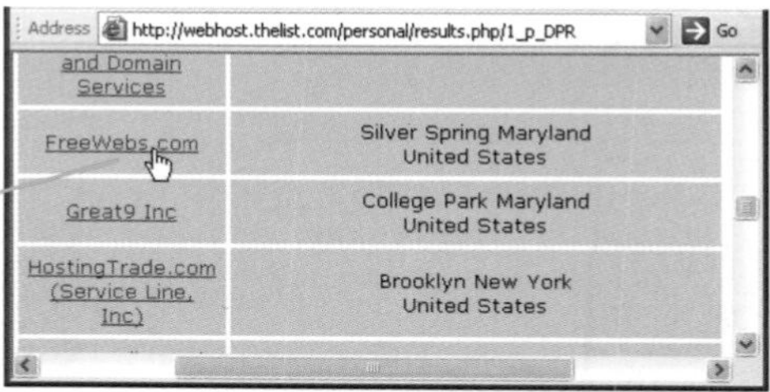

If you want to find a WPP that offers support for FrontPage-enabled Web sites, you'll find help at Microsoft's Web site.

To view the current list:

Don't use the Publish Web button, since this will automatically use the last destination defined, even if that was just for backup to your hard disk (see page 88).

3 Select File, Publish Site and click Remote Web Site Properties. Then select the link to the Web Presence Provider search page.

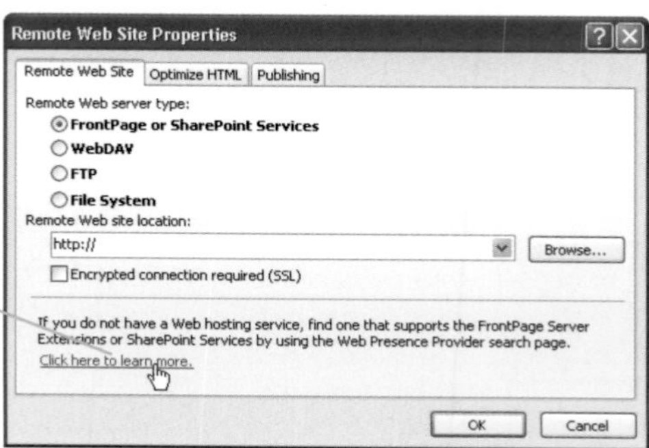

The WPP list was not immediately updated after the release of FrontPage 2003, but the Web site will be updated as suppliers are qualified for the 2003 WPP program.

4 Click the link for one of the registered WPPs that provide support for all features of FrontPage, to get details.

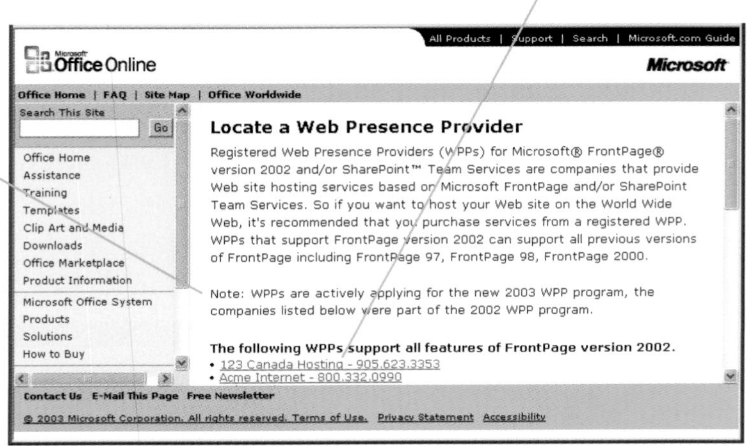

You can fill in the ISP name, the services required or the location to find other WPPs (USA or Canada) which provide support but have not yet been formally tested.

5 For example, you'll find full FrontPage 2003 support, including Server Extensions and SharePoint Team Services at Interkey.net.

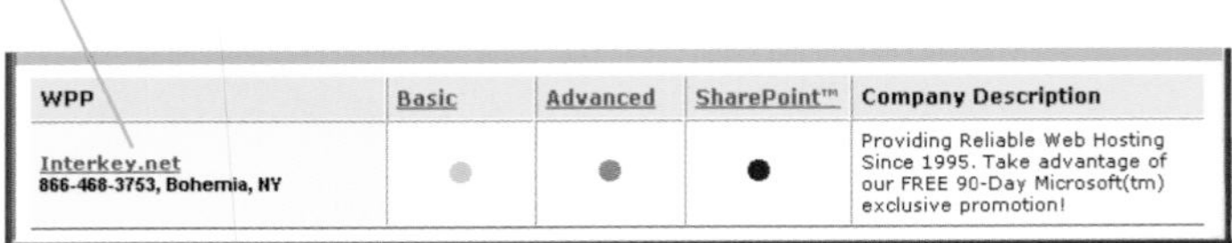

WPP	Basic	Advanced	SharePoint™	Company Description
Interkey.net 866-468-3753, Bohemia, NY	●	●	●	Providing Reliable Web Hosting Since 1995. Take advantage of our FREE 90-Day Microsoft(tm) exclusive promotion!

If you do not find a suitable WPP listed by Microsoft, try searching for other WPPs that support FrontPage-based Web sites, using Google.com for example. They may already be updated to support the current version, even if they are not on Microsoft's list.

6 Not all the available services choose to be listed by Microsoft. For example, Hypermart.net which supports server extensions and provides low cost Web site hosting (and a 30 day free trial), but hasn't been listed.

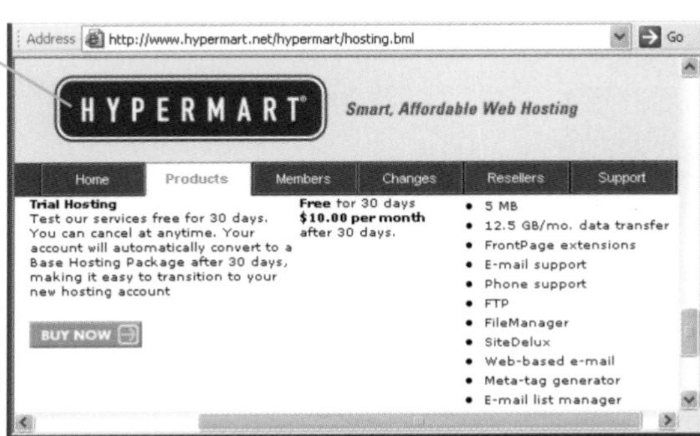

Hypermart.net specialize in Web site hosting and do not provide dial-up support. You can use any Internet Service Provider to give you access to the Internet, and you can manage your Hypermart Web site from that ISP.

Publish with FTP

Although FreeWebs.com has FrontPage support, it is limited to FTP for publishing, since it does not support server extensions.

This is the method to use if your WPP does not have explicit support for FrontPage 2003 server extensions.

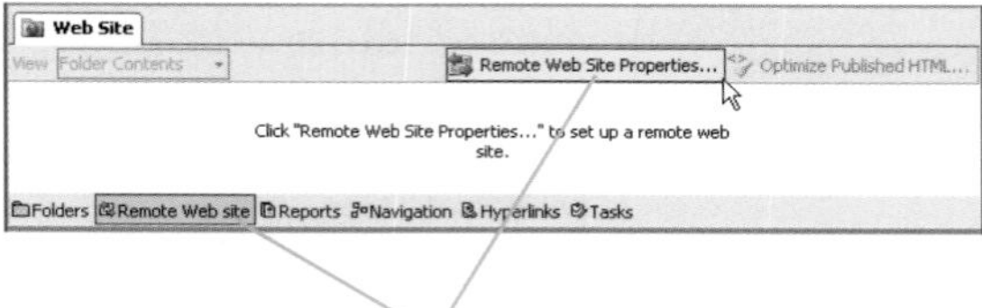

1 Open the Web site, click Remote Web Site and click Remote Web Site Properties.

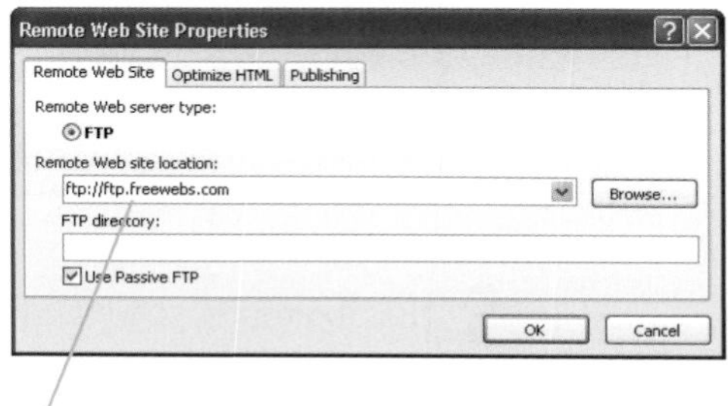

2 Enter the FTP address for the Web server providing the Web site space.

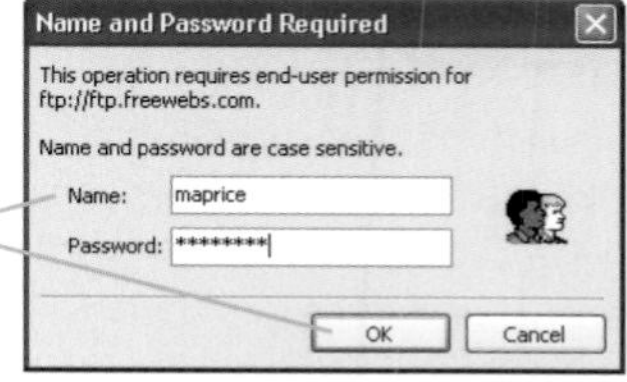

3 Enter the account ID or user name and the password, and then click OK.

4 FrontPage connects to the Internet, and opens the folders in the Web site and identifies which files need updating.

There may be pages already at your Web site, even if it is new. For example, there may be a page called Index.html, created as a placeholder by your ISP.

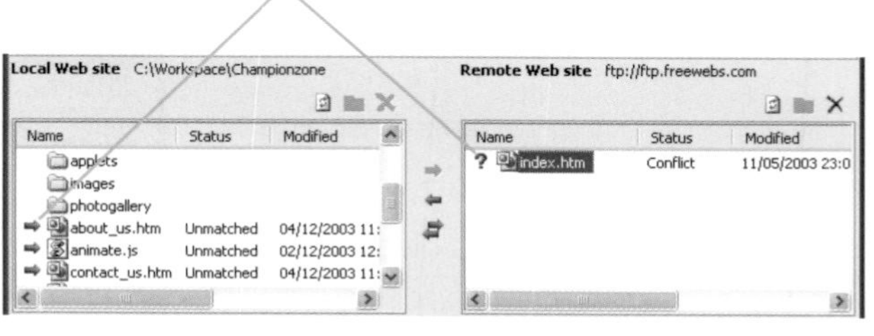

Try asking your WPP (or your network administrator for an Intranet) to install the features. At least they'll then know that there is a demand.

5 Select Local to remote, and click Publish Web Site to transfer the files from the local Web site on the hard disk to the Remote Web site at the Internet server.

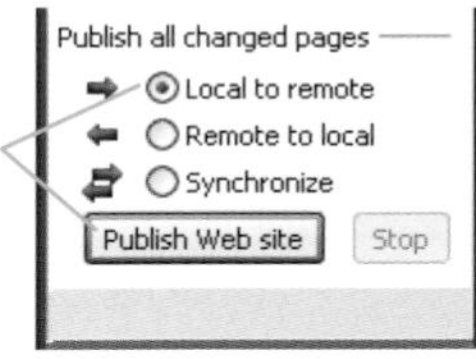

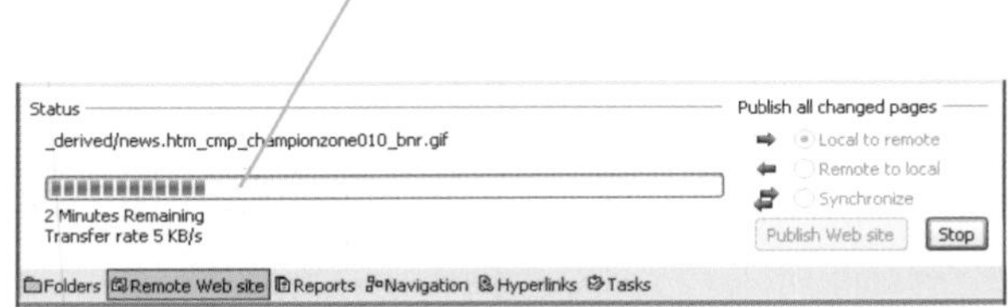

6 FrontPage will detect that the server does not support FrontPage server extensions and warns you of any pages that rely on them.

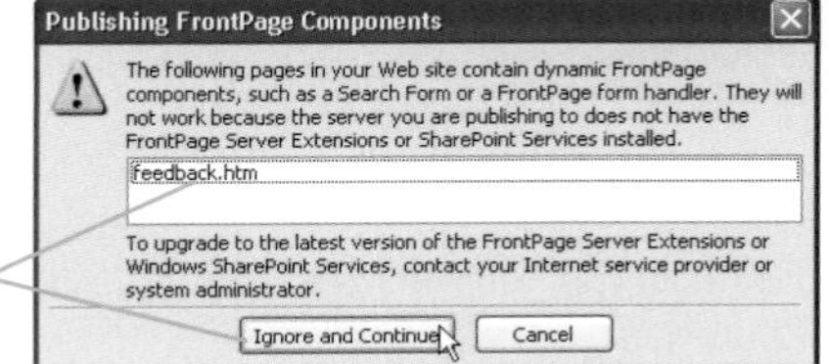

7 When all of the files have been transferred, the Web site status is updated. Note that the FTP transfer may change the date and time stamp on the files, causing FrontPage to detect file conflicts.

Because you have used FTP to publish the site, FrontPage cannot offer the link. Use your domain name, or the subdomain address provided by your ISP to view the Web site (do not use the FTP address).

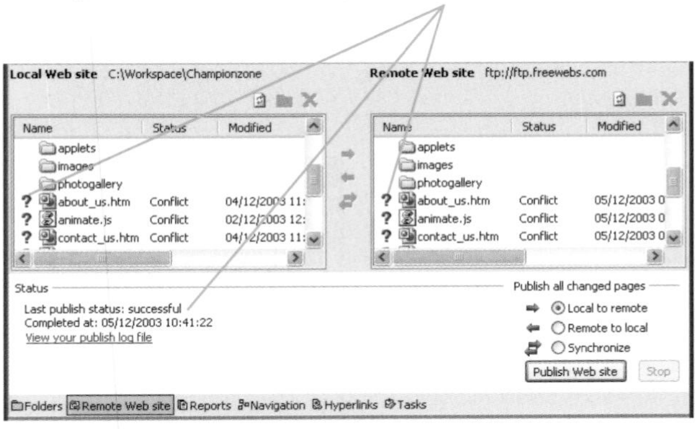

8 Open the browser and enter the URL for the Web site, and check out the hyperlinks.

Try the form

Dynamic features such as FrontPage forms may appear to work but won't complete properly without the server extensions. *See pages 102-103* *to see how the form operates when the server extensions are supported.*

Various Internet sites offer Guest Book facilities that manage responses for you without requiring special functions on your Web server.

Alternatively, you can take advantage of email to get responses.

Re step 2 – you'd need to change the page to use a different method that does not depend on the extensions. For example, insert a MailTo address hyperlink so you can get responses via email.

Feedback

Please give us your comments and suggestions.

Contact the Championzone Webmaster

1 Display the Feedback page. Even without server extensions, your browser will allow you to complete the fields in the form.

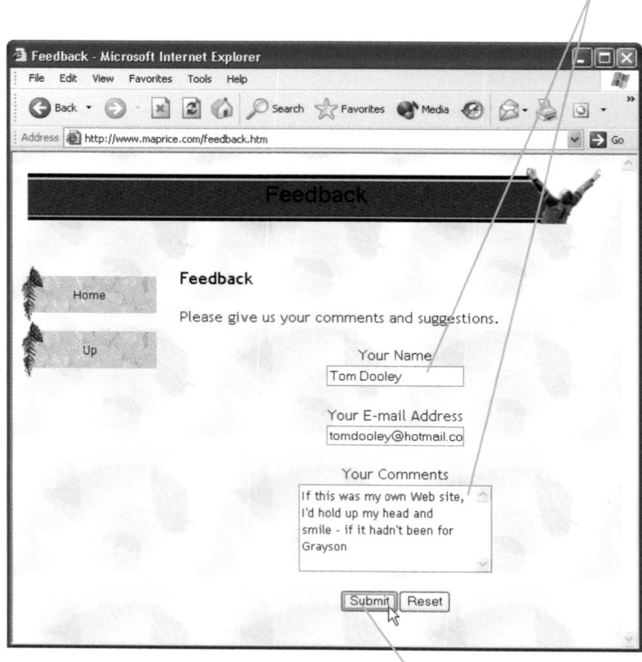

2 However, when you press the Submit button, if there are no server extension to process the form, you get an error message.

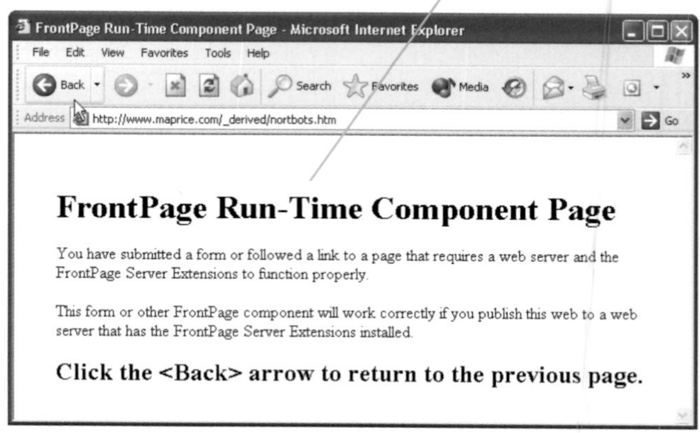

Set up FP Extensions

FrontPage server extensions allow you to use the publication feature and dynamic page elements available in FrontPage.

If your WPP supports the FrontPage server extensions, you can use HTTP for the transfer. In fact this is the recommended method, to keep the Web sites fully in sync. Before you do this however, you must enable the extensions for your Web site. The details may vary between WPPs but the main steps will be similar. For the Hypermart.net hosting service:

Site Tools is the Web-based administration interface which allows you to control all aspects of your Web site hosting account, including security, scripts and FrontPage extensions.

1 Sign on to your account, then in the Members Area, locate the Online Control Panel, and click the link for FrontPage Extensions.

2 Click the Enable button to install the FrontPage Server Extensions on your Web site. They will be activated, after a short delay.

Once you have enabled the FrontPage extensions on your Web site, you will no longer be able to upload your files by FTP. Selecting the option to Disable the Server Extensions will restore FTP access.

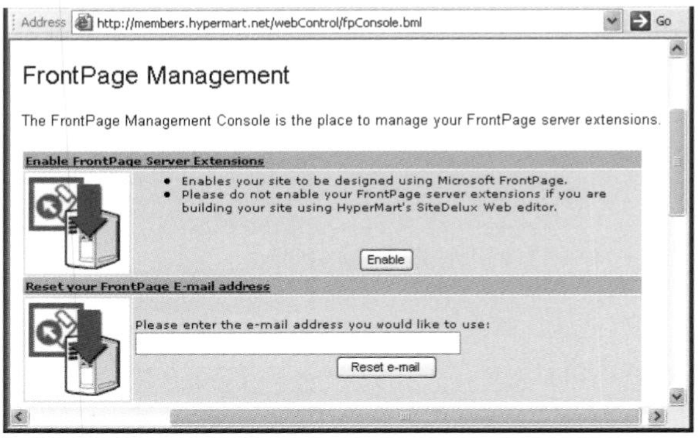

3 From the FrontPage Management Console you will now be able to Tune-Up, Reinstall or Disable the FrontPage server extensions for your Web site.

Publish with HTTP

This is a similar process to publishing with FTP (see page 96), but you use the Internet HTTP protocol rather than the File Transfer Protocol.

1 Open the Web site, click Remote Web Site and click Remote Web Site Properties.

FrontPage checks that the extensions are enabled at the target site, then asks you to sign on.

2 Select FP Services and enter the URL address for your Web site.

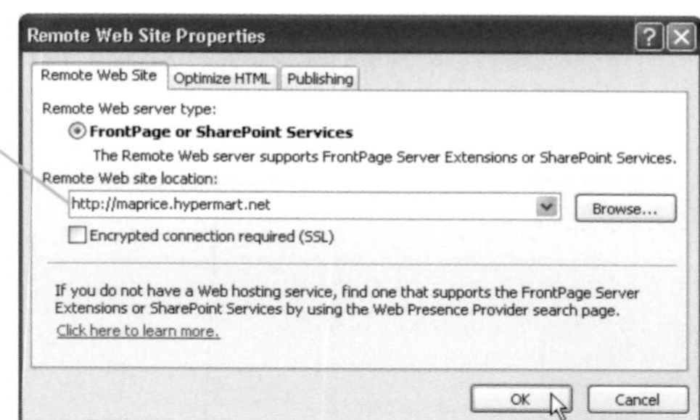

3 Enter the account ID and password for your WPP account, and then click OK.

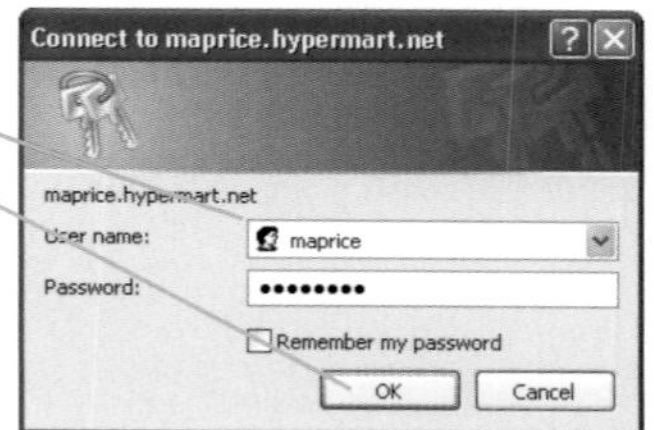

Note that the Web site is shown with Realm: FrontPage Extensions, indicating that these are available on the server, as required to publish the Web site using HTTP.

FrontPage compares the files on the source and the destination, and decides which files need sending to the server.

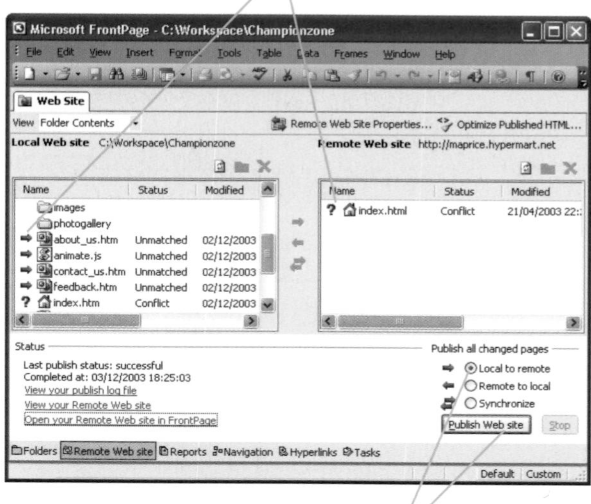

With Options you can choose to send changed files only, comparing the source and destination versions by time stamp or by contents.

4 Select Local to Remote, and click Publish Web Site to transfer the files from the local Web site on the hard disk to the Remote Web site at the Internet server.

5 FrontPage connects to the Web server hosting your site, and transfers copies of all the folders and files of your Web site.

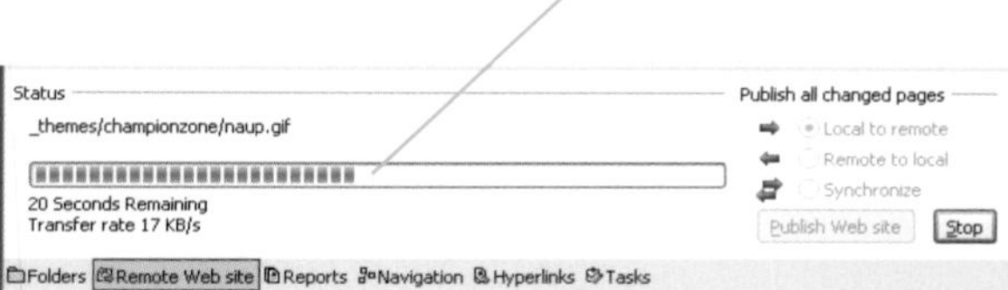

If there are already pages at the Web site, FrontPage checks to see if they have the same names, and warns you before it updates them with newer versions.

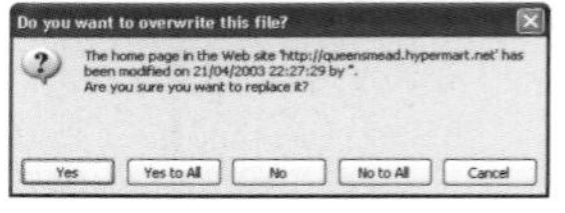

6 Click the link to view your remote Web site in the browser. You can also choose to view the files and folders in FrontPage.

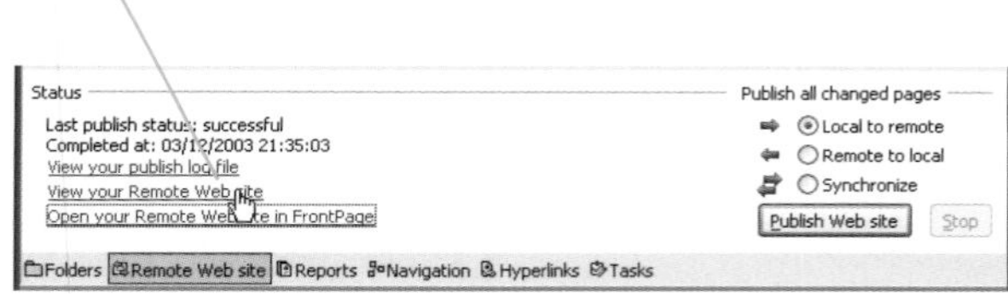

The Home page for your Web site is displayed. When you open the site, all the pages and features of your Web site should operate just as they did with the ISP setup. However, this time you should be able to use the form on the Feedback page to collect observations left by visitors to the site.

There are several caches where copies of your pages may be stored, in addition to the main copy in the Web site space. Some of these copies may not be updated immediately so you may get different results if, for example, you assume the default home page name, or if you explicitly say Index.htm. These copies will be synchronized after a few hours or so.

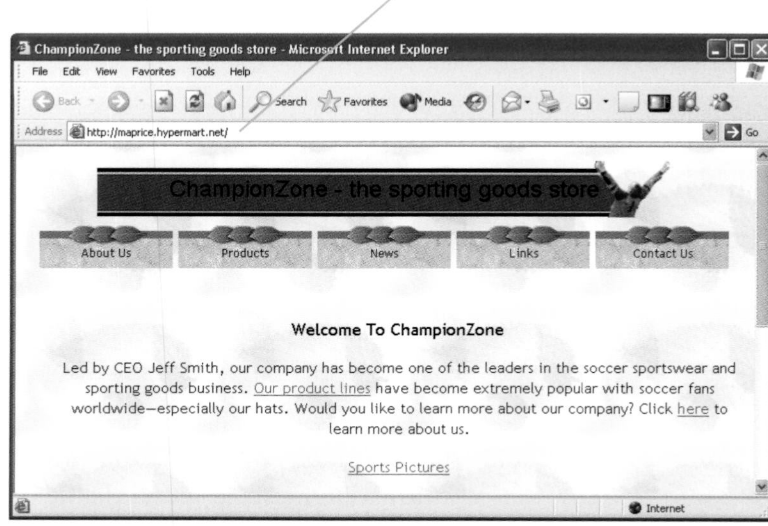

WPP form

If the WPP supports FrontPage extensions, and you have enabled the feature, the dynamic features such as FrontPage forms will now operate correctly.

1 Click the Feedback button on the Contact Us page to display the FrontPage form.

2 Click in the first box and type your name. Press Tab and enter your email address, press Tab again and put your comments.

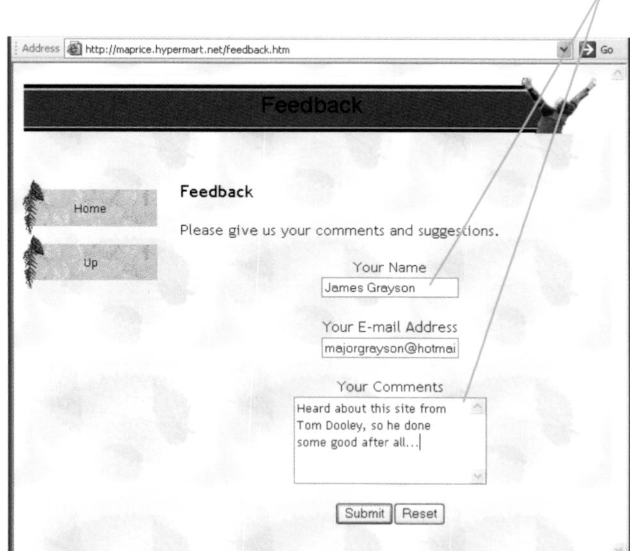

The form contents are written to a file in the Web site (see page 103 opposite).

The message can be made as long as the user scrolls to accommodate the extra text.

3 Remember you can create as long a message as you want, using the scrolling text box.

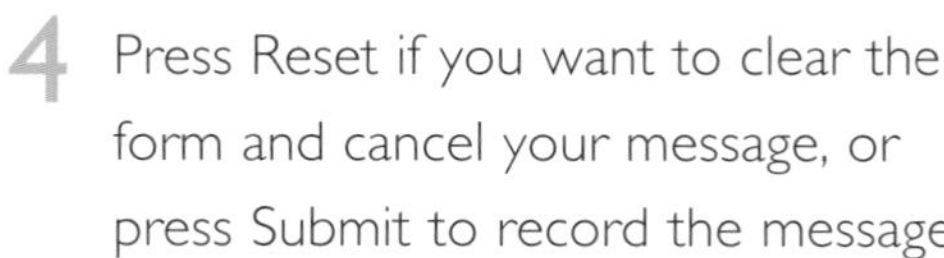

Your Comments

might encourage us when we think about the day when it will be an American soccer team that is in the number one position...

Submit Reset

4 Press Reset if you want to clear the form and cancel your message, or press Submit to record the message.

When you submit the form, the details are written to file, and a confirmation message shows the fields recorded.

By default, FrontPage forms use simple field names such as T1, T2. You can choose meaningful names when you create the form, using form field properties (see page 76).

5 Press the browser's Back button or click the Return to the form link to re-display the Feedback form.

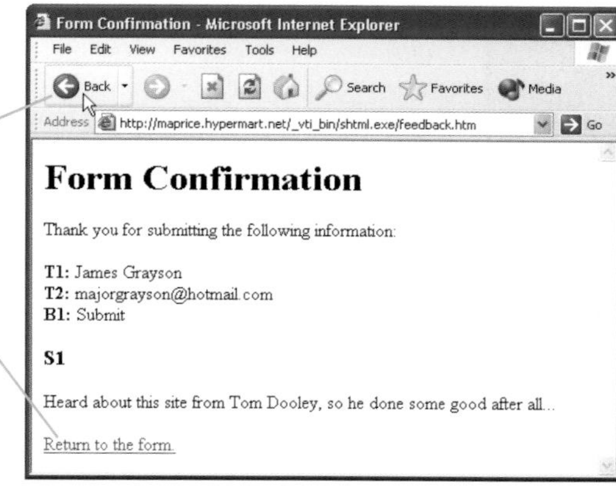

6 Click Remote to Local, open the _private folders in both copies of the Web site, and click the arrow to publish just the form_results.csv file back to your hard disk copy of the Web site.

The results are saved in the _private folder on the Web site, in a file called form_results.csv. The Web site owner or someone with the proper password and file permissions can access the results file. However, it is easier to access the local copy.

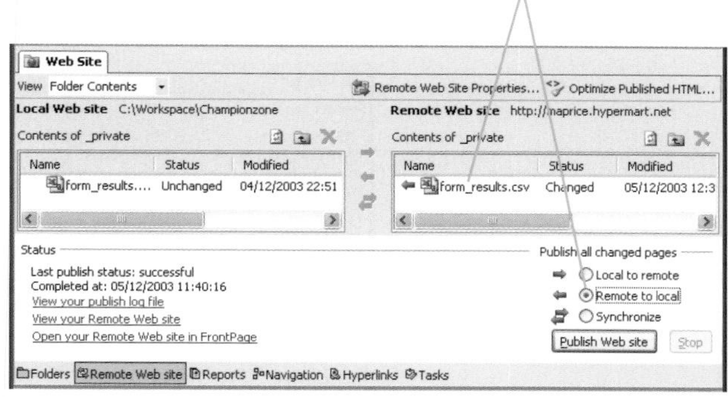

7 Double click the file entry, to open the form_results.csv file at the local Web site and display the records of comments.

When you save results files to the hard disk copy of your Web site, you must be careful to avoid republishing the results file and thereby overwriting new responses. See page 104.

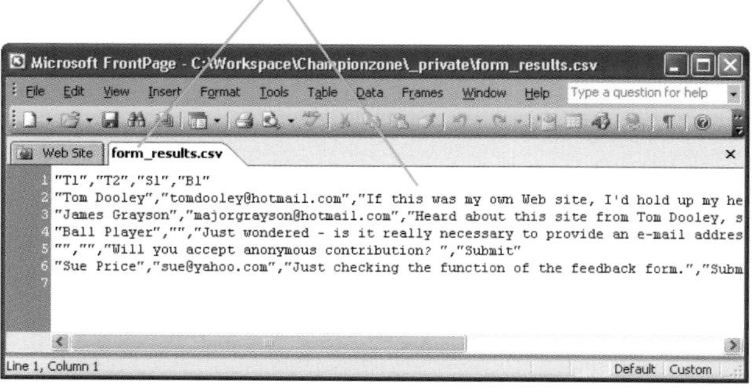

Selective publishing

You may need to restrict publication of some parts, for example while they are still under development.

When you first publish your Web site, you usually publish all pages. FrontPage then automatically switches to publish only files that have changed. It compares the files in the Web site on your hard disk to the published files on the Web server. Only newer versions of files are published.

FrontPage also looks out for files that have been deleted or relocated on your hard disk copy, and synchronizes the files on your local Web site with the published files on the Web server.

Some files are published only once, e.g. comments, guestbook entries or hit counters, to avoid overwriting collected data.

When there are incomplete pages that are still under development, or files that are not currently part of the Web site, you may want to prevent publication of particular files.

1. Select View, Reports, Workflow, Publish Status and choose the file or files that you want to protect from update.

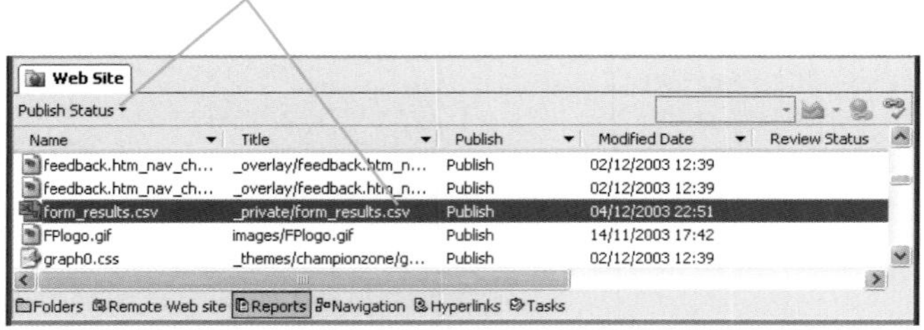

You can right-click the file icon from the Folder List in any view, click Properties on the shortcut menu, and then click the Workgroup tab. However, using the report allows you to select files from multiple folders at the same time.

2. Right-click the selection, choose Properties and then click the Workgroup tab.

3. Click Exclude this file when publishing the rest of the Web, and click OK. Despite the wording, it can be applied to multiple files in a selection.

4. To re-enable, select the files and clear the Exclude... box.

Promoting the Web site

The best design won't help if nobody knows about your Web site, so you need to provide the information that will get your URL added to the search sites, to encourage visitors and references for your Web site.

Covers

Chapter Seven

Will you be seen?

Sending your Web site files to a Web server does not guarantee visitors. You have to make certain that you will be noticed.

Designing an exciting Web site and publishing it to a server is really only half of the job. You have to ensure that other Internet users know about your site. Then you will get visitors to enjoy your work, and perhaps some suggestions for improving the site.

There are many ways in which people might find particular Web sites, for example:

- Follow links provided by their ISP.
- Follow links found on other Web sites.
- Find a Web site using a search engine or directory (Google, Yahoo!, Infoseek etc.)
- Click on a banner heading or in a secondary window.
- Find out a URL address by word of mouth.
- See a URL address in a review, advertisement or brochure.
- Receive an email with a Web site URL address.

Some of these methods apply to the larger business, but many may be equally applicable to the small business or the personal Web site.

To get started with promoting your Web site, consider the following options:

- Make use of the facilities offered by your ISP or WPP for raising awareness of your site.
- Tell your family, friends and business associates, with an email announcement.
- Make sure that you are listed by the search sites, with a good description and in the right category.
- Run a small ad or issue a press release to a local newspaper or to a magazine dealing with your particular topic.

Your ISP or WPP

ISPs and WPPs are usually eager to encourage visitors to their account holders' Web sites, and will provide tools and facilities to help. FreeWebs.com for example have a Site Promotion section with lots of advice to help you add Meta tags, submit to search engines and add your site to Internet Directories.

Some ISPs will ask you to complete a form giving title, description and category for your Web site, and will then register your Web site at various Internet search engines.

FreeWebs.com also features example Web sites and if you believe your site would be of interest to other users, you can apply to have your site included in one of the lists.

Some WPPs will organize their users into groups, much like the Yahoo categories, so that visitors can easily find Web sites that meet their interests.

Announcement

This may be all you need to promote your personal Web site to the people who are most likely to be interested.

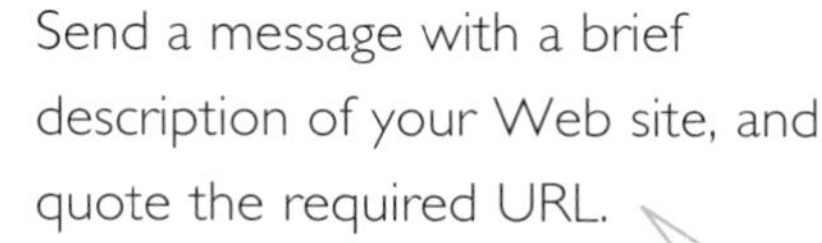

1 Send a message with a brief description of your Web site, and quote the required URL.

Make the announcement text sufficiently detailed to interest and intrigue, but don't include so much of the content that curiosity is satisfied without a visit. If it is appropriate, include an email address or telephone number for queries. Remember that the email address you use for sending the announcement will be attached to that message. Your email program should have a "send using" option, so you can select a suitable email address.

Think of it as a public message, like a small ad in a newspaper, which can be seen by just about anyone.

Put the Sender addresses in the Bcc box, to avoid distributing all your contact addresses with the announcement. Don't make the announcement message too personal to the recipients. It should be general purpose enough that your contacts feel able to forward it to their contacts. You can always send separate, personalized notes to introduce the announcement.

2 Add your Web site URL to your email signature, to act as a reminder to your contacts whenever you send email.

3 Add the message to newsgroups that deal with topics related to the content of your Web site.

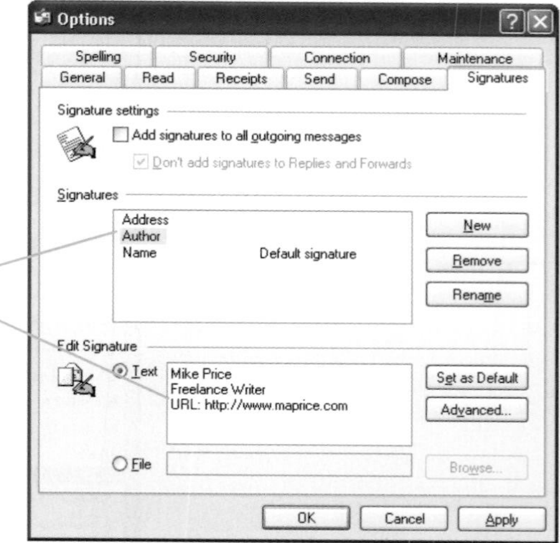

How sites are found

Extend beyond the limits of your immediate circle and appeal to the Internet as a whole.

To find a Web site, page or other element, you choose a search engine such as Google and enter the details of your query in the form provided. This is the way most people locate Web sites that may be of interest to them.

1 Select the type of item you want to find – images, directories, Web sites or just a general search.

Advanced search options let you state your query more precisely, to minimize the number of inappropriate matches.

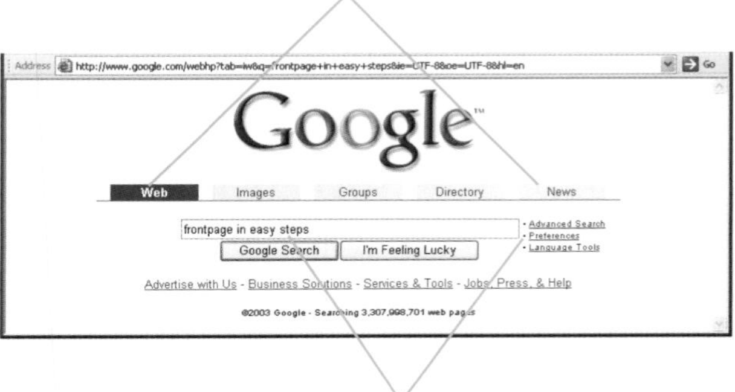

2 Type keywords or phrases defining the item, or enter a question. You can limit responses to a particular language or geography.

3 Click Google Search and await the results. There may be a long list but better matches are closer to the start of the list.

You should note that there are three types of search site. These are:

- *search engines that use robots*
- *directories that use people*
- *hybrids that are a mixture*

You want to be sure that searches for topics related to your Web site will include your URL in their results, near the top. This can only happen if the search engines know about your site.

Search sites may rely on being told about URLs, and their staff visit and review the Web pages, to decide whether to add the URL, and what categories to use. Others send out Web robots that roam around the Internet looking for new or updated Web pages. The URL, page title, and selected text from the pages are sent to the search site. Some search sites use both methods.

To increase your chances, you can register your URL with specific search sites, or include meta-variables in your Web pages, to feed data to the search robots.

Search sites

There are very many different search sites, directories and search engines, for general and special purposes.

The table shows some of the main search services (based on general popularity and usage). These search engines are the ones that are more likely to be well-maintained and upgraded when necessary, to keep pace with the growing Internet.

•	AllTheWeb.com	http://www.alltheweb.com
•	AltaVista	http://www.altavista.com
•	AOL Search (external)	http://search.aol.com
•	AOL Search (internal)	http://aolsearch.aol.com
•	Ask Jeeves	http://www.askjeeves.com
•	Google	http://www.google.com
•	HotBot	http://www.hotbot.com
•	Inktomi	http://www.inktomi.com
•	LookSmart	http://www.looksmart.com
•	Lycos	http://www.lycos.com
•	MSN Search	http://search.msn.com
•	Netscape Search	http://search.netscape.com
•	Open Directory	http://dmoz.org/
•	Overture	http://www.overture.com/
•	Teoma	http://www.teoma.com
•	WiseNut	http://www.wisenut.com
•	Yahoo	http://www.yahoo.com

Sites may combine but the old name will usually work. For example, if you switch to the old Infoseek site at: http://www.infoseek.com you'll automatically be redirected to the replacement site which is: http://infoseek.go.com

You can find details of these and additional search engine sites at the search engine watchers site: www.searchenginewatchers.com

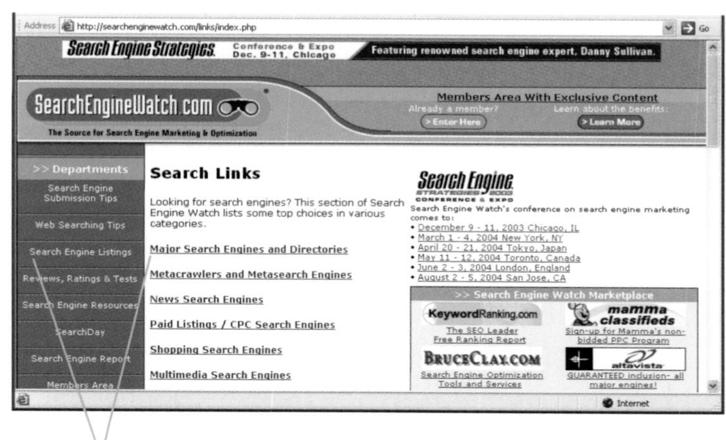

For details of these sites and to find out how to register your URL with them, visit www.searchenginewatchers.com the search engine watchers site, and click the Search Engine Listings link.

Register your URL

Search sites will include a link to let you submit your URL. It may say Add URL, Register URL, Suggest a Site or similar text. See page 110 for a list of search sites.

Originally these facilities were all free, but it is now becoming common for the search sites to charge a fee for registration. So check the terms before adding your details.

You can find this page from the main Google page by selecting "Jobs, Press & Help" then clicking "Submitting your Site", though these links may change over time, so the search is a better option.

Google adds your URL to the list that it will be reviewing. It does not guarantee to add all submitted URLs to its index.

Registering your site with a search engine or directory is usually free of charge, if you can locate the right Web page. The procedure for each search site may vary, but the examples of Google and Yahoo illustrate the main techniques. To register with Google:

1. Open the search site at http://www.google.com and search for "Add URL to Google"

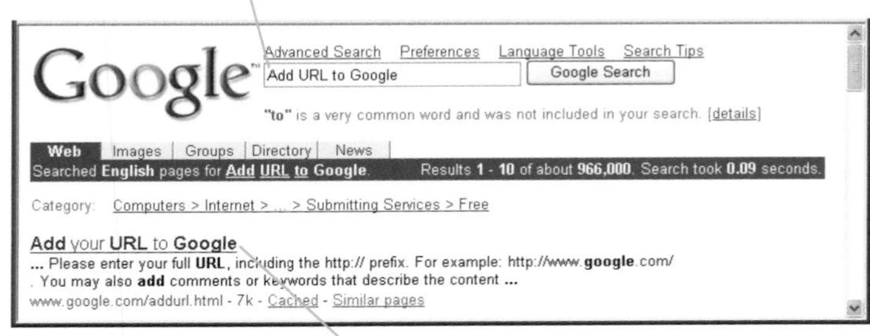

2. Open the AddURL Web page to find information about registering your site. Scroll down to the registration form:

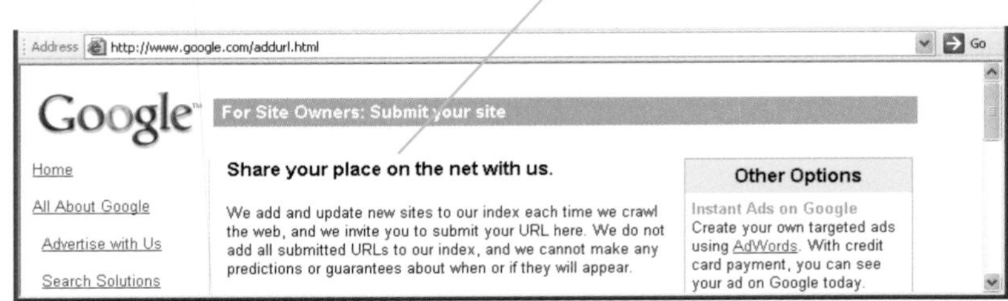

3. Enter the URL for your site, and a comment or keywords related to your Web site, then click the AddURL button.,

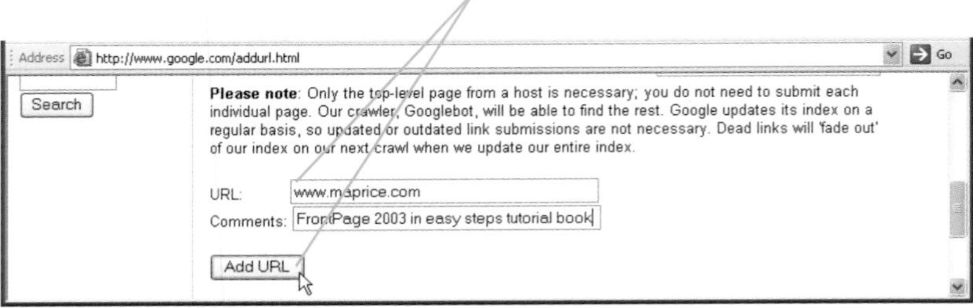

Suggest your site

With directory sites such as Yahoo! you should select one of the predefined categories and subcategories, then click the Suggest a Site link. You can add your URL to Yahoo! for no charge, or use the quicker Yahoo Express, at a one time charge of $299.

1 Select one of the 14 main Yahoo categories, and follow the subcategory links to identify the most suitable one for your site.

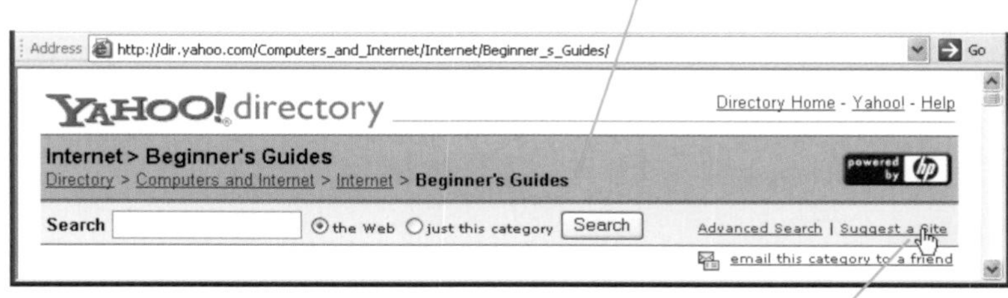

2 With the appropriate category selected, scroll down the page until you can find and click the Suggest a Site link.

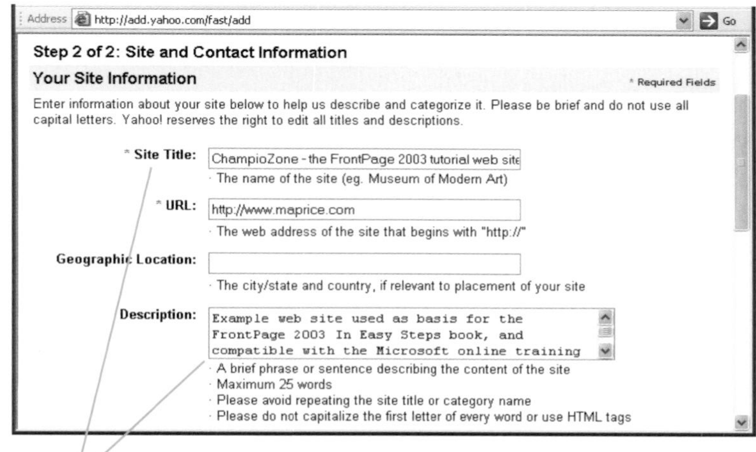

The topic and path will be filled in for you, if you pre-select your category.

3 Complete the registration form with the title, URL, location, description and any other requested information about your site.

When you submit the request, it is sent to the directory staff for evaluation.

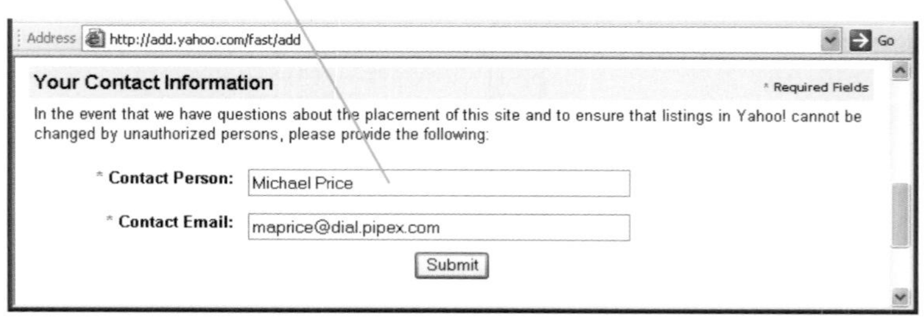

Meta-variable tags

You do not need Meta tags in all the pages in your Web site. It is usually enough to define the Home page, and leave the rest to the search site robots.

Some search sites make use of Meta-variables to collate indexing information, although this is now less common. If you wish to add metadata, the following user variable types are most applicable for use by search sites:

Description: A concise definition of the page contents. Aim to provide about twenty or so words.

Keywords: Terms and synonyms related to the topic of your Web page. Choose the words you think that visitors are likely to enter into a search. Separate each word with a comma.

Author: The author or company name, if you want, this could be the target of a search.

Resource-type: Put Document for an HTML page. This is the only tag that you need to put in for indexing purposes.

Include common misspellings or include different word forms, to increase the chances of your page being selected in a search.

To add Meta tags to your Web page:

1. Open the Index.htm page in Page view, select File, Properties and select the Custom tab to create or change meta tags.

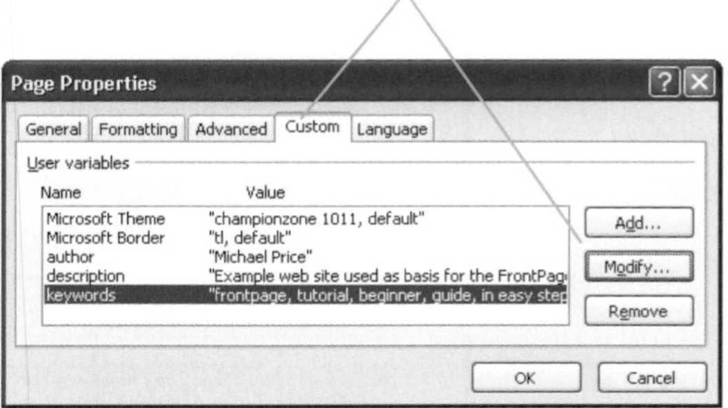

Some of the items in the list may have been added automatically by FrontPage, so don't change or delete an item unless you are sure where it came from.

2. Click Add, or select an existing entry and press Modify. Enter or amend the Name and Value for the variable, and click OK.

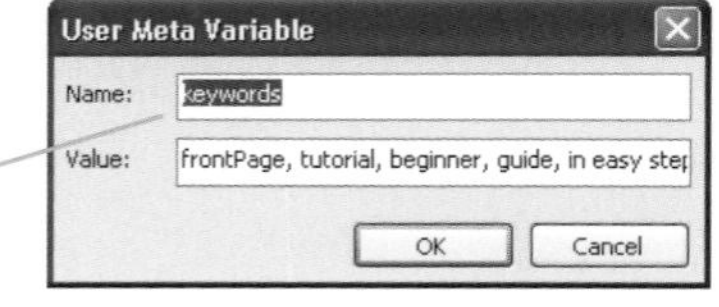

When you have added all the Meta tags, republish the Web page.

Registration services

There are services that will register your Web site on your behalf, usually for a fee, but some offer free services also.

While it is easy enough to register your Web site with a few of the main search engines, it can become quite time-consuming if you want wider coverage. The answer may be a registration service such as AddPro which will do most of the work for you.

1. Connect to the www.addpro.com Web site, and select *Automatic Service,* and then *Free Search Engine Submission*.

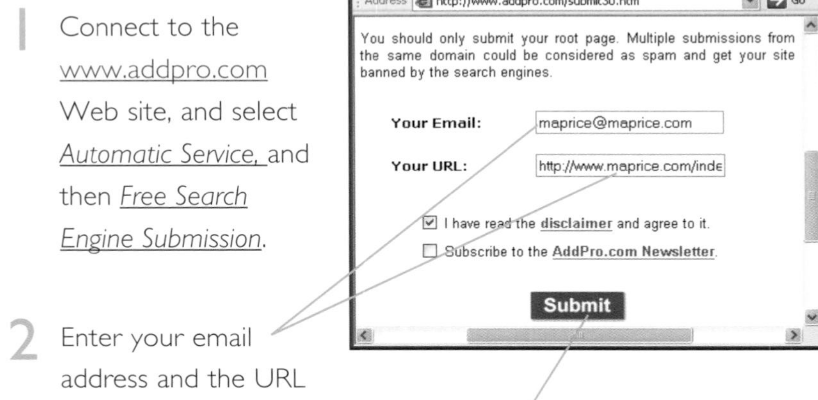

2. Enter your email address and the URL for your home page. Click the Submit button to register your site.

AddPro.com offers a link and button that you can add to your Web site, though you are not required to display the link.

You may get a variety of responses from the twenty search sites, ranging from timeouts to Web page not found.

3. AddPro sends your URL to each of the 20 search sites, and displays all the replies that it receives back.

Check your email for responses from some of the search sites, since they may ask you to confirm your URL before they add you to the list.

4 Some of the search engines may contact you via email to confirm that you want your entry added to their index.

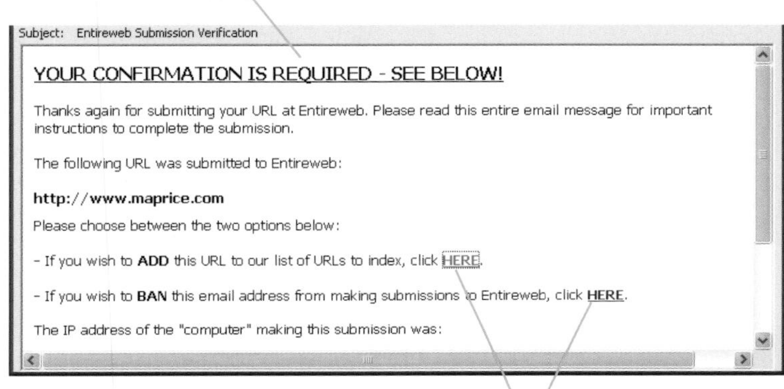

5 With EntireWeb.com for example, you can confirm the entry, or ask for the submitting email address to be blocked.

It may take several days for the search site robots to locate your Web site and collect the details from the text within your pages, and there's no guarantee your site will be listed.

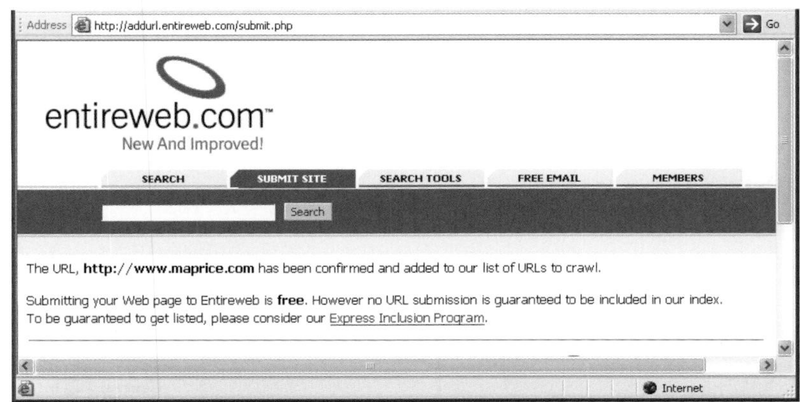

The sites may also take the opportunity to offer you other related services, and they may also add your email address to their promotional list.

A number of the sites are Meta Tag search engines. This means your site will not be added to their indexes unless it has title and description tags as a minimum. Some of the sites offer facilities to check and edit the tags on your Web page, or you can check the tags yourself using Meta Medic (see page 116) or an equivalent product.

Checking your Web site

If you do use Meta tags, it may be worth checking them before the search engines begin reviewing your site. However, many search sites have abandoned the use of Meta tags because of misuse.

To be sure that your Web site will be properly recognized by the search engines, you can use Northern Web's Meta Medic to check your Web site's Keyword and Description Meta Tags.

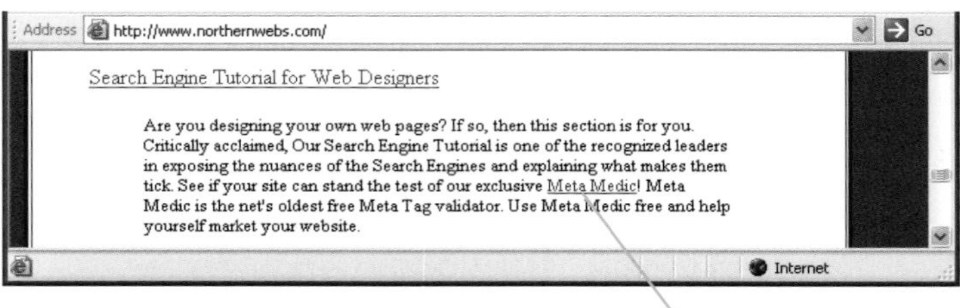

This will check the structure and the contents of the two main Meta tags, and advise you on how to improve them to increase your visibility to search engines that use Meta tag data.

1 Open http://www.northernwebs.com and click the *Meta Medic* link to open http://www.northernwebs.com/set/setsimjr.html. You'll find Meta Medic at the foot of the page.

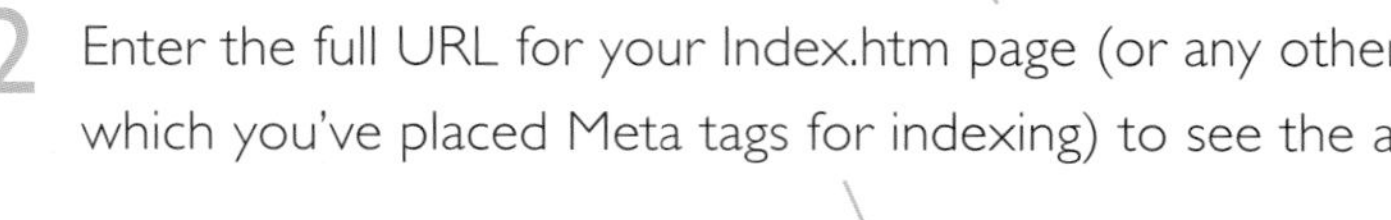

It may be wise to periodically re-check your tags if you do change them.

2 Enter the full URL for your Index.htm page (or any other page on which you've placed Meta tags for indexing) to see the analysis.

Meta Medic also checks how effectively your keywords represent the content of the target Web page and suggests that you consider the Meta Medic Pro version if you want to improve this.

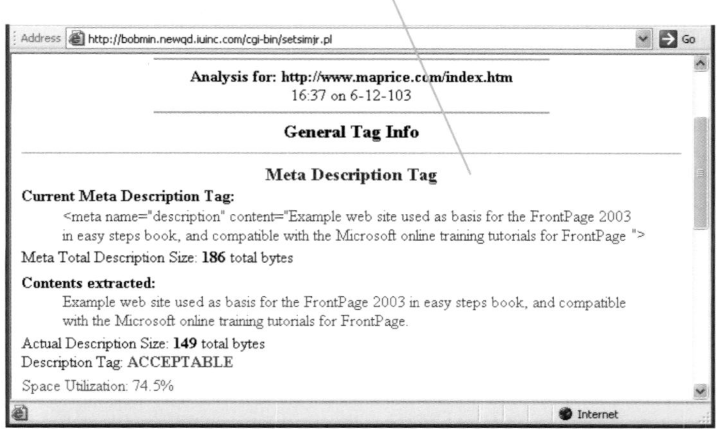

Bells and whistles

When you have published and registered your Web site, you can start adding features to make sure that visitors find the site worth revisiting and worth recommending. You'll also need to measure the rate of success that you achieve.

Covers

Chapter Eight

Counting on success

To show that the search sites are doing their job, you need some means of checking how many visitors you have had to your site.

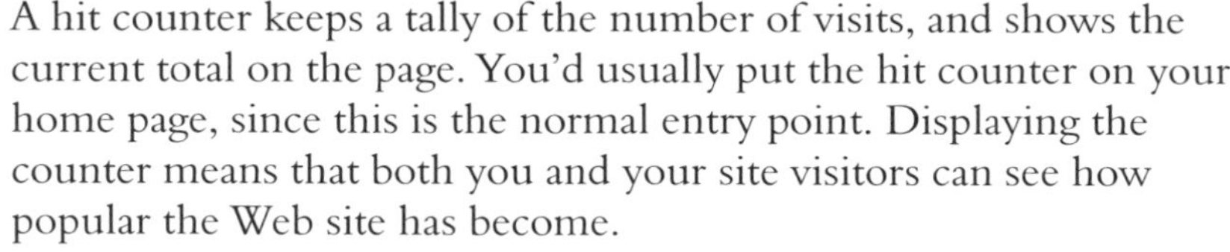

A hit counter keeps a tally of the number of visits, and shows the current total on the page. You'd usually put the hit counter on your home page, since this is the normal entry point. Displaying the counter means that both you and your site visitors can see how popular the Web site has become.

To add a counter:

1. Open the Web site and the Index.htm page, and position the cursor where the counter should appear.

To use the FrontPage Web components, you must have a Web server that supports FrontPage Server Extensions. In the examples in this chapter, Interkey.net is used as the WPP for the domain FPineasysteps.com, since it fully supports FrontPage 2003.

2. Select Insert, Web Component. Click Hit Counter and then Finish.

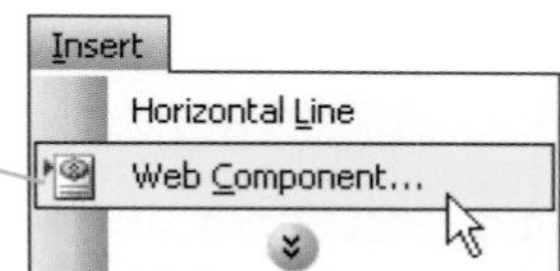

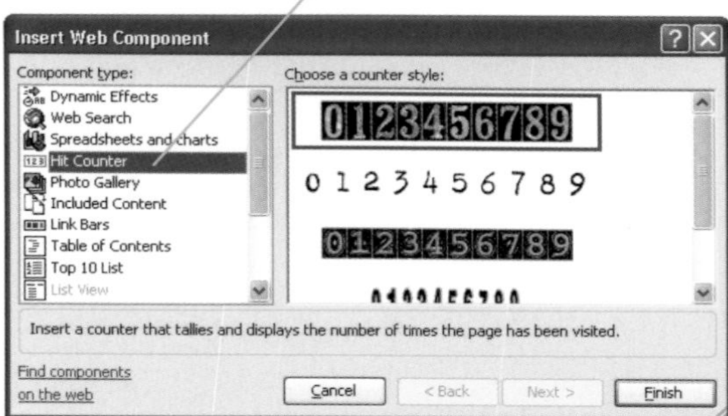

3. Double click the Hit counter to set properties:
   - Choose counter style
   - Set an initial counter value
   - Set the number of digits
   - Click OK to apply changes

You can reset the counter again when you have finished your testing, or if you introduce a new set of topics to the Web site.

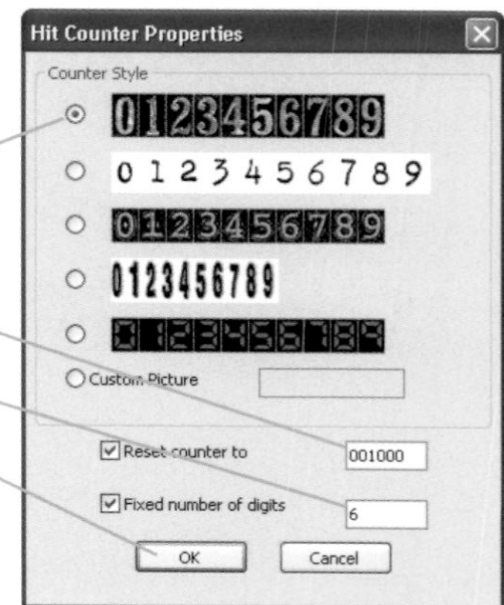

4. Save the page, and re-publish the Web site to the Web server.

5 You could type an explanatory note at the side of the counter. Click Preview to see the changes.

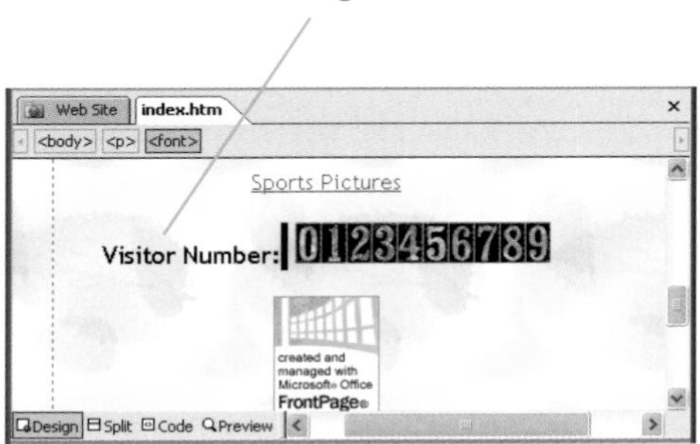

You might wish to add the date when the counter was reset as a comment or as a displayed entry, to put the count into context.

6 Preview displays a [Hit Counter] placeholder. Preview in Browser also has a placeholder.

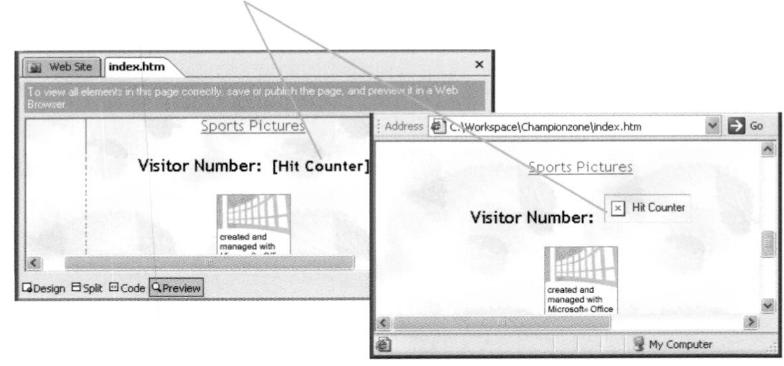

When you reset the counter, the initial value is saved in the _private folder, in a file called Index.htm.cnt. This is published to the Web server, where the server extensions increment the value on each visit. To see the count in the Local copy, you must synchronize the Local and Remote Web sites.

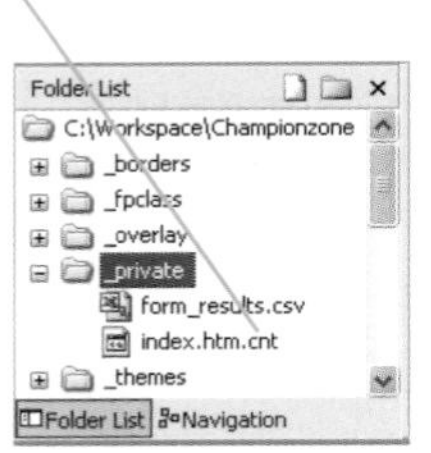

7 Save the page, re-publish the Web site to the Web server, and view the Remote Web site, where you'll see the counter, updated each time you visit the site.

Add a time stamp

You can time stamp one or more pages, but it is more effective to put the stamp in the bottom margin, and a stamp will appear on every page.

Add a time stamp to a page to display the date or the time and date that the page was last published. This tells visitors that the site is up to date and active, and encourages them to pay return visits and to recommend your site to others.

To add the time stamp:

1. Open the Web site and the home page and select Format, Shared Borders.

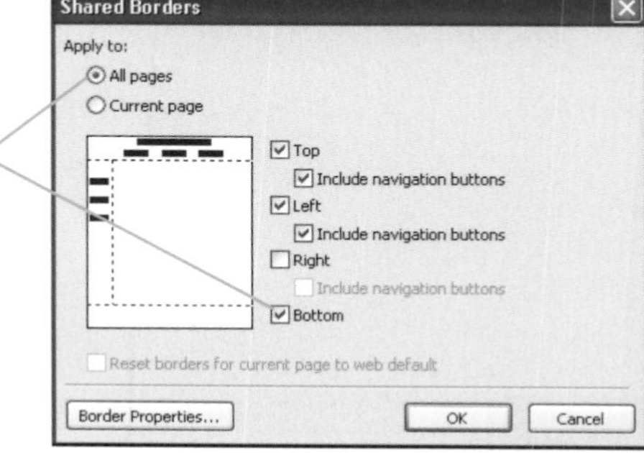

2. Check that the All pages option is specified, and click the button to add a bottom border.

3. By default, the bottom border contains the date and the time, with time zone. Click the text to highlight the field.

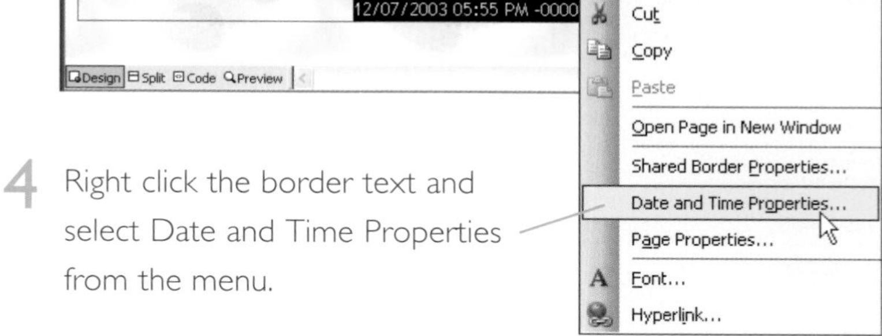

You can choose the Date Last Edited, or the Date Last Updated by FrontPage (the date published).

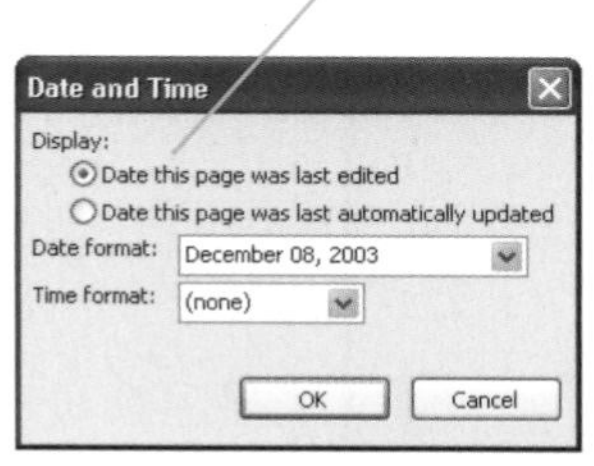

4. Right click the border text and select Date and Time Properties from the menu.

5. Choose a date format with the month shown alphabetically, to avoid confusion. If you want the time, use a TZ (Time Zone) format so the time will be shown in local time for the visitor.

The time shown in Normal or Preview views will be the local time for the PC on which you are running FrontPage.

6 Add an expression such as *Date this page last updated:* to explain the meaning of the border value.

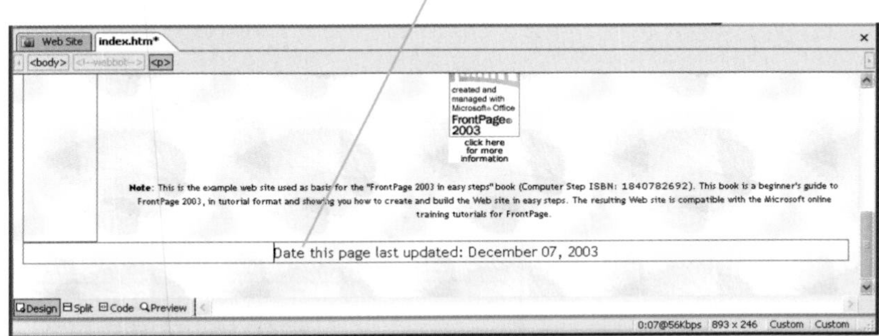

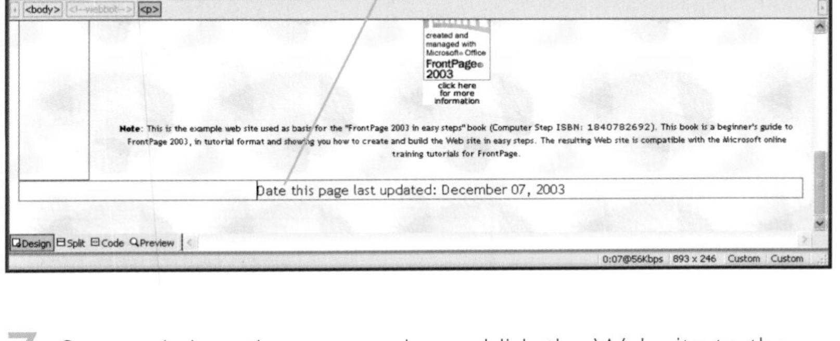

If the Web site is already open in the browser when you publish an update, press Refresh to rebuild the screen.

7 Save and close the page, and re-publish the Web site to the Web server. The home page and borders are transferred, and the borders in all the other pages are updated.

The date and time shown in the browser will be the local time for the server, which may not be the same as your time zone.

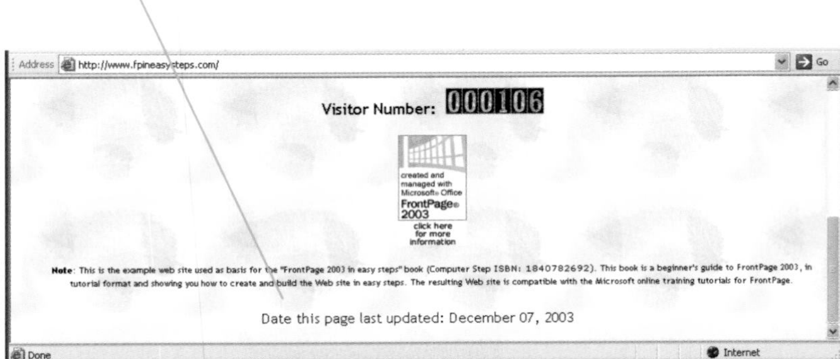

Make a practice of editing the important pages on the Web site, or the time stamp will get out of date and spoil the effect of your Web site.

8 Switch to any other page in the Web site, and you'll see the same bottom border but with the date applicable to that page:

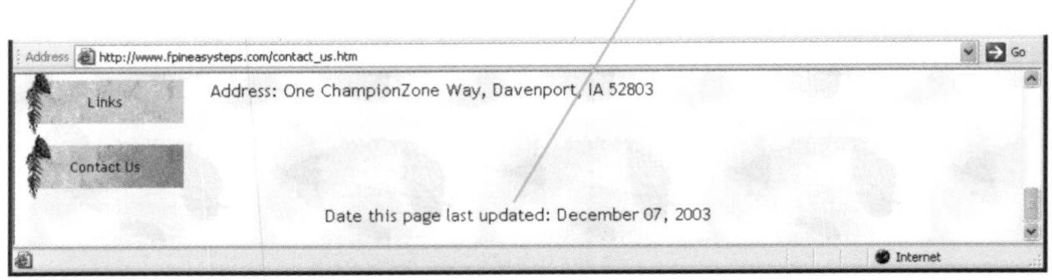

Horizontal lines and images

In FrontPage 2003, horizontal lines are plain and simple, though you can make changes to their properties.

You can add a horizontal line to a page, to separate items or add effect. For example, to add a line above the time stamp:

1 Open the Index.htm page in Design view, position the cursor before the text and select Insert, Horizontal Line.

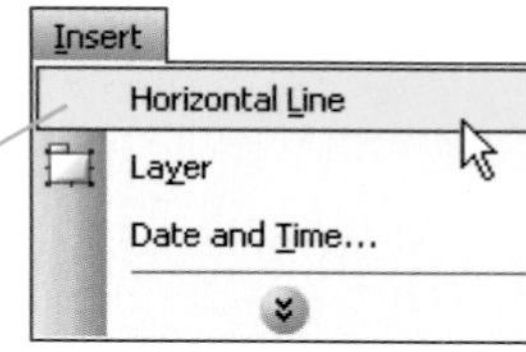

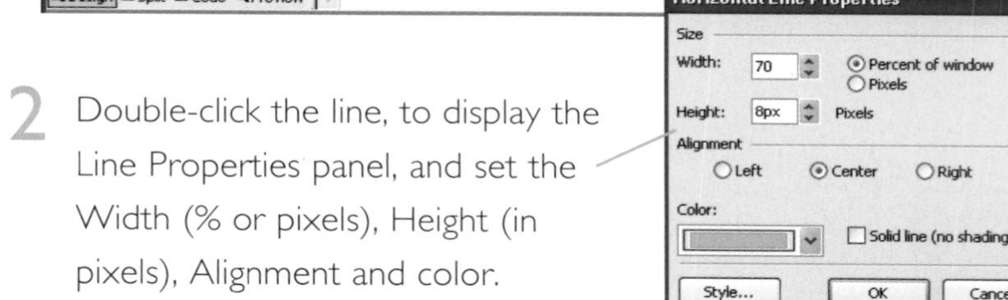

You don't have to press Enter, since a line break is automatically added before and after the horizontal line.

2 Double-click the line, to display the Line Properties panel, and set the Width (% or pixels), Height (in pixels), Alignment and color.

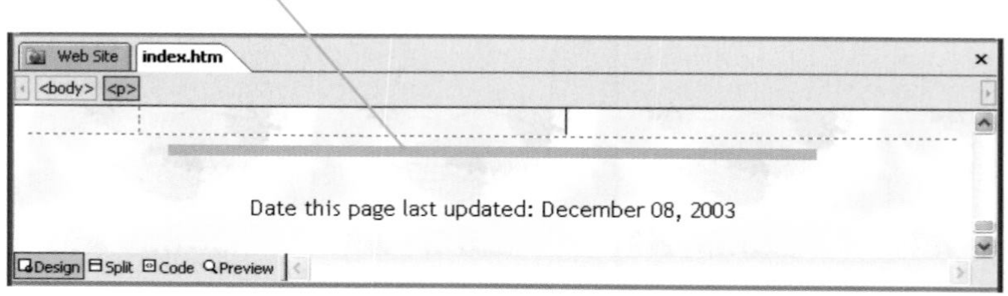

In previous versions of FrontPage, when you added a horizontal line to a page with a theme specified, the line could be a graphic. In FrontPage 2003, you can insert a picture to get a similar effect.

3 Insert an image to get a pictorial horizontal line, and adjust it using Picture Properties.

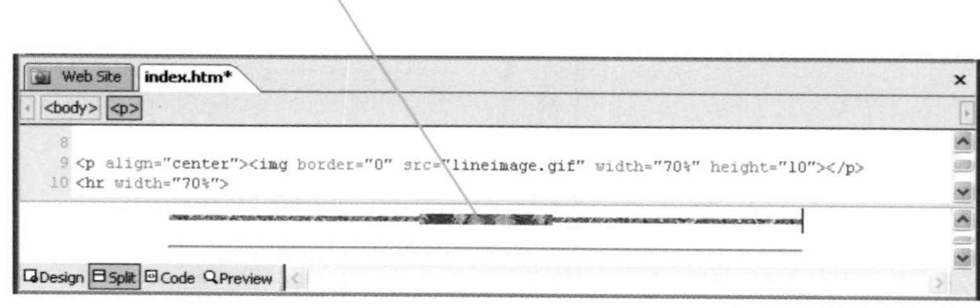

Background sound

This is not supported by all Web browsers. Remember also that some visitors may be deterred by audio effects.

You can set a background sound which plays when the visitor opens the page.

To specify the sound:

1. Right-click the page, and select Page Properties and then the General tab.

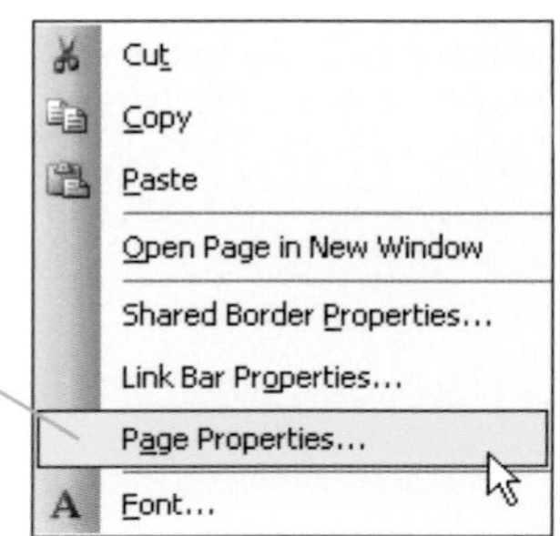

2. In the Background sound Location box, type the path and name for the sound file you want to play (or click Browse to find the file).

You can use .WAV files or the compressed .MP3 files for short sound extracts, but if you have Midi files for music, they are much better because they are so much smaller.

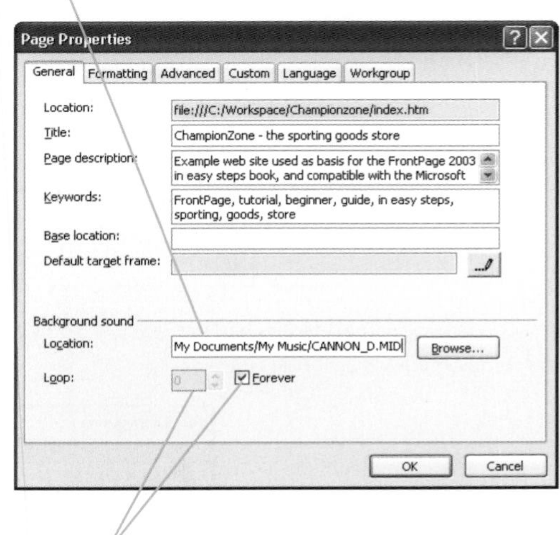

When you save the Web page, you'll also be asked to import the sound file. Store this in the Web site folder, in a Sounds subfolder if you have one set up, so that the file will be available to online visitors.

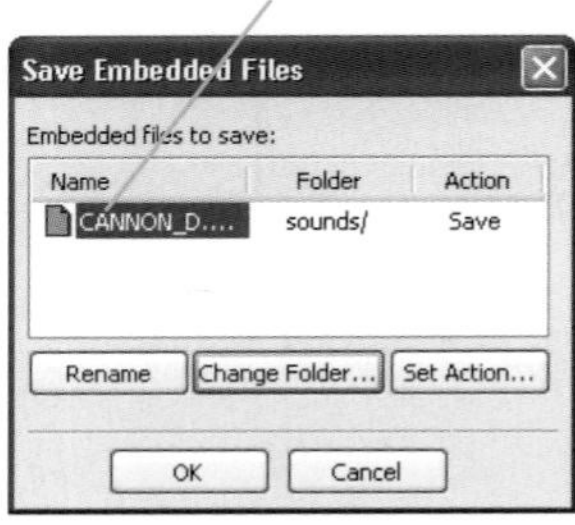

3. Clear Forever and select 1 or more plays in Loop if you want the sound to play for a limited time.

4. Save the Web page and Preview in Browser to check the sound.

5. Re-publish the Web site, and the sound will play each time that the associated page is selected.

List effects

Format lists to make the data on the page easier to view and analyze. You can create lists of many types, including bulleted, numbered, definition, directory and menu lists.

1 Open the Links page. Organize the links by inserting suitable category headings.

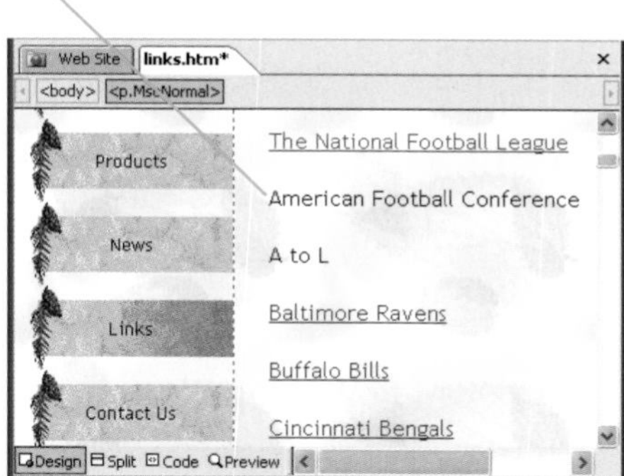

2 Select the links and headings and click [icon] to create a single level list.

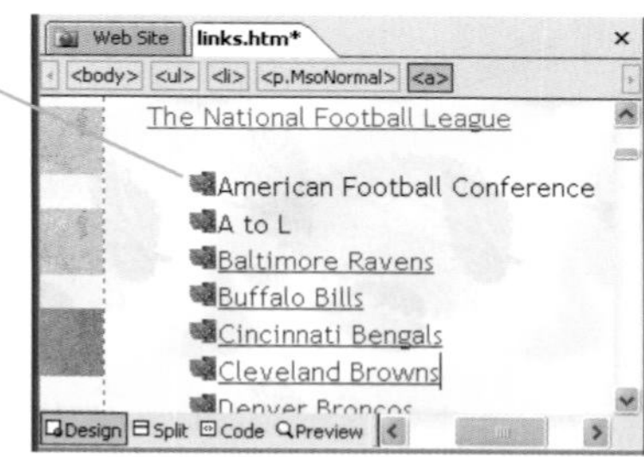

3 Select the group of links beneath a heading, and double-click [icon] to introduce another level in the list.

If the page uses a theme, the list will use the styles defined for fonts and picture bullets (see page 125).

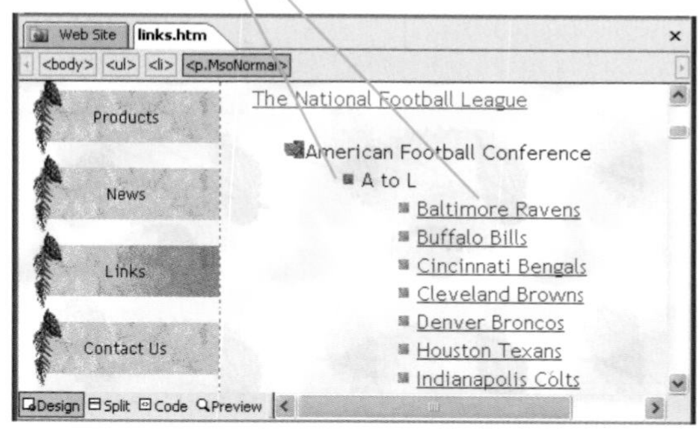

4 Repeat for each subheading in turn, until all the groups are indented to the appropriate levels.

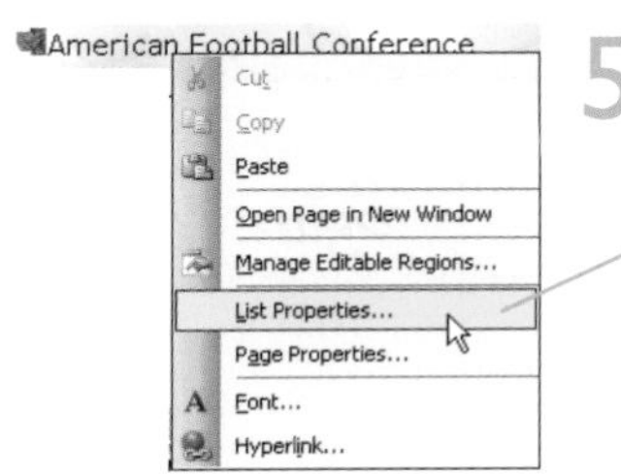

5 Right-click the top level heading and select List Properties. Click the Picture Bullets tab, and choose Enable Collapsible Outlines, and set them as Initially Collapsed.

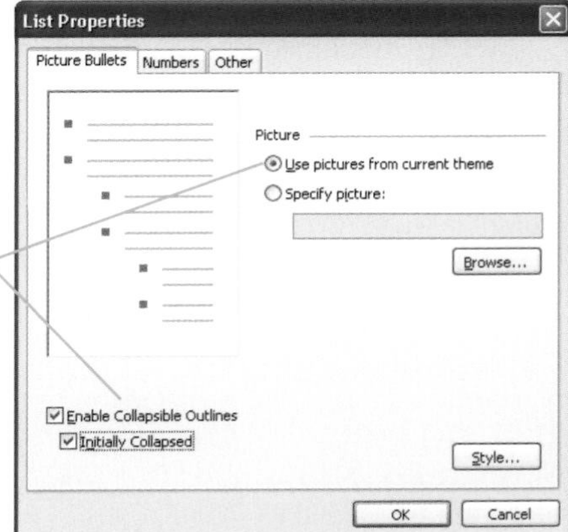

Collapsible lists are supported by Microsoft Internet Explorer 4.0 or higher, or other Web browsers that support Dynamic HTML.

6 Save the changes to the page, and click Preview in Browser to see how the page appears to visitors.

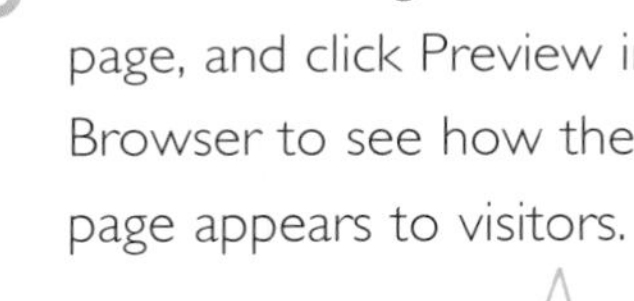

The list is shown collapsed initially. Click on any level to expand it to show the next level of detail. Click again to contract it and hide the detail.

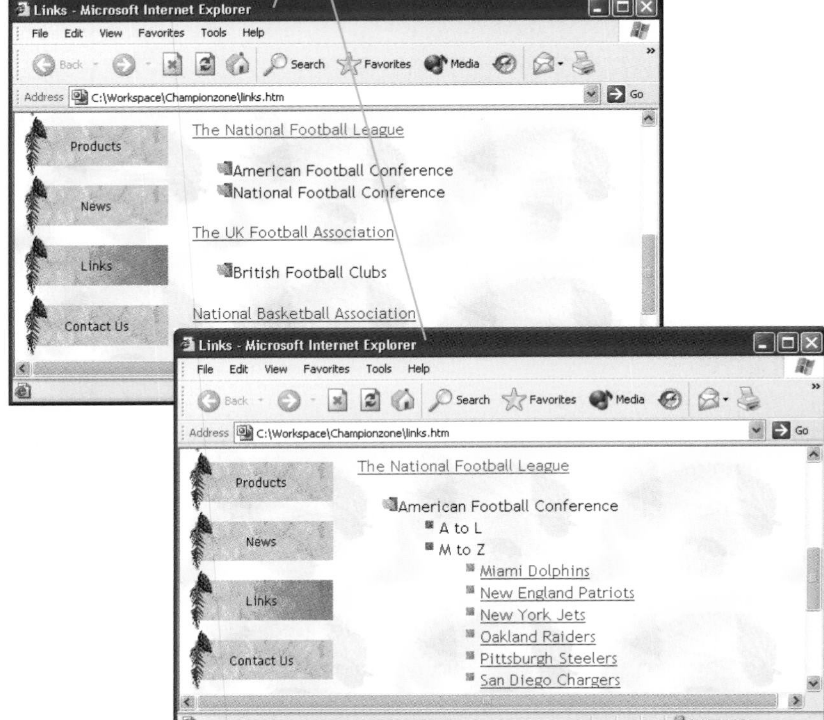

You may wish to add a note on the page to explain to the visitor about the collapsible lists and how to activate them.

Display form results

You can let your visitors share the feedback from other visitors. To do this, you need to save the results to a HTML file.

1 Open the Feedback page, right-click the form, select Form Properties, and click the Options button.

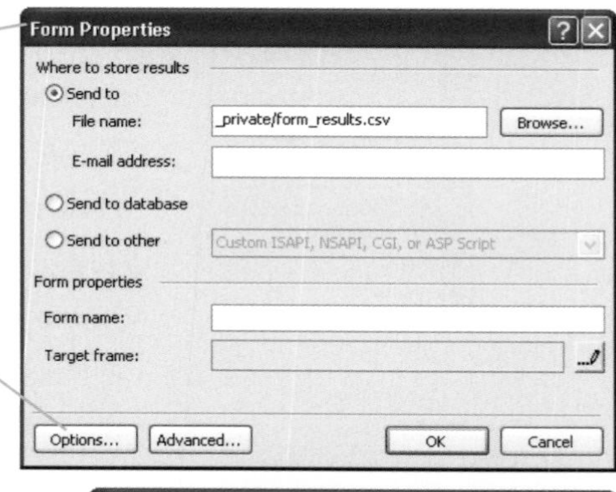

2 Specify the file name for the optional second file, and choose the HTML format. The file will be stored in the root of the Web site. Clear the boxes to exclude the field names and to show latest comments first.

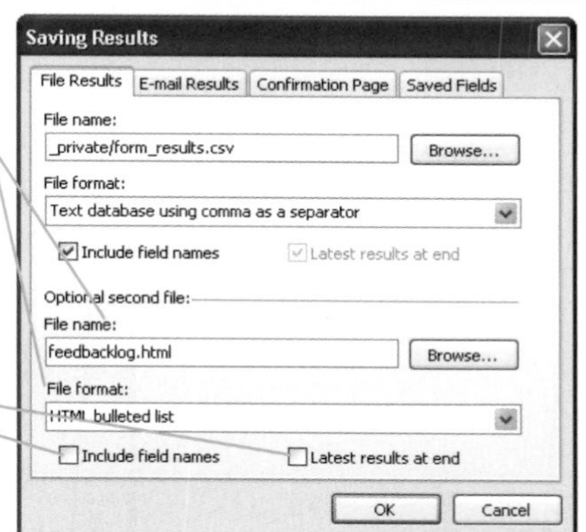

You can save the form results to two files. One could have all the data fields, for your confidential records, and one could be a subset of the fields, for display.

3 Choose which of the fields to show on the results. For example, you may decide not to display T2, the email address. In any event, you won't want to show B1, the button field, which has no associated data value.

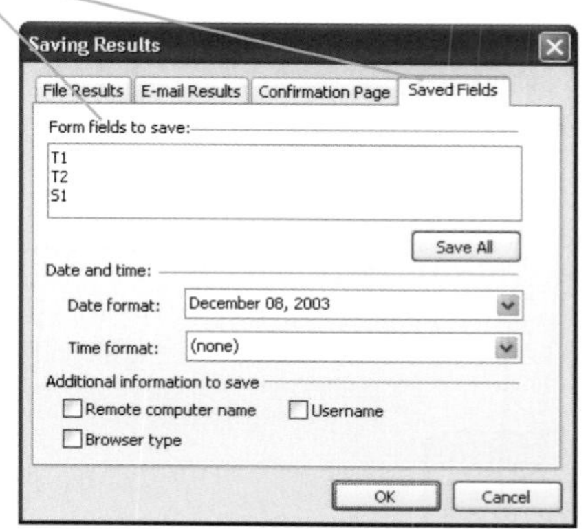

You can collect extra data, such as the type of browser used by the visitors (but only if they leave feedback).

4 Add a hyperlink to the Web page, targeted at the new results file, with an appropriate text message. Save the Web page and republish the Web site.

Feedback (Click here to see comments)

Display the feedbacklog.html file

Please give us your comments and suggestions.

5 Connect to the Internet, open the Web site, switch to the Feedback page, and click the link to see comments from visitors.

The results are displayed as a HTML page. Note that the late comments entered may not appear immediately – it depends on how the data is cached on the server. Press the Back button to return to the Web page.

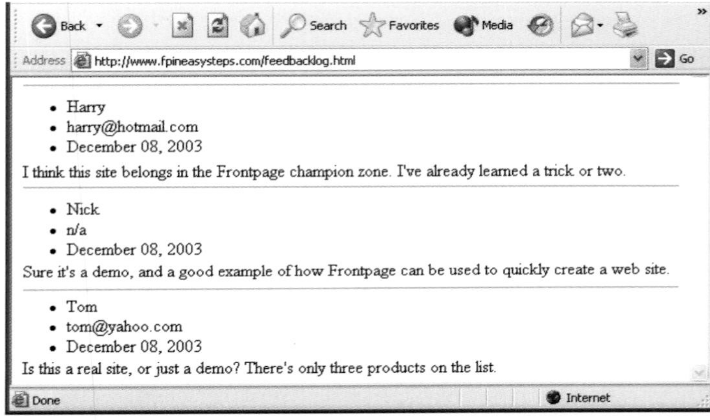

Guest Book

If all you want is to capture visitor comments and make them available to everyone, without any additional data, you can use the pre-defined Guest Book template.

The Web Site and Web Page templates will provide many of the most needed features, and you can always tailor the pages to add your own particular requirements.

6 Select New, Page or Web, and select the Guest Book Web page. This provides a comments area, and saves the data in a log file.

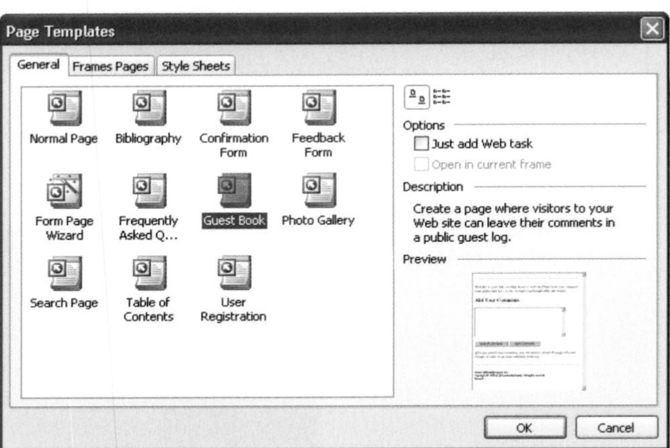

Using color

When you select color depth, allocate colors to Web components or choose a theme, try to imagine what different types of visitors will see, and make choices that will encourage them to revisit your site.

A picture may be worth a thousand words, but everyone may not get the same message. There are differences between video adapters and monitors, not just the settings chosen, but in the way they portray colors. Browsers may reinterpret color schemes, and different types may not follow the same rules. There is also a wide variation in the way individuals perceive colors.

PCs can display colors selected from over 16 million combinations, using the true color 32-bit setting. In practice many users will restrict their display to the de facto standard for Windows and the Internet, choosing the 8-bit, 256 color setting.

GIF image files can use 256 colors only, but it could be a different set of 256 for each image.

The GIF file image format uses 256 colors, so when you save an image to GIF, the graphics program may use dithering. This mixes some of the available colors in a mottled or checkerboard effect, to approximate other colors. Also, if the PC is set for 256 colors, the browser will use a fixed 256 color palette and may simulate missing colors by dithering. These changes may degrade the image, especially with large blocks of single colors.

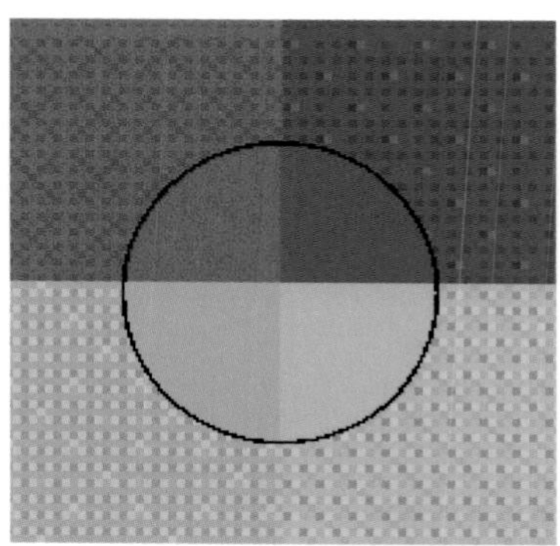

Note that four colors from the Web site palette are not rendered correctly in Internet Explorer and should be avoided if possible. These are (two greens and two blues):

- *00FF33*
- *33FF00*
- *0033FF*
- *3300FF*

To avoid the effect, you should create or modify the image to use the same 256 color palette as one of the main browsers. Netscape uses six shades of red, green and blue (0, 51, 102, 153, 204 and 255) to give 216 colors, known as the browser-safe palette. Internet Explorer also honors this set of colors. See Lynda Weinman's site http://www.lynda.com/hex.html for a full discussion of Web colors.

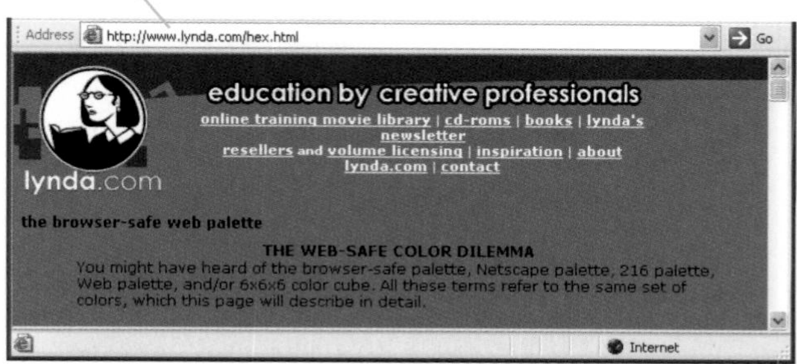

Choosing a transparent color

To enhance the effect of your graphics and images, use a transparent color to make them stand out, especially when your page has a background picture or pattern.

1 Open the Web page in Design view and Insert an image. Then click the image to display the Pictures toolbar.

If the Pictures toolbar doesn't appear when you click the image, select View, Toolbars, Pictures.

2 Using the pointer, select the color you want to make transparent. The image gets integrated in the background.

You can choose any suitable color, it does not have to be white. You should choose a background color that is not vital to the integrity of the image.

You also use transparency color to create a background, partially transparent image to act as a watermark on the page, and overlay it with text or other images.

3 When your changes are complete, save the page, storing the modified image in the Images folder, and re-publish the Web site.

Print a page

When you print the current page to the Windows printer, the results depend on which view you start from.

You can print any FrontPage HTML file from Page view, including the results of forms that have been saved in HTML format.

1 In Page view (Design or Split) select File, to get Page Setup, Print Preview and Print, and click Print Preview to see the page content.

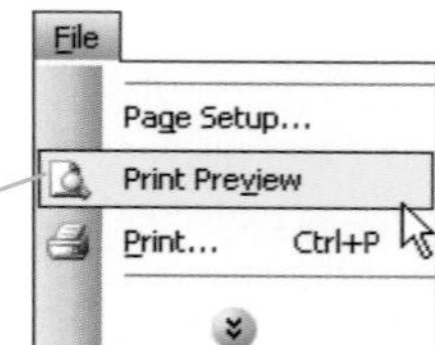

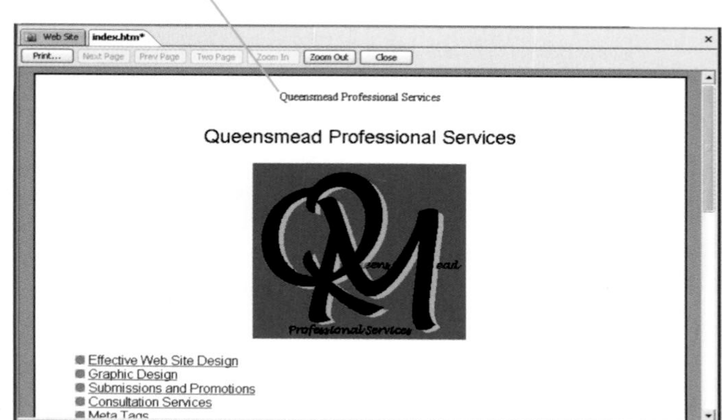

When you print from Design view, you'll find that collapsible lists are printed in their fully expanded form.

2 Click the Code tab and File, Print Preview (or File, Print) will show the actual HTML code that generates the Web page.

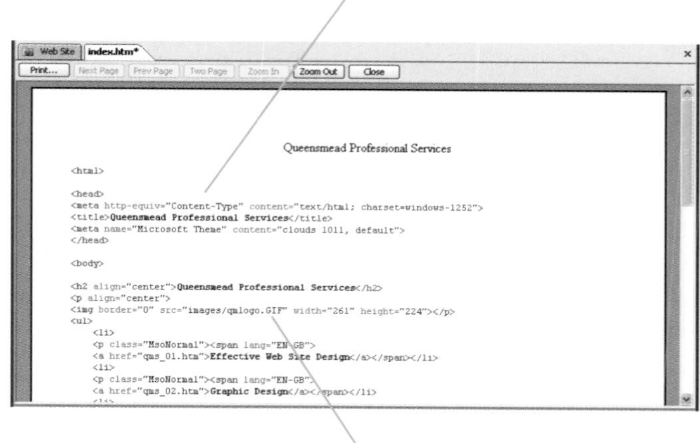

If your Web site uses Frames (see page 140), you can only print individual frame pages in Design view. You must Preview in Browser to print the whole page.

You won't see any of the images that belong to the Web page, but you will see the file names and the HTML control statements.

3 Click the Preview tab and you'll find the File, Print and Print Preview options disabled (grayed out). You'll need to Preview in Browser to print the page.

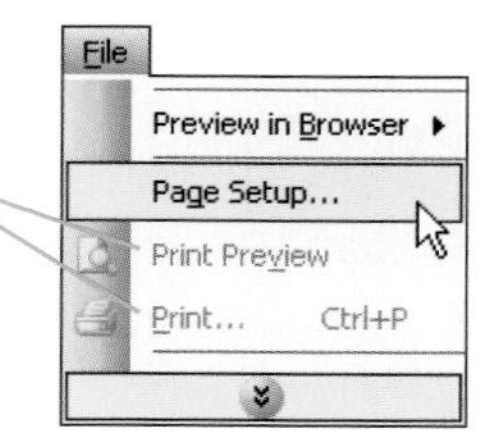

Preview in Browser will print the page as visitors will see it, showing for example collapsible lists in the state selected by the visitor. By default, they will be fully collapsed.

4 The Browser File, Print options available depend on which browser version and level you are using. This shows File, Print Preview in Internet Explorer version 6.0

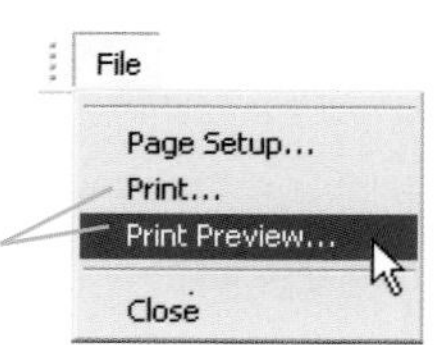

When you switch to Web Site, only the Navigation View offers File, Print or File Preview options. It lets you print the structure of the Web site, as defined in that view.

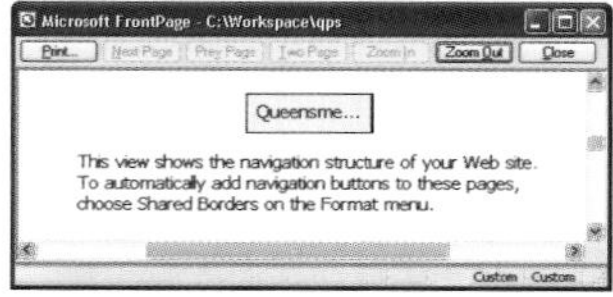

5 Select File, Print Preview to see the additional printing options that are provided.

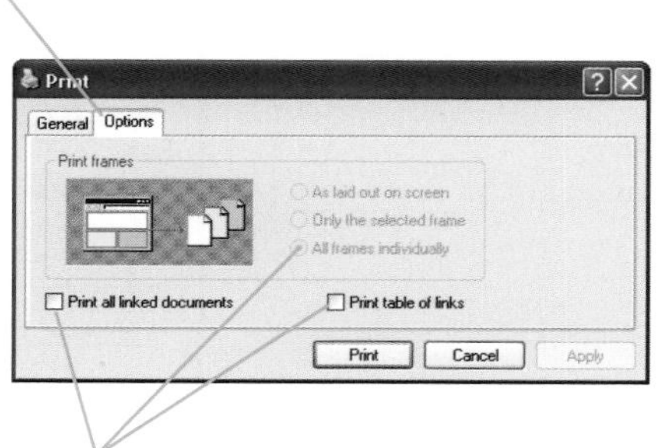

You can print specific page frames if applicable (see page 140), or all linked documents (note that this could be a large amount), or a table of all the URLs on the Web page.

Fixing errors

FrontPage uses temporary files on your hard disk to store data about the Web site. This speeds up the process of opening a large Web site. However, if you have several authors developing different parts of the Web site, these files can get out of sync.

To rectify errors that may arise with your Web site, follow these steps in sequence until Web site reports show everything is correct.

1 If updates don't show in the browser, click the Refresh button on the toolbar.

2 In FrontPage, select Tools, and click Recalculate Hyperlinks. For large Web sites with many hyperlinks, this process may be time-consuming.

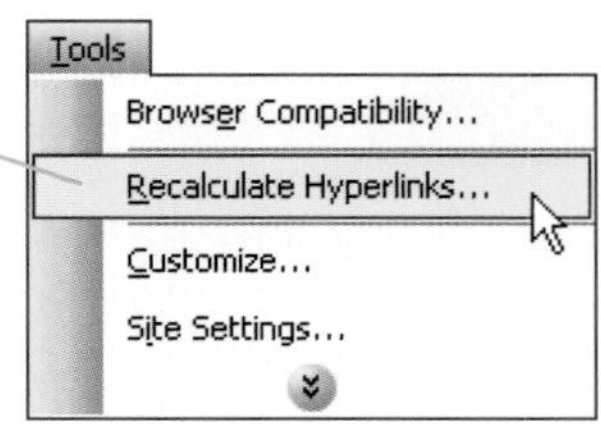

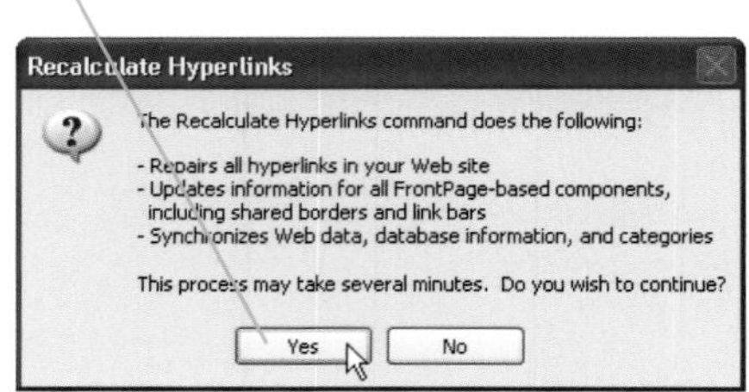

Apply the steps in turn, until you reach the position where your reports show full and correct information about the Web site.

3 In FrontPage, click Site Settings from the Tools menu, click the Advanced tab, and then click Delete Files.

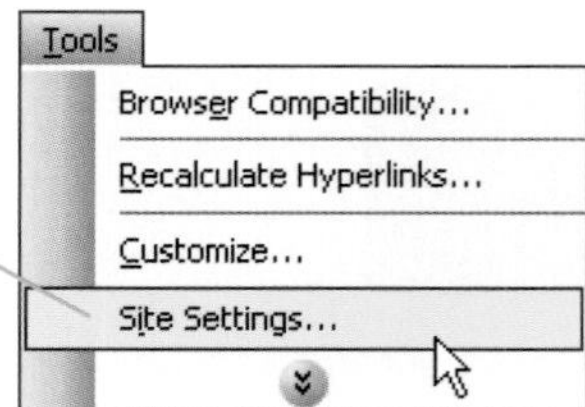

The next time you open the Web site on the server it may take longer, since FrontPage must copy the Web site information from the server to recreate your local temporary files.

Upgrading Web sites

If you have an existing Web site, it can take advantage of FrontPage 2003 design and publishing features, even if it was created in a previous version of FrontPage, or in a totally different HTML editor. If your Web server has the FrontPage extensions, you can upgrade the Web site to exploit them.

Covers

Chapter Nine

Import the Web site

If you have an existing Web site that you want to upgrade, import it as a FrontPage 2003 Web site.

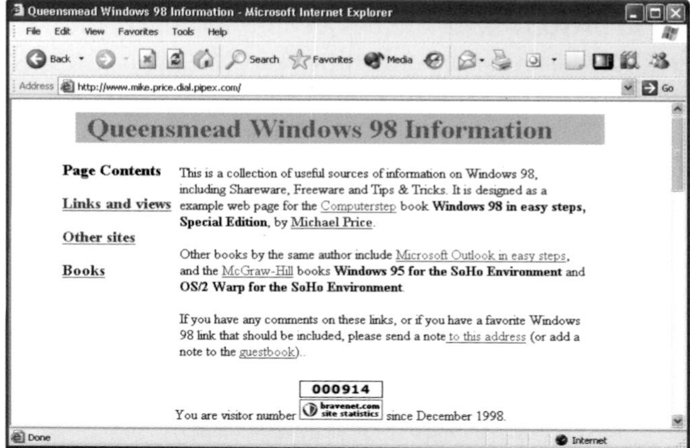

You can import pages from any Web site on the Internet, not just the sites you own or manage. This can be a useful way to obtain Web site components, but do be careful to avoid infringing copyrights.

1 Start FrontPage, close any open Web sites, and select File, Import.

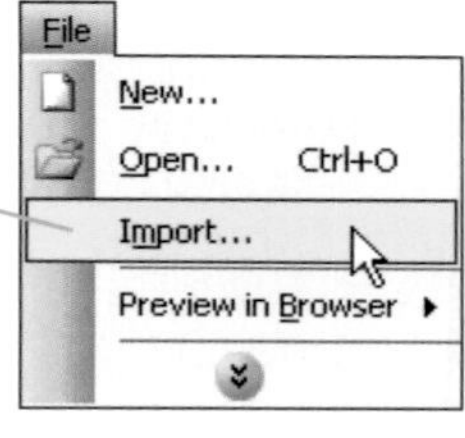

2 When the Import Web Site Wizard starts, select the location, and enter the path for the Web site you want to import.

You can import the original source files and folders from the hard disk, or the Web pages and components from the Web server on your network or on the Internet.

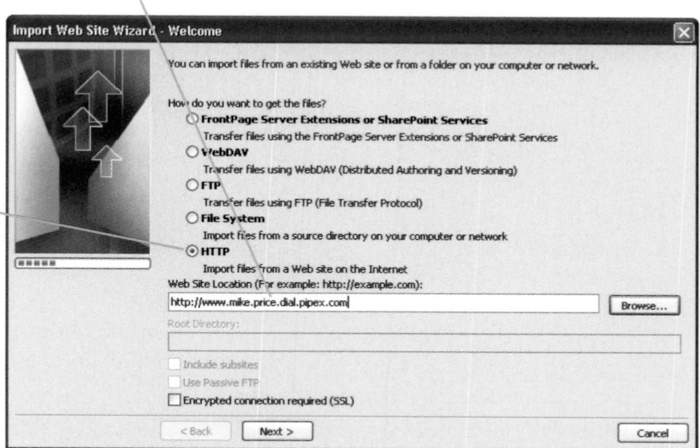

For a source directory, specify the folder on your hard disk or network drive. For a Web site on the Internet, specify the full URL.

3 Specify where you would like to create the local copy, and the name for the new Web site.

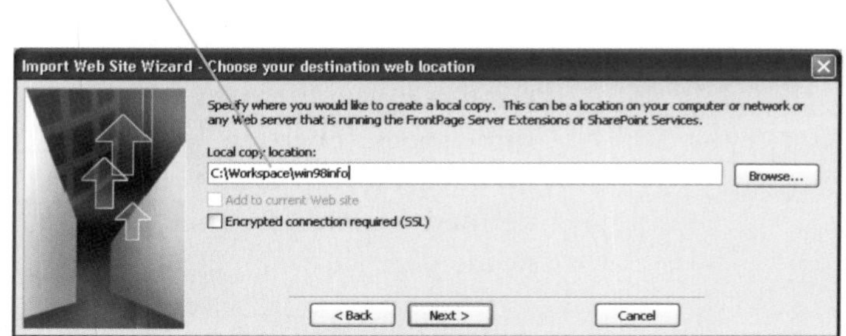

The starting page can be any page in the Web site, not just the home page, and it will follow every link to the depth specified (but avoiding cyclical references). Note that you will only be downloading the pages that belong to this Web site, and not pages referenced through external links.

4 Specify the number of levels below the starting page and a limit on how much disk space to use. Choose to import text and images only, or all files referenced on the pages selected.

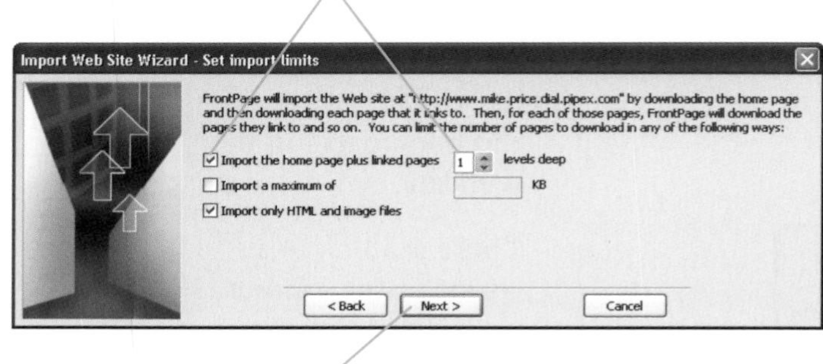

5 Click Next, and the pages and images from the original Web site are copied to the hard disk as a new FrontPage 2003 Web site.

The new Web site will be shown in FrontPage, ready for you to review or edit as appropriate.

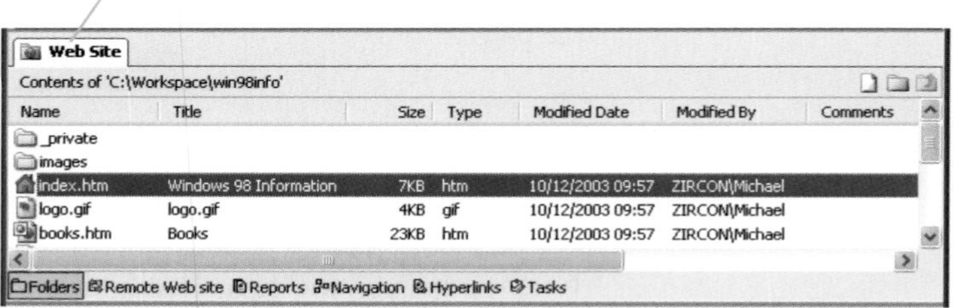

Analyze the Web site

Review the style and structure on the Web site, to decide what changes are appropriate to bring it up to the FrontPage 2003 level.

The downloaded Web site has been given a FrontPage 2003 folder setup, but all of the files are in the root. It has five image files and three pages. There is no navigation structure defined – only the home page shows.

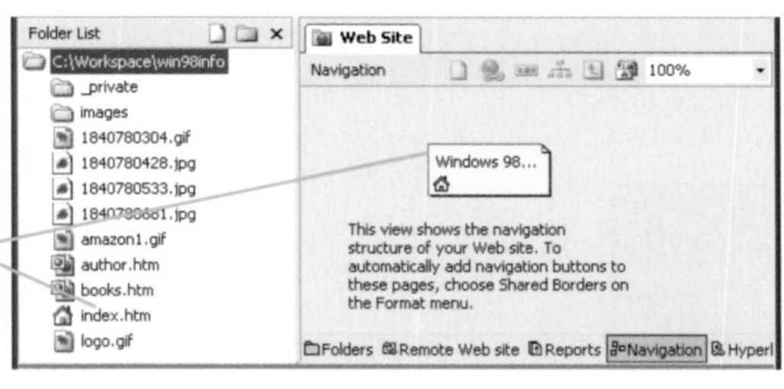

This is typical of the simpler Web site designs. It uses tables to organize and position text, graphics and links.

One table contains a simulated Navigation bar, linking to pages and bookmarks in the Web site.

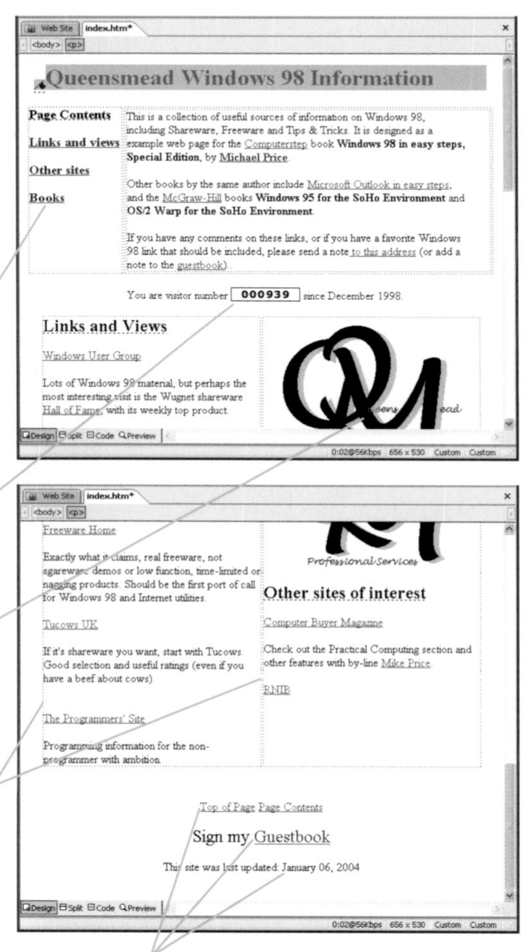

There is a link to a visitor or hit counter.

The hit counter and guest book facilities are maintained and managed by external Web sites.

The graphical image is positioned within a cell of the table, to control its relative placing.

The text tables give the effect of a magazine by simulating columns on the page.

The page is long, so when you scroll down, the navigation table disappears. To make up for this, more scrolling links are provided at the foot of the page. There's also an edit date, that can be maintained by FrontPage, and there's a link to a Guest Book.

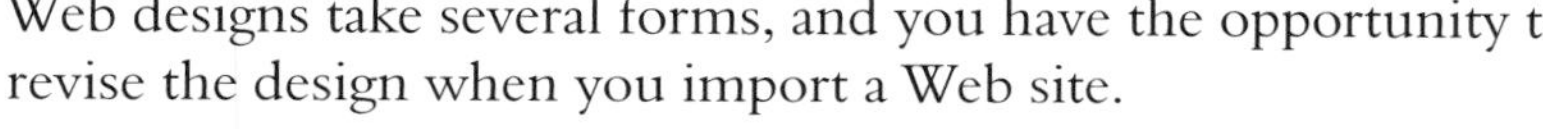

Your Web site could use tables, shared borders, frames, or two-dimensional positioning to lay out Web pages. Each method has its own pros and cons.

Web designs take several forms, and you have the opportunity to revise the design when you import a Web site.

Table structure

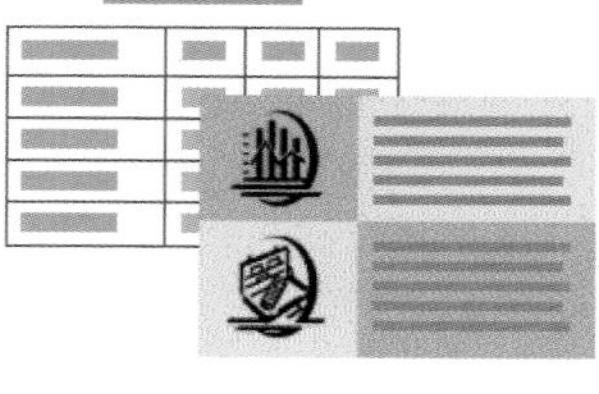

This is the simplest and most universal design. Tables provide an easy way to get columns, and align graphics with text. Your visitors don't even see the table because you can hide its borders. Using tables to organize text/graphics on the page means just about any browsers can display your Web site. However, it will limit your use of the more advanced Web site functions.

Visitors who use non-graphical browsers or screen readers may have difficulty with tables or with positioning, since it is impossible to present the page contents in sequence.

Shared borders

Shared borders are useful when you want the same items to appear on each page, for example, a company logo or a page banner. They also support navigation bars, as described for the ChampionZone Web site, where FrontPage creates and maintains links between the pages. However, they are not very flexible when you want something other than the standard layout.

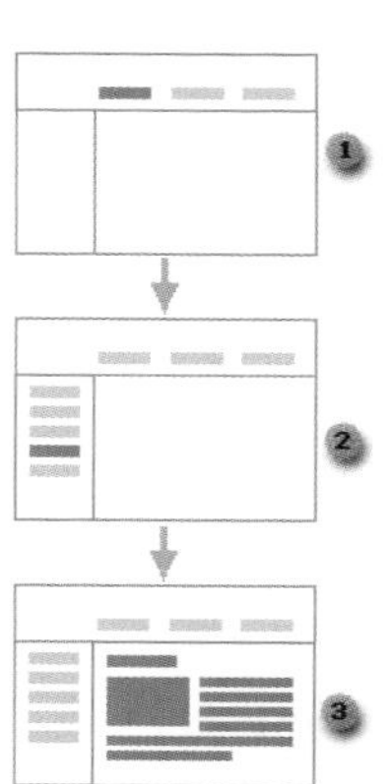

Frames

Frames allow you to display multiple pages dynamically on one page. They let you display some data continually, such as a list of hyperlinks, and to display a large amount of data that can be scrolled without interfering with other components on the page.

Requires CSS 2.0, so older browsers do not support positioning and will not display the page correctly.

Positioning

Relative and absolute positioning allow you to place text/graphics elements anywhere on a page, independent of paragraph marks, specify layers so that you can overlap text and graphics, and group elements to treat them as a unit. It is the most flexible method, which can match any requirement but is the hardest to maintain.

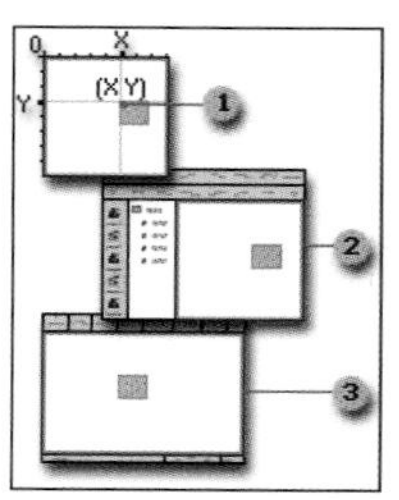

Upgrade the Web site

FrontPage manages Web sites you import, without needing changes to their structure, yet you can still make use of the reporting and maintenance functions.

You do not need to make significant changes to the imported Web site, in order to upgrade it to FrontPage 2003. In fact, just saving the pages is sufficient. It will support the original design, whether table or frame, and you can use the FrontPage 2003 facilities to manage the Web site, make editorial changes to the contents as needed, and publish the upgraded Web site back to the Web server.

To check the accuracy of Web site hyperlinks:

1. With the imported Web site open, select Web Site view and the Reports tab, and click Unverified Hyperlinks on the Site Summary.

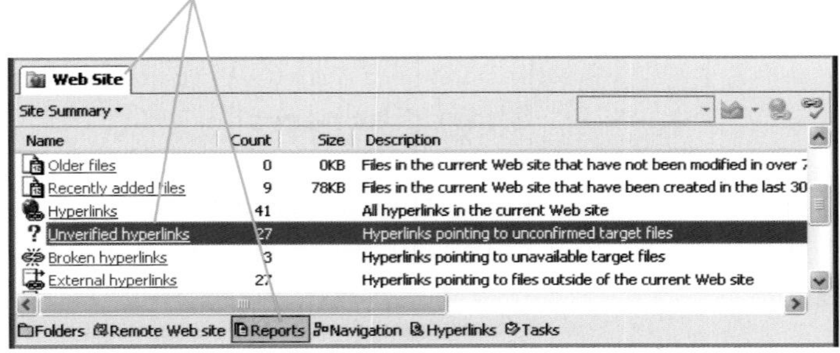

2. Click Yes and FrontPage will check all the external hyperlinks. You must have an active Internet connection.

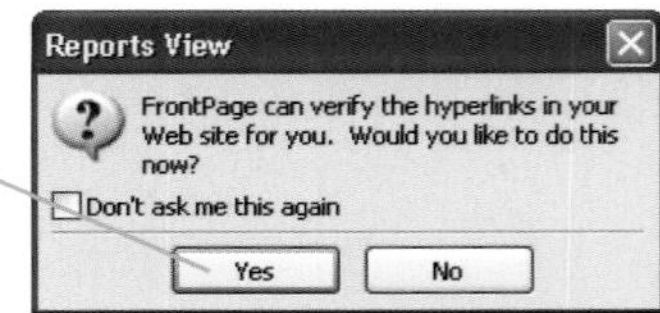

Click the Status header to sort the hyperlinks, and put all the broken links at the top of the list.

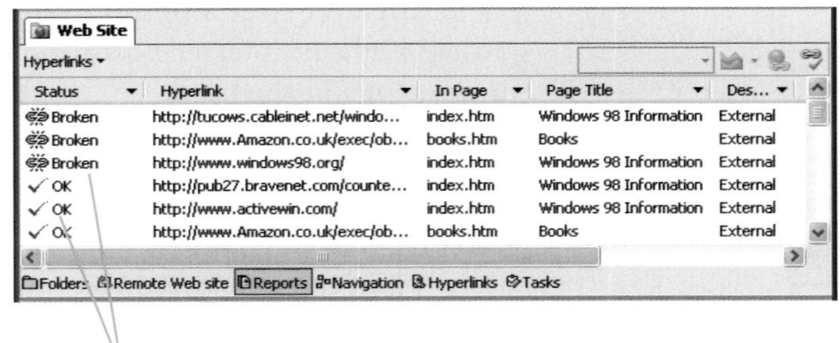

3. The Hyperlinks report shows the status for all the hyperlinks, so you can identify and correct all broken or invalid links.

You may need to move files to a more suitable folder, e.g. the image files to the Images folder.

4 Press Ctrl and select all the image files. Drag them, and drop them into the Images folder.

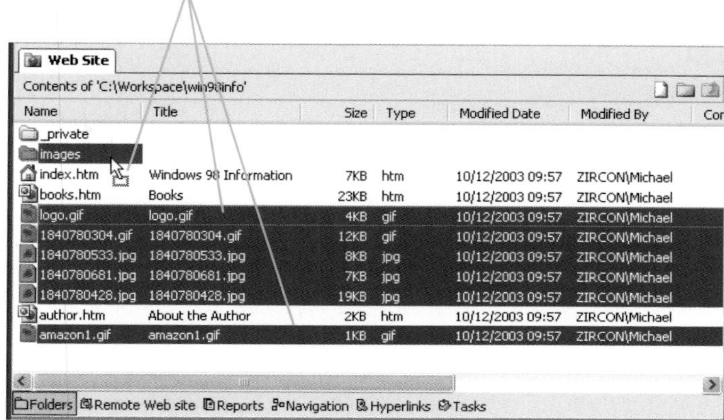

Some changes will be required, if you want to convert to shared borders.

5 Select the Navigation view, click the Home page, and drag the second level page files to the appropriate position in the navigation structure.

If the Web site you have downloaded includes manual navigation data, you can change to the FrontPage Shared Borders and Navigation Bars, to ensure that the links will be automatically managed in future.

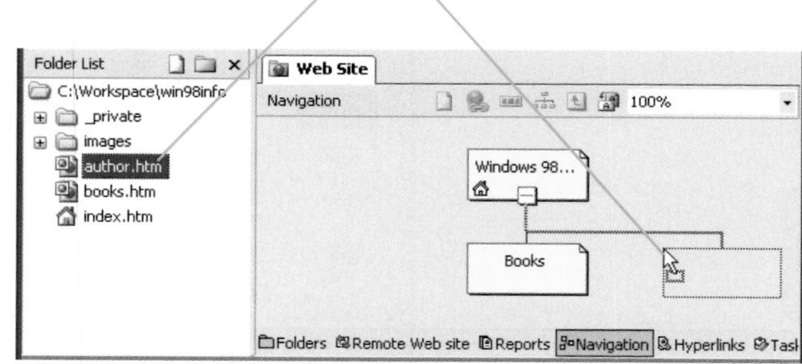

Avoid the use of navigation bars if you are planning to use frames (see page 140), since the combination creates confusion in navigating the Web site.

When you've completed the structure in Navigation view, you can use Shared Borders and Navigation Bars as described on pages 62–63, to automate the links between the pages. Remember that when you've completed the upgrade, you should remove any manual navigation table data that is included in the text of the pages.

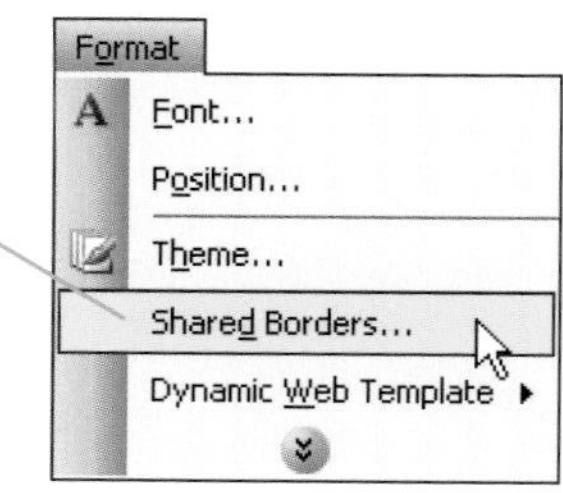

Frames page

The frames page itself contains no visible content. It is merely a container that specifies which other pages to display and how to display them. You click a hyperlink on a page in one frame, and the linked page is displayed in another frame, the *target* frame.

A frames page is a special kind of HTML page that divides the browser area into different areas called frames, each of which can display a different HTML file. You create a frames page using one of the frames page templates provided in FrontPage. These have the navigation between frames already set up.

1 First rename the *index.htm* file to *main.htm* – the frame page will be the new *index.htm*.

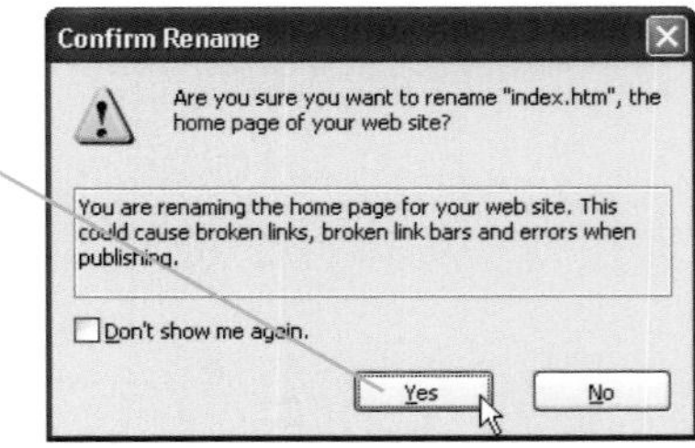

2 Select Page view and click File, New, Page, Page Template.

3 Click the Frames Pages tab, and preview the templates. It gives a description and preview when you click on any of the templates.

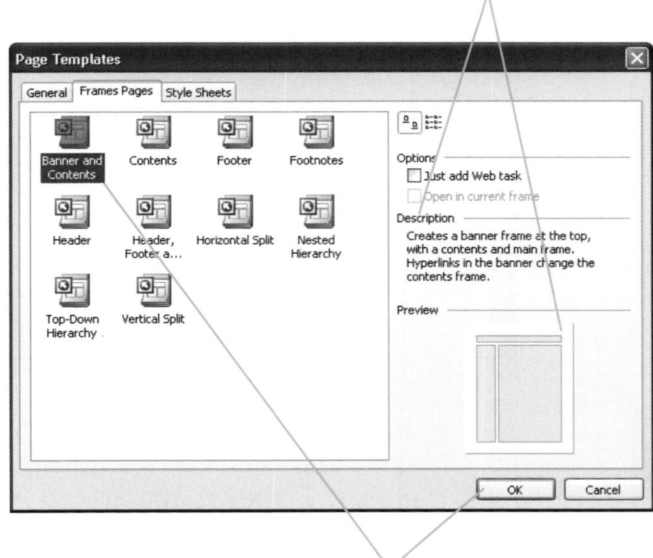

You must rename the home page to something other than "Index.htm", before you start building a frame version of the page.

4 Select the Banner and Contents template and click OK. This will create a frames page with three frames, ready for you to set the initial page, or define a new page in each frame.

Select or create the pages to display initially in each of the frames.

5 Save the frames page as *Index.htm*, and select New Page for the top banner frame.

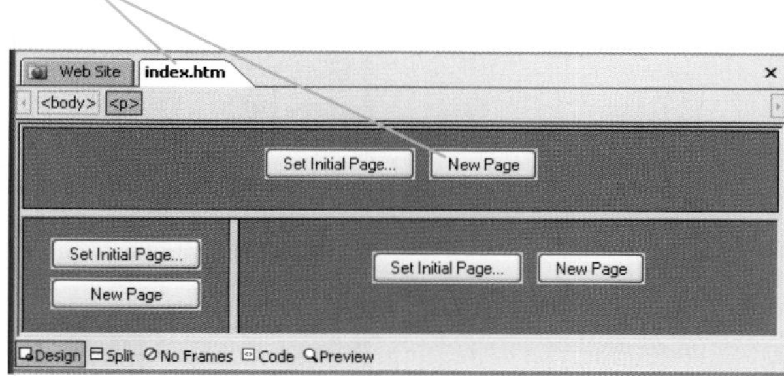

6 Enter the banner title for the Web site, format the text as Heading 1 and Center, and save the page as *Banner.htm*.

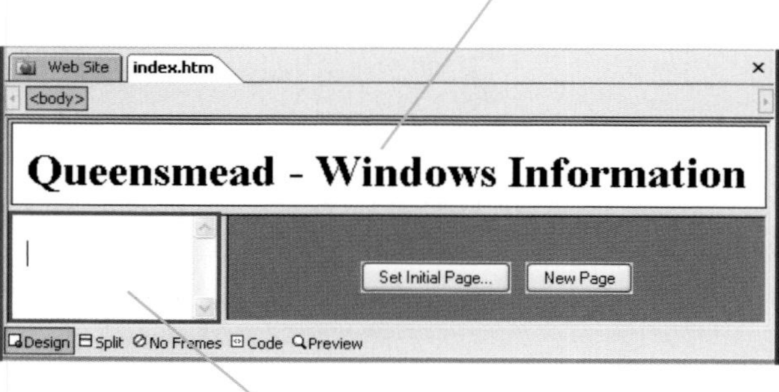

You must specify the starting page for the TOC, and select the rules that will apply e.g. don't show unlinked pages, and recalculate the table when other pages are edited.

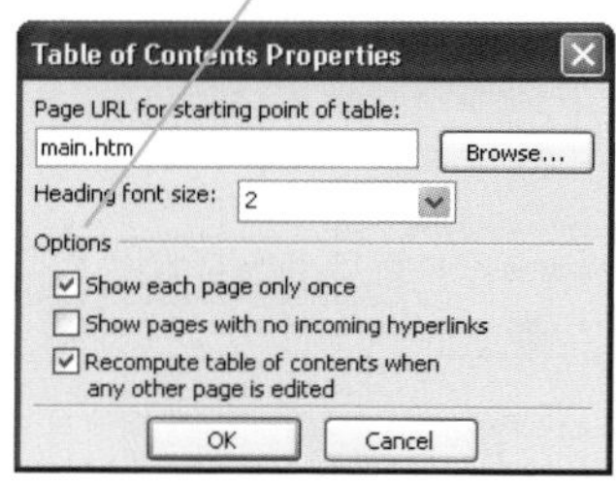

7 Click New Page on the left, save it as *Contents.htm*, and click Insert, Web Components, Table of Contents.

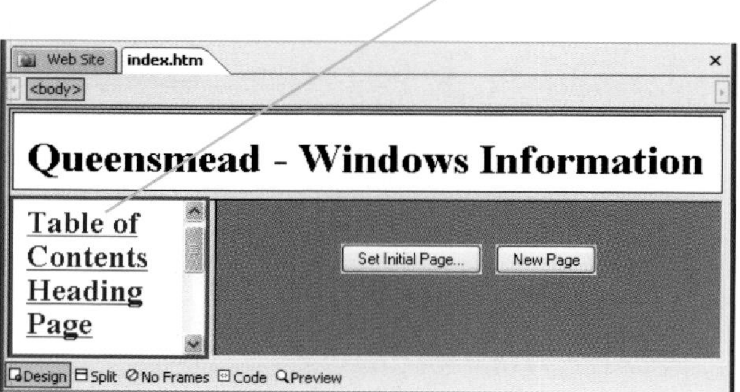

The main page

The main page and any other pages in your Web site will be displayed in the right-hand frame.

1 Click Set Initial Page in the right hand frame, and specify the page file *Main.htm* (the original *Index.htm*).

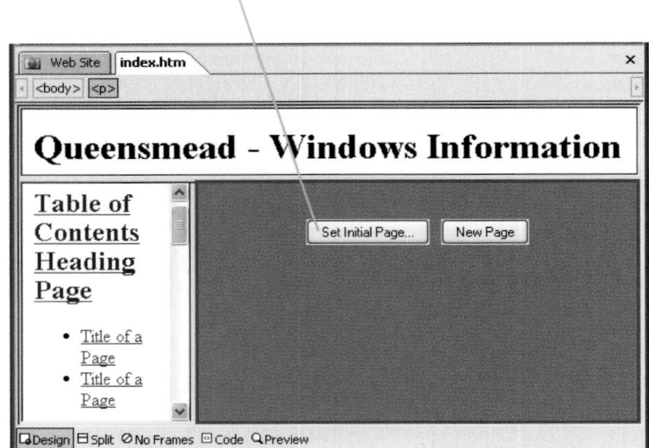

The changes needed will vary from Web site to Web site, but you need to apply changes to remove such items as contents links which are handled by other frames. You also need to rearrange the text to work with frames.

2 Edit the page, remove the components no longer required, split the text to create new pages, taking advantage of frames facilities:

Remove banner text.

Remove contents table.

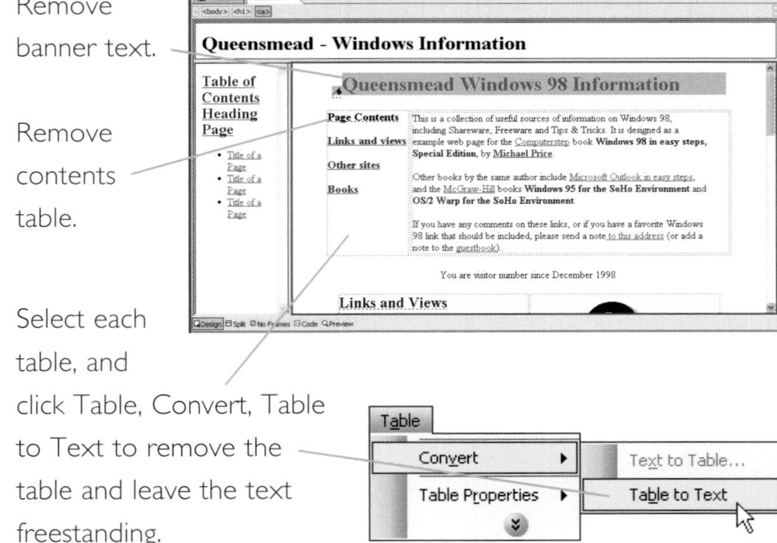

You should also create new Web pages to hold the Links and Web sites referenced in your Web site.

3 Select each table, and click Table, Convert, Table to Text to remove the table and leave the text freestanding.

Add the new pages in Navigation view, to show where they fit in the Web site structure. This does not add the pages to the Table of Contents. Pages must be linked, directly or indirectly, from the starting page.

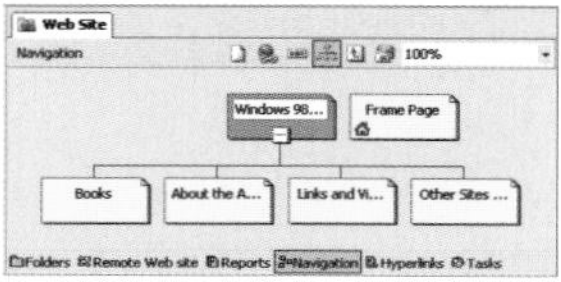

4 Add links to all the pages at the foot of the Main page, and copy these to all the pages (for users who can't display frames).

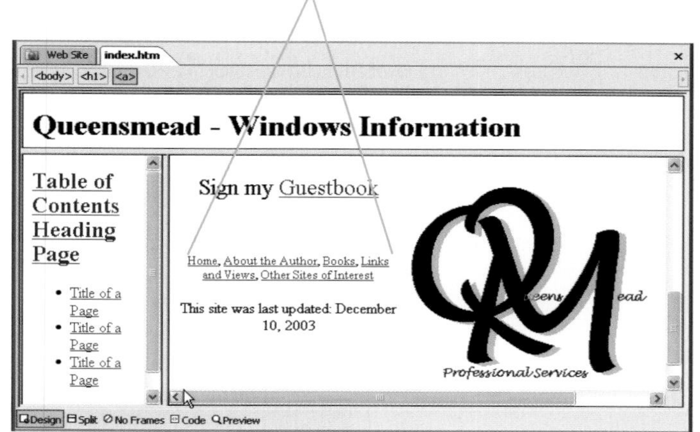

Adding links to all the pages will help visitors with older browsers that do not support frames (see page 77).

5 Save the changes, and press Preview in Browser.

Linked pages are listed in the Table of Contents as well as at the foot of the page.

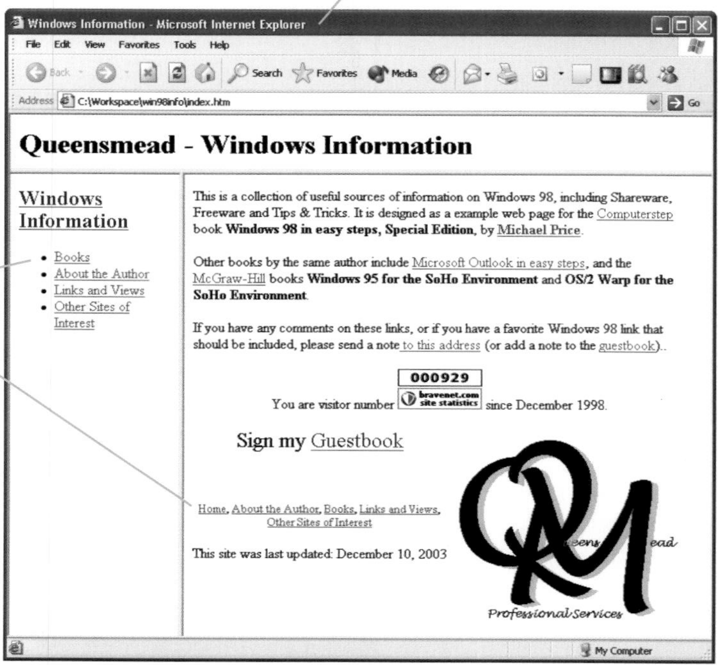

Inline frames

Inline frames are similar to frames pages except that the inline frame and its contents are embedded in an existing Web page. Anything that you can put on a regular page you can put in an inline frame. Inline frames can also be customized in the same ways as regular frames.

The advantages of using inline frames is that you don't need to create a separate frames page in order to have embedded content.

FrontPage 2003 supports inline frames, which allow you to embed another Web page and its contents in an existing page. One advantage of inline frames is that you can have embedded content without having to create separate frames pages.

To embed another Web page and its contents in an existing page using inline frames:

1. In Page view, click in the Web page at the position where you want to insert the inline frame.

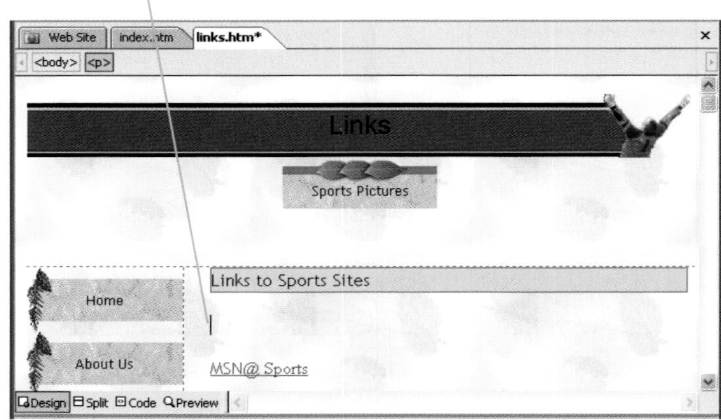

2. Select Insert, Inline Frame from the menu bar and click the Set Initial Page button to find and insert the required Hyperlink.

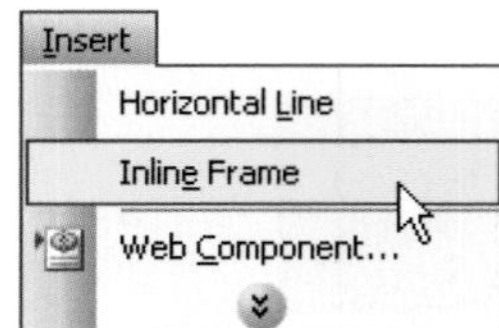

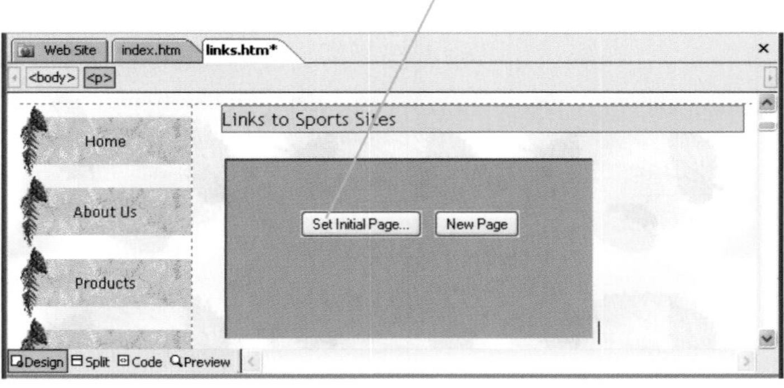

To embed a new page, click the New Page button. A new page will open and you can enter the text and graphics for the page.

You can insert a page from your Web site, or you can insert any URL from the Internet, to give your Web site a dynamic effect. Here for example, we provide a live link to the Masters page on the ESPN sports Web site.

3 From Insert Hyperlink, press Browsed Pages to locate the required Web page on your site or on the Internet. Click OK.

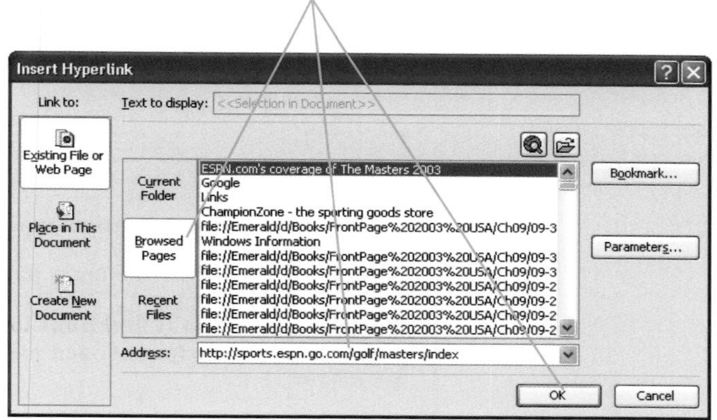

4 Save the page. If you had specified New Page instead of Initial Page, you'll be prompted for a name for the new page file.

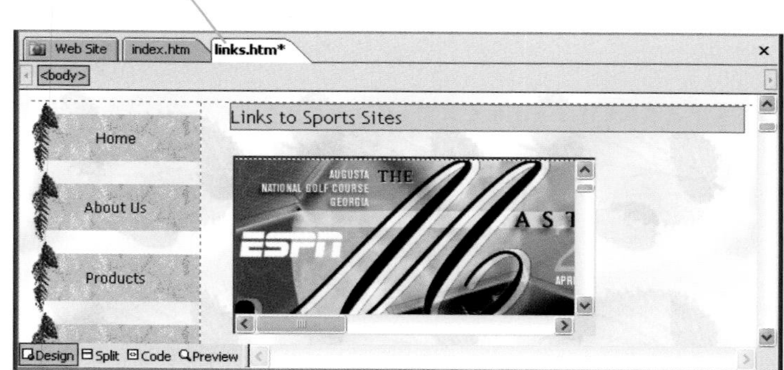

You can make changes to the Name, Initial page, Frame size, Margins, Alignment, Scrollbars and Show border. You can also specify alternate text to show if the visitor's browser does not support frames (see page 146).

Alternate text:

Your browser does not support inline frames or is currently configured not to display inline frames.

5 To make changes to the inline frame, move the cursor over the top border of the inline frame until it changes to a left-pointing arrow, then click to select it, then right-click and choose Inline Frame Properties.

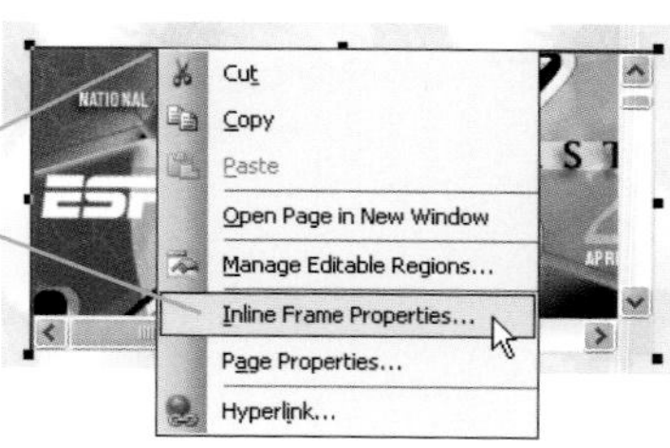

No frames

Some visitors are unable to view Web pages that use frames, due to their use of older browsers such as Internet Explorer 2 and Netscape 2 which do not support frames pages. FrontPage handles this situation by displaying a simple message to warn the visitor of the problem.

If you added links to the pages (see page 143), you can tell the visitor to use these links to view the contents of your Web site.

Restrictions on Web TV (MSN TV) will also place limitations on what functions on your Web site visitors may be able to use.

To display the default No Frames message:

1 Open the Index.htm frames page and click the No Frames tab at the bottom of the display.

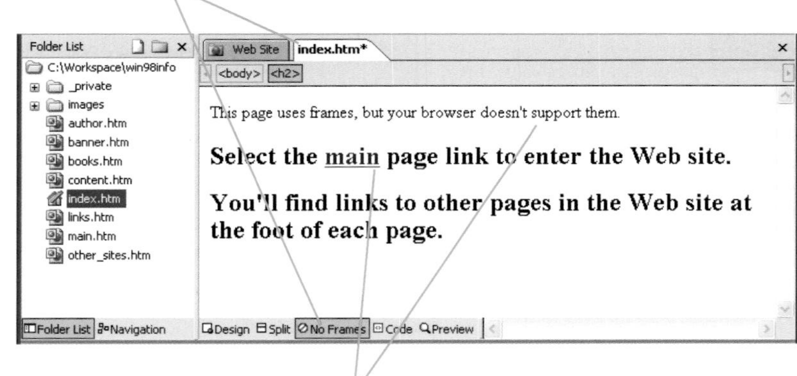

2 The first line shows the default message, which provides no alternatives. Add a text message with a hyperlink to a no-frames page, for example the *main.htm* used for the Frames display.

Web TV constraints

Download the Web TV viewer to check if the content on your Web site is suitable for users of MSNTV. You will find it at http://developer.msntv.com/Tools/msntvvwr.asp.

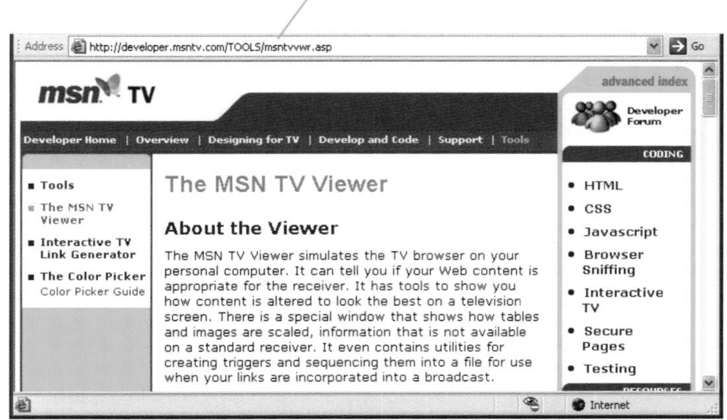

Web designs

Chapter Ten

You may want several Web sites at the same ISP, for personal and business use, or for different members of the family, or to suit different browsers. Subsites make it easy to manage such varying needs.

Covers

Web page size

There's no right or wrong way, just a number of pros and cons. Short pages are easier to scan, and you can update sections of data at a time. Long pages are better for concentrated research, and you have fewer files and links to maintain.

Your Web site could have just one page or many pages. It depends on how much information you have, and how much you put in each document.

There's no maximum size as such for a page, but you can only display a screenful at a time. If you have a lot of reference material, you should help the visitor to find the main items on the page.

1 Bookmarks can be used to highlight items of interest, point to sections that are off-screen, and return you to the top of page.

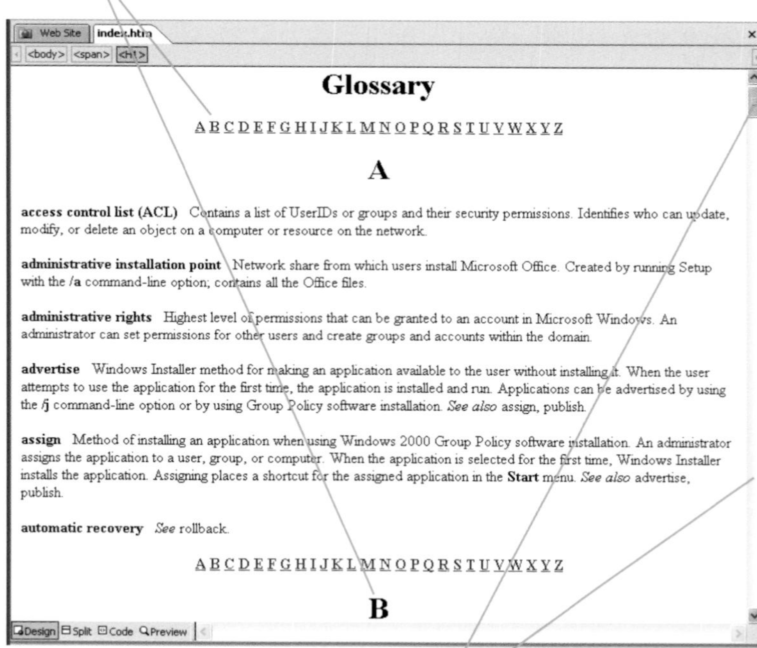

The size of the scroll bar section indicates the amount of data that is off the screen.

2 Scroll bars allow the visitors to select a different portion of the page, or to swiftly scan the page contents.

The concern with long pages applies in particular to visitors who are casually browsing or surfing the Internet.

However, long documents take more time to download, and visitors may fail to spot items that would interest them.

The default screen size is normally assumed to be 800 x 600 pixels. You can split the page up into a number of smaller pages, each providing a screen of information, with little or no scrolling.

3 Each page may link Forward and Back to the next and the previous pages, or may carry links to all the other pages.

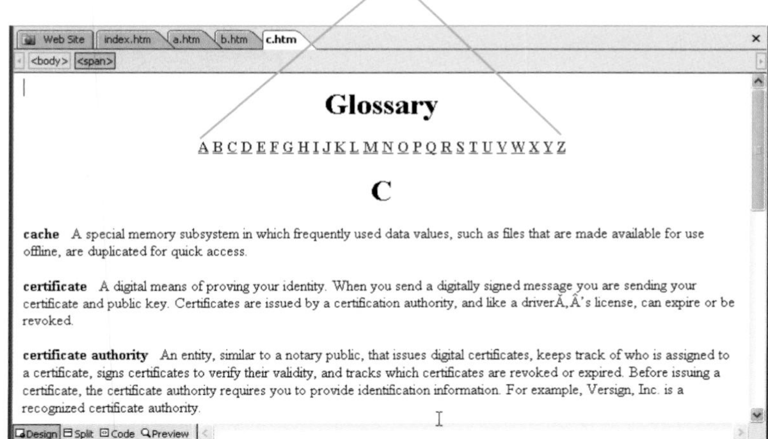

An overall index page may be used to set the pages into their proper context.

You can arrange the links in navigation bars or tables of contents, if you use shared borders (see pages 62–63) or frames (see pages 140–141).

Choose the page size and style based on the type of information and the type of visitor you expect. There is no single right answer, but there are some guidelines you can consider:

- For overviews and presentations, don't make the page longer than the default window size.
- Use scrollable screens for longer pages, with text or reference lists.
- For general purpose pages, keep the size around one or two screens, and don't hide important features like Continue buttons below the edge of the initial display.
- Consider preparing a separate, single page version of your Web site for printing/downloading or non-graphical browsers.
- If your Web site uses frames, consider a separate entry point for users without frame support.

Some users need screen reader software which may need to rearrange the screen content to present it in a logical sequence.

Web structures

Web space providers and ISPs cater to the standard Web site structure which is really designed for the single owner situation.

The typical single user personal Web site has one home page and a number of lower level subsidiary or child pages.

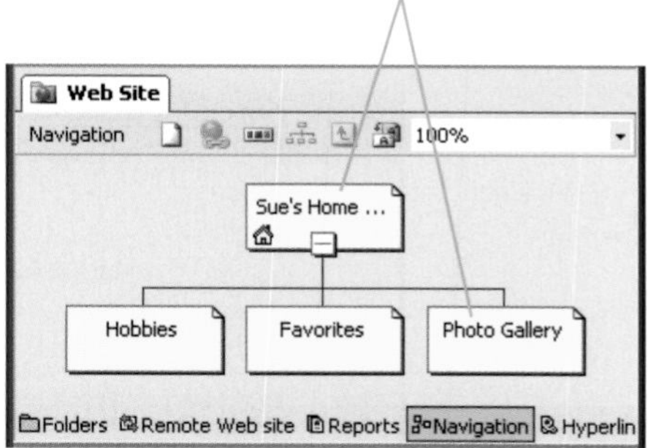

If you are sharing the Web site space with others, you might require separate home pages for each user, yet want to manage the site as a single unit from the same WPP.

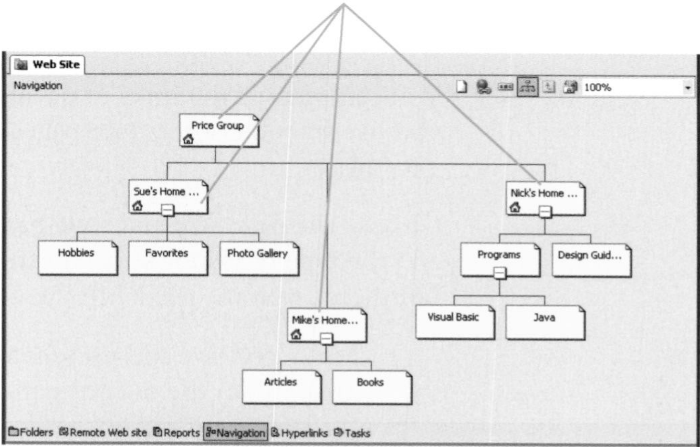

This is in effect what FrontPage offers you, through the subsite facility. You create a master or parent Web site, and build your independent subsites within it. Each subsite can have its own settings and themes, and be separately edited. However, the set of subsites can be published and maintained as a group, to a single ISP or WPP account.

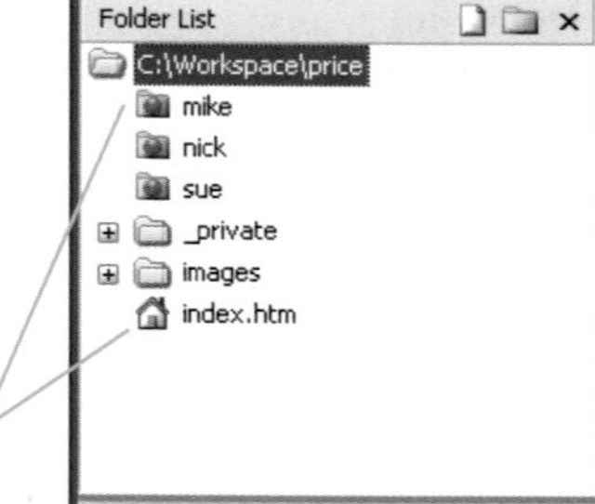

Create the parent

Create a Web site to act as the entry to the subsites that you want to create.

Any type of Web site, including an existing Web site, can be used as the parent Web site for a subsite.

It is not essential to put hyperlinks in the parent Web site, since you can address the subsite directly from the browser. However, for default entry through the parent home page, you do need to add suitable links to the parent.

1 Start FrontPage, close any open Web sites and select File, New and click the More Web sites templates link on the Task Pane.

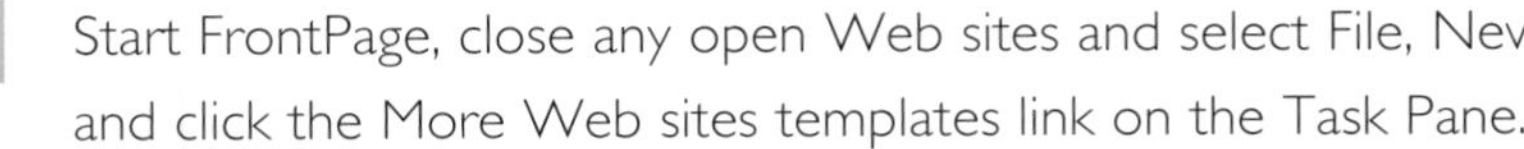

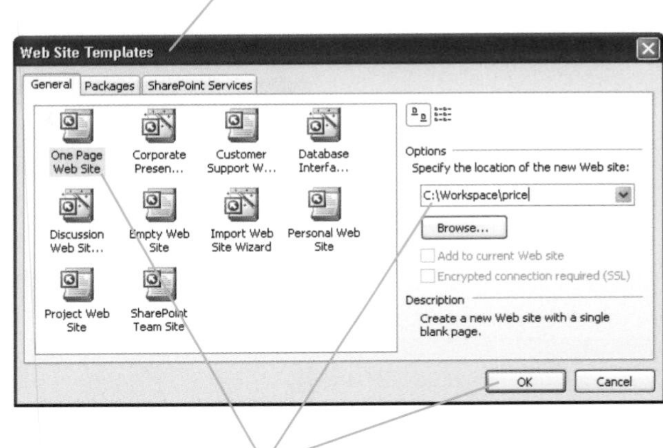

2 Select the One Page Web Site template, specify the location and the name for the Web site, and click OK.

The Web site will be generated with a single blank Web page named Index.htm, plus the usual FrontPage folder structure.

3 Open Index.htm in Page view. Add a page title and some text placeholders for the hyperlinks to the subsites you plan.

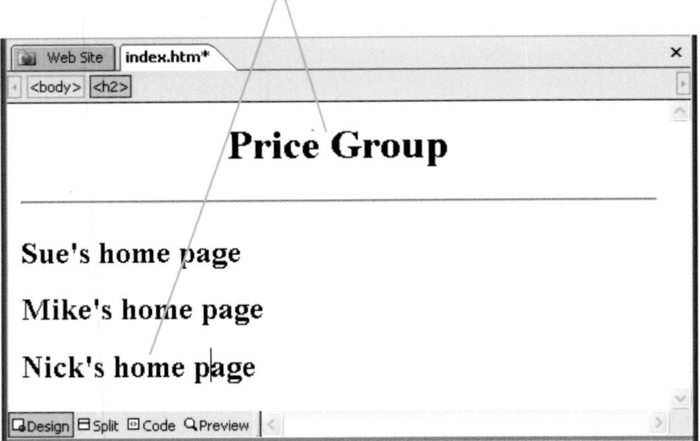

Create subsites

If the contents for the subsite already exist in another Web site, then choose the single page Web site template, and publish the existing Web site to this new subsite.

1 Open the parent Web site. Select File, New, click More Web site templates, and choose the template (e.g. Personal Web Site). Specify the location as the parent Web site plus subsite name.

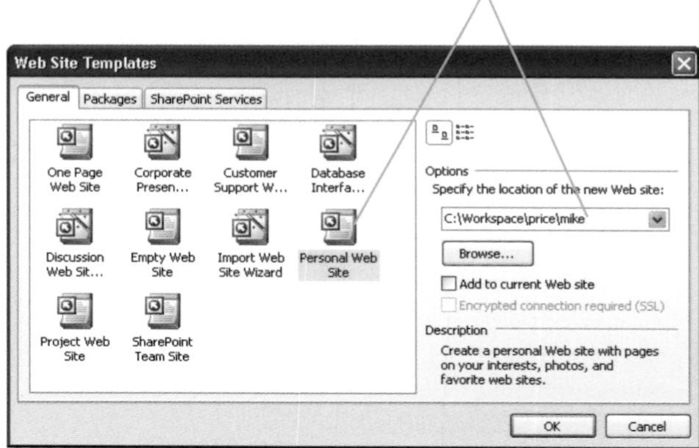

The subsite is created within the parent Web site, and starter versions of the *Index.htm* page and any other pages will be created.

If you update the Web site this way, the Web site settings from the original Web site will be retained, so you'll have to reapply shared borders and themes.

2 Create the Web pages or, if there is an existing Web site elsewhere, you can publish the contents to the new subsite.

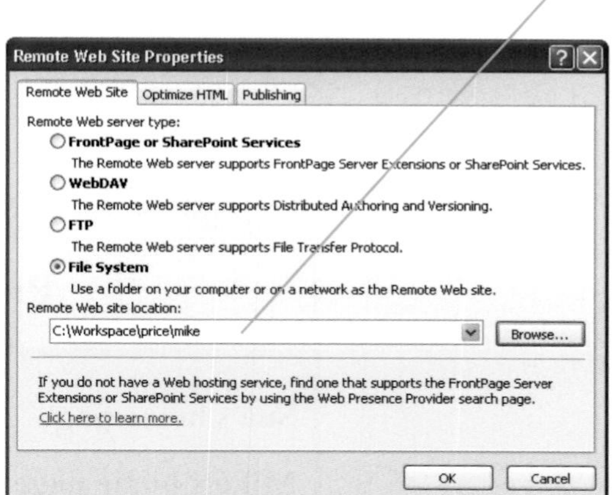

3 Repeat the process for each of the remaining subsites in turn, to install them below the parent Web site folder.

Complete the parent Web site

The subsites appear as Web site folders within the parent Web site folder. You can open the subsite by double-clicking the folder. A new instance of FrontPage will be launched for the subsite; you can edit the files or review the reports, as with any Web site.

1 Open the parent Web site, edit the home page *Index.htm*, and highlight a subsite hyperlink placeholder. Click Insert Hyperlink.

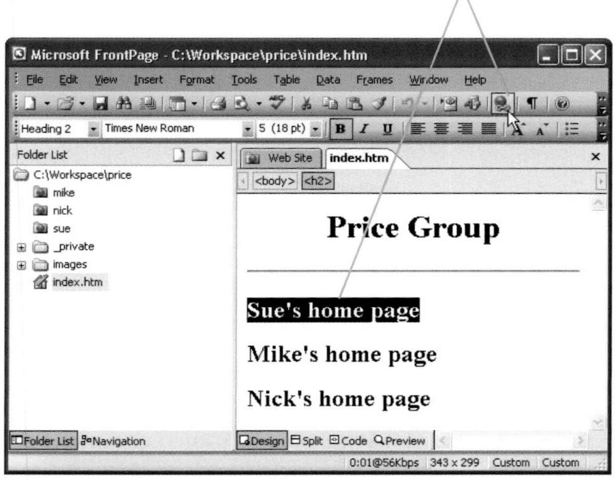

You should provide hyperlinks from the parent to the each of the subsites that you have defined (see pages 150 and 152).

2 Click Existing File or Web Page, and select the appropriate subsite. Click OK to accept the subsite name and title.

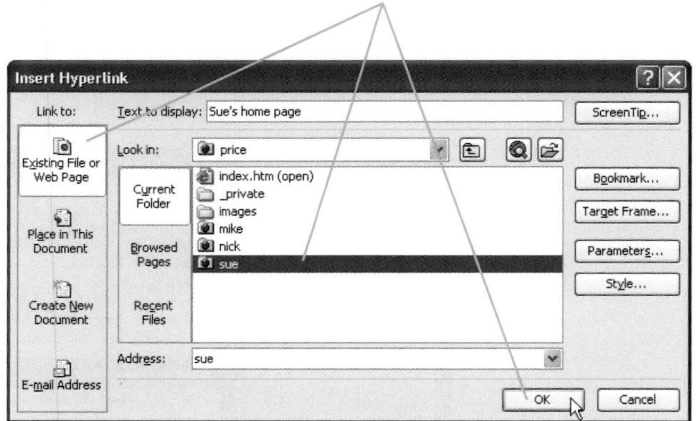

You can specify just the subsite name, or put the full URL for the home page. However, your choice does affect the way the Web site appears in browser previews (see page 154).

3 For one of the subsites, double-click the subsite to open it, and select the home page Index.htm explicitly and press the OK button.

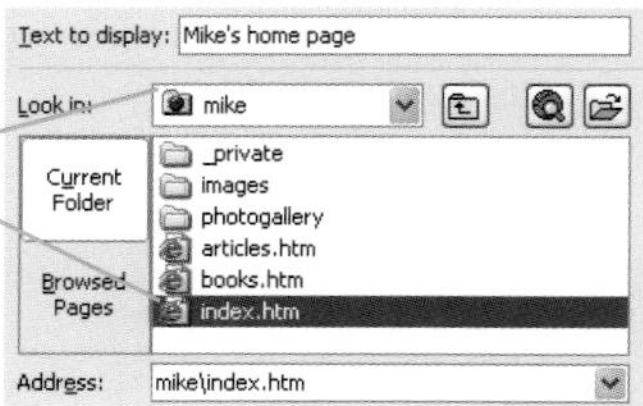

Preview the Web sites

1. Open the parent Web site, open the home page and press Preview in Browser.

2. The home page for the parent Web site is displayed. Click a subsite hyperlink of each type – name only or full home page.

If you specify just the subsite URL, Preview in Browser will open the folder rather than the Web site.

When you are online, specifying the Web site URL with or without the home page will open the Web site just the same.

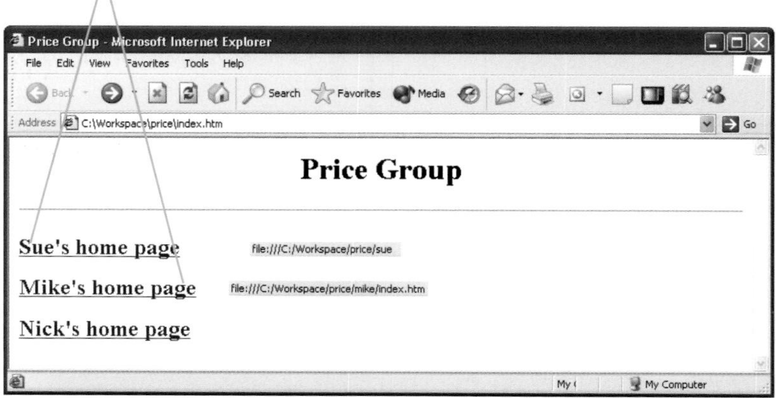

3. The Web site folder is displayed with subsite name only, but the Home page displays if the full URL is defined in the hyperlink.

You can still access the Web site. Double-click the icon for the home page to open the subsite in the normal Internet Explorer manner.

Publish the Web sites

When you have subsites defined within your Web site, you can publish them individually to your Web server.

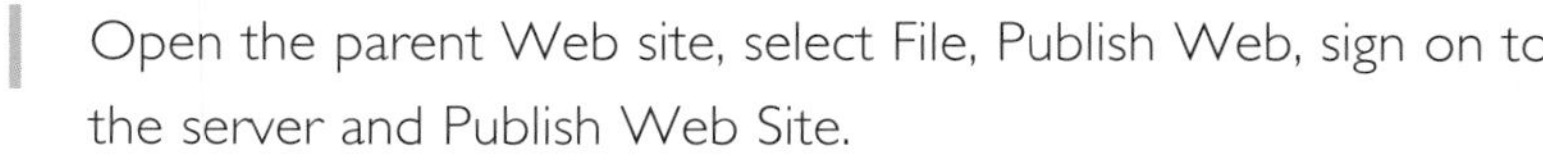

1 Open the parent Web site, select File, Publish Web, sign on to the server and Publish Web Site.

2 Open one of the subsites, specify the FTP server and enter the FTP directory, which is the same as the subsite name.

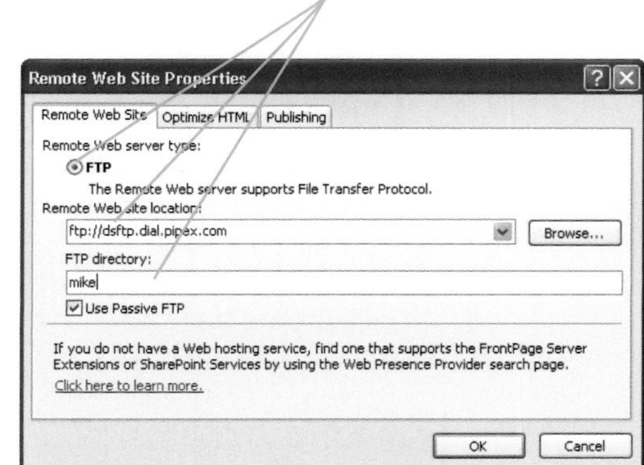

If you are publishing via HTTP, the subsite name can be appended to the main Web site URL address, for example, you could have: http://www.maprice.com/mike Again, you'll be prompted to allow FrontPage to create a Web site folder.

3 Since this is a new folder, you'll be prompted to allow FrontPage to create a Web site folder at the remote location.

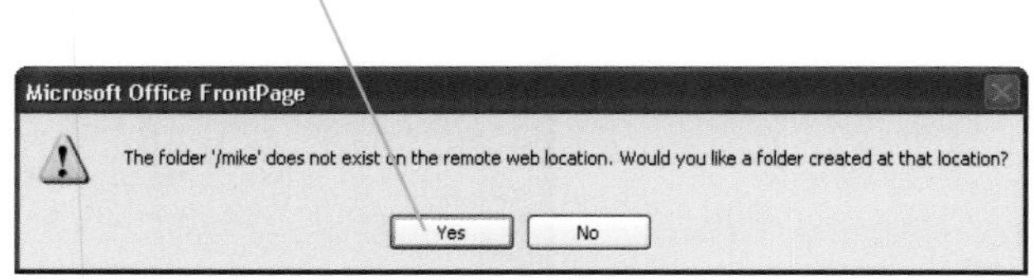

You must specify the folder name for each of the subsites in turn, and publish the individual subsites to the Web server.

4 When the new subsite has been created, click the Publish Web Site button to transfer the files and folders.

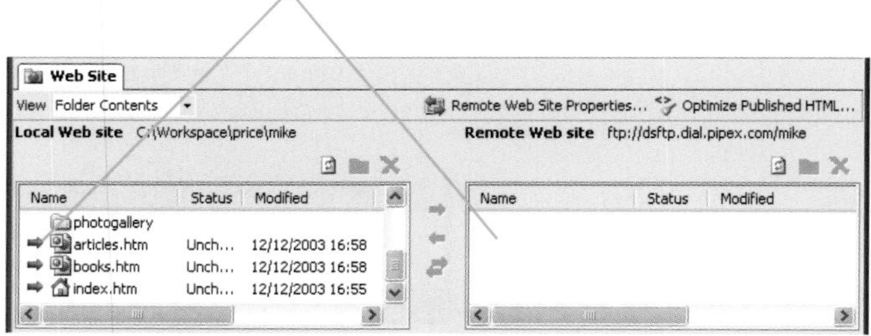

Visiting subsites

You can visit subsites by selecting hyperlinks from the parent site, or by entering the URL for the subsite in the browser address bar.

1 Select the Web site in your browser while connected to the Internet, to display the parent home page.

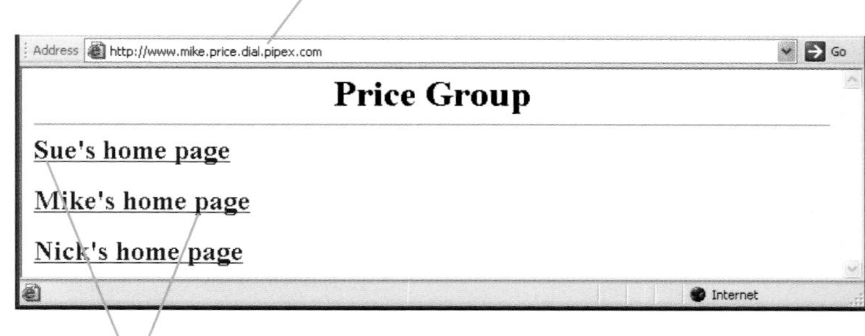

2 Click on the hyperlink to display one of the subsites. You'll get the home page even if the link has no page name specified.

When you provide a URL without a page name, the browser tries the standard names for home pages, and displays the first match it finds, in this case "Index.htm".

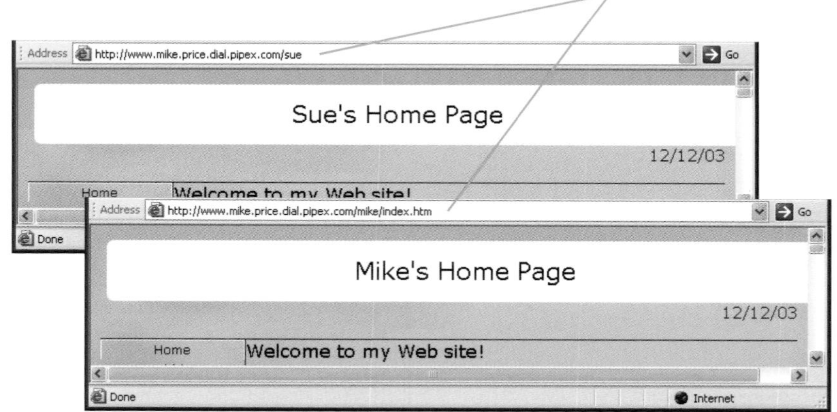

The Web site folder name usually doesn't matter because it is not published. However, when a Web site becomes a subsite, the name and its case become an issue. It is best to name the Web site folders with lower case names – the normally expected format.

3 You can also display the subsite by entering the full URL, e.g.
http://www.mike.price.com/nick/index.htm
however, you must be sure to specify the proper case, or the address may not be found.

Editing the Web site

If the Web server supports FrontPage Server Extensions, you can view the Web site folders and make immediate changes.

View and edit the contents of the Web site folders, at the Web server, when the server supports the FrontPage Server Extensions.

To view the folders:

1 Select File, Open, specify the Web site URL and choose Open as Web Folder.

2 You will be asked for your Login name and password to confirm your authority to make changes to the contents of the Web site.

3 The Web site folder is displayed, allowing you to locate the Web page or Web page element you wish to modify.

This is useful if you need to make a change to your Web site when you are away from your usual system, but the original copy on your hard disk will not be updated. You'll have to synchronize the Web site from the Web server to your hard disk to refresh your copy.

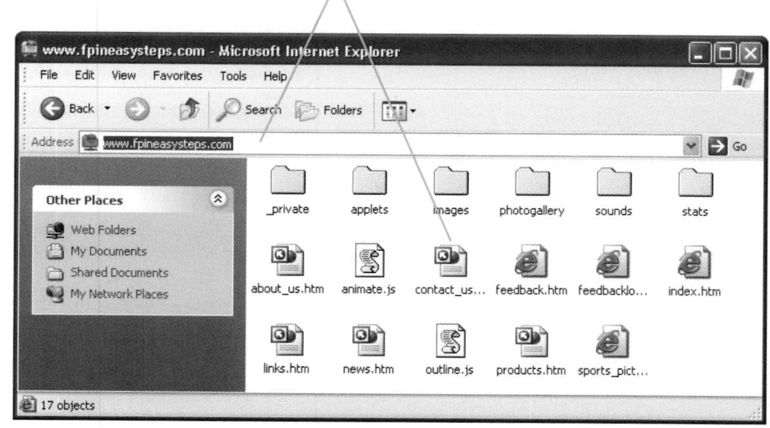

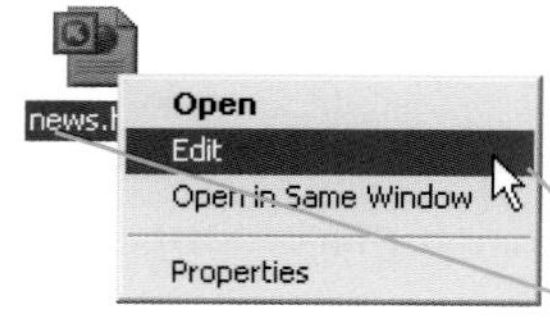

4 Right-click the page file and select Edit to open it in FrontPage and make changes, then choose Save, Close to update the file at the Web server.

Switching sites

When you change Web site space providers and move your Web site to a new Web server, you can redirect your visitors to the new location.

1 Replace the existing home page for the old location, with an explanatory message, and a hyperlink to the new location.

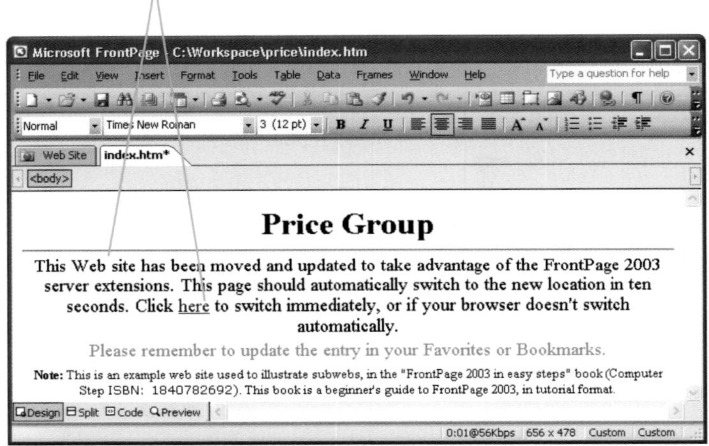

You can use the same technique to redirect visitors to pages within your site, when you reorganize and rename pages, since visitors might bookmark any page on your site, not just the home page.

2 Right-click the page, select Page Properties, Custom, and Add a system meta-variable to refresh the page after ten seconds.

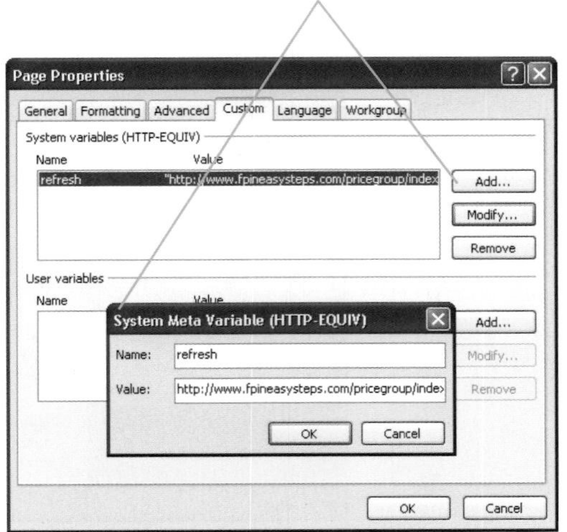

See pages 113 and 116 for more details on meta-variables.

When visitors select your old Web site or Web page, they will see the message and get an automatic transfer to the replacement.

Tables, images and forms

A more detailed look at the features of FrontPage, including the use of tables, the design of image maps and the creation of a SharePoint Team site for interaction and collaborative working.

Covers

Chapter Eleven

Creating tables

Tables are used in Web pages for two different purposes. They are used as a method for arranging text and graphics, as discussed on page 137, and they have their more usual function of presenting text and numeric data.

FrontPage provides several ways of creating tables. You can create a simple table by specifying the number of rows and columns. To create the table, in Page view select the insertion point and:

1. Click the Insert Table button to display the table selector. Click to expand the toolbar if the table button doesn't show.

2. Move the cursor down and across until you've selected the required number of rows and columns. The selector expands as necessary.

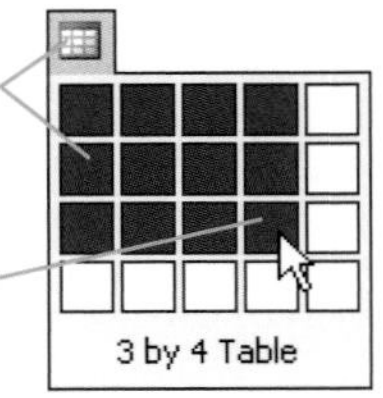

3. Click the bottom right cell to generate the table with default properties set.

You can modify the properties of the table after creating it. See opposite for examples of layout properties.

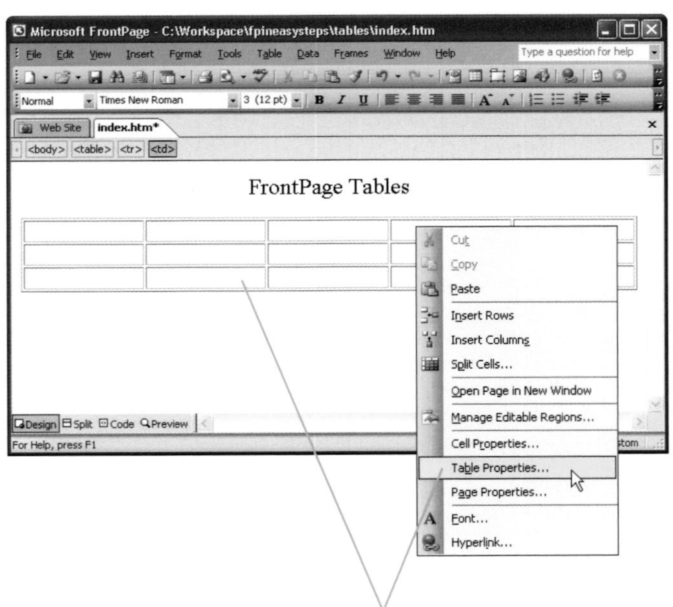

4. Right-click the table and choose Table Properties to adjust table settings such as Alignment, Padding, Spacing or Color.

Create from menu

If you click the Table button, you get default properties. But you can specify properties for your table as you are creating it, and make these the new defaults if required.

1 From the menu bar select Table then select Insert, and then Table.

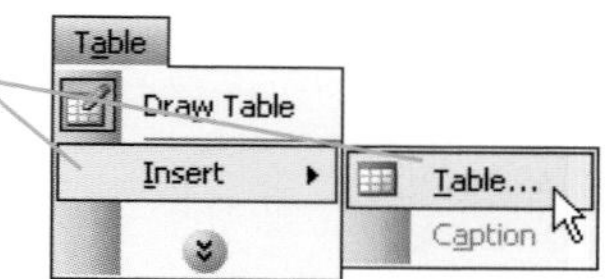

2 Select the properties of the new table:

- Number of rows and columns
- Alignment on page
- Float (text flow around table)
- Padding (space within cell) and Spacing (gap between cells)
- Border size and colors
- Background color and background picture
- Width and Height (in pixels or percents)

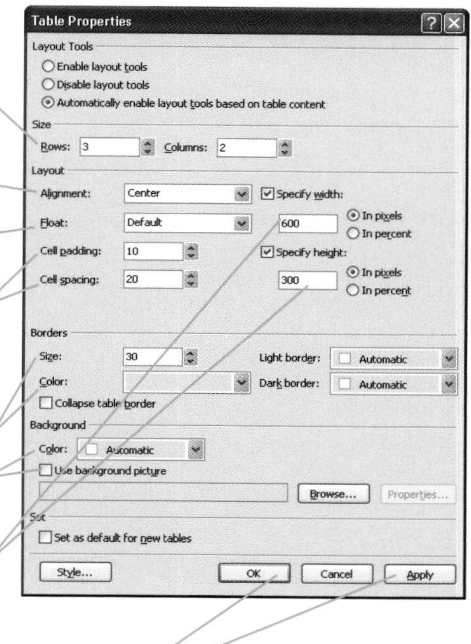

Note that you can specify the width of the table in pixels or as a percentage of the screen or frame width.

Layout properties that you specify for the table will be used as the default properties the next time you create a table.

3 Click OK or Apply to create or amend the table.

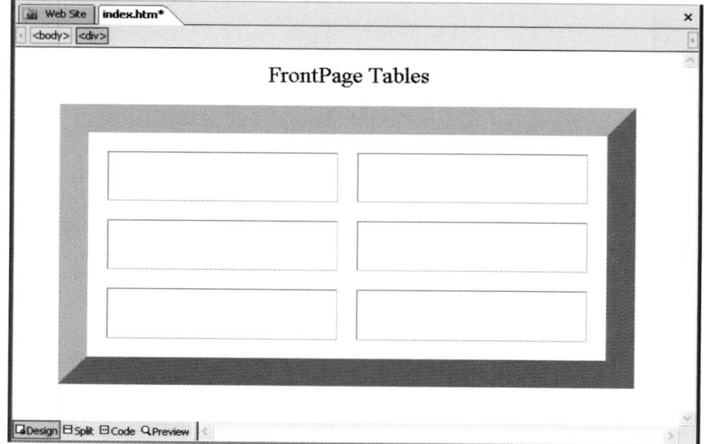

You can increase the number of rows or columns in an existing table by changing the properties, but you cannot decrease the numbers.

Draw a table

If you want a complex table, with different sizes of cells and varying numbers of columns and rows, you can draw it the way you want, no matter how irregular.

1 In Page view, select Table, Draw Table, and FrontPage will open the Tables toolbar.

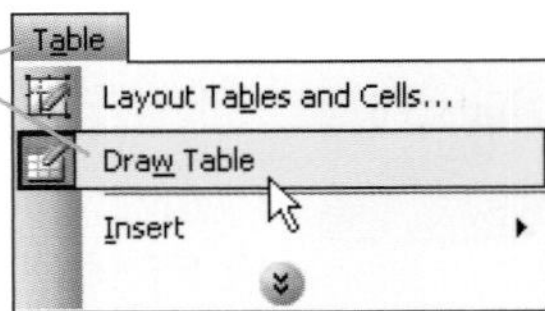

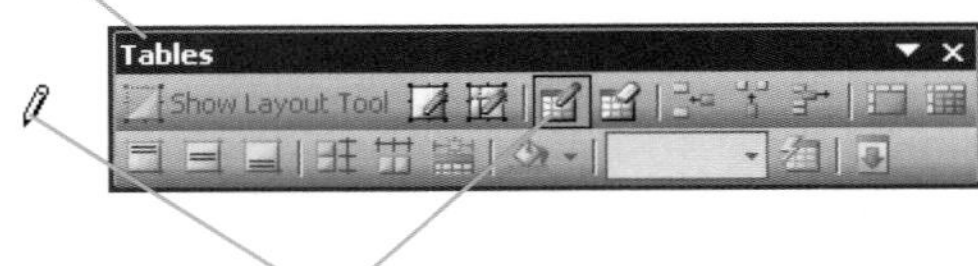

2 Select the Draw Table tool, and draw the outside border of the table by dragging from the upper-left corner to the lower-right.

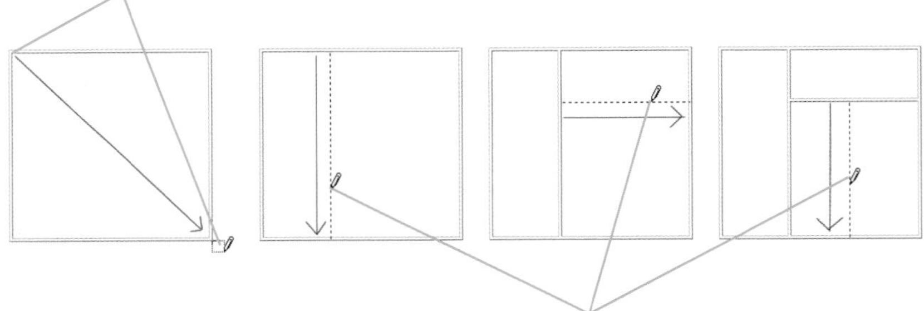

3 Draw vertical and horizontal lines, to create columns and rows in the table, nested within cells.

Click Draw Table on the Tables toolbar, to de-select the button and end table drawing.

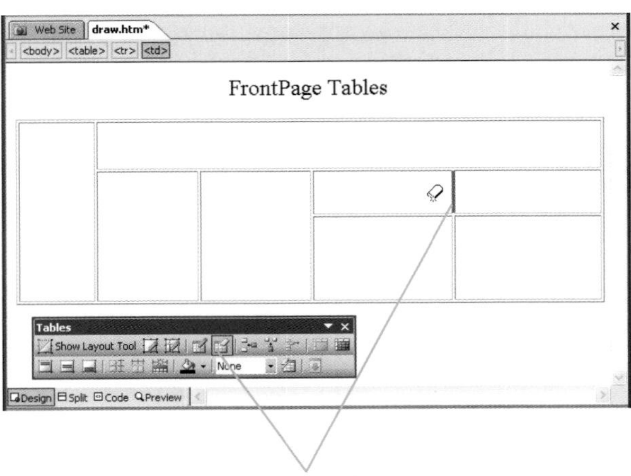

4 Click Eraser on the toolbar, and drag across an unwanted line. When the line turns red, release the mouse button.

Convert text to table

You can convert text into a table if it has been delimited – separated into rows and columns. Use a separator character to mark column boundaries, and the end of line (paragraph marker) to indicate rows.

HTML does not directly support tab characters, so avoid using tab characters as your text delineator.

If you select None, all the text will be placed in a single cell table, for example to keep all selected text together when you use tables for page layout.

The current default values will be used for borders and spacing, but you can change properties, and resize the cells and the columns.

The Office 2003 Basic Edition is designed to be pre-installed on some PCs, and is not available separately.

1 Open the Web site and open the page in Page view. Type or copy the text onto the page.

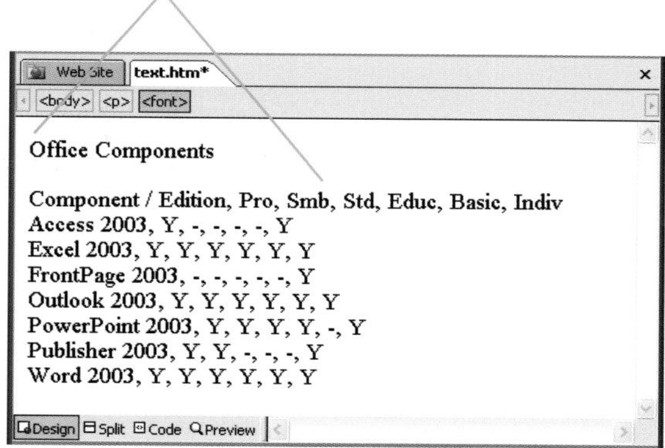

2 Highlight the text (excluding the title) and select Table, Convert, Text to Table.

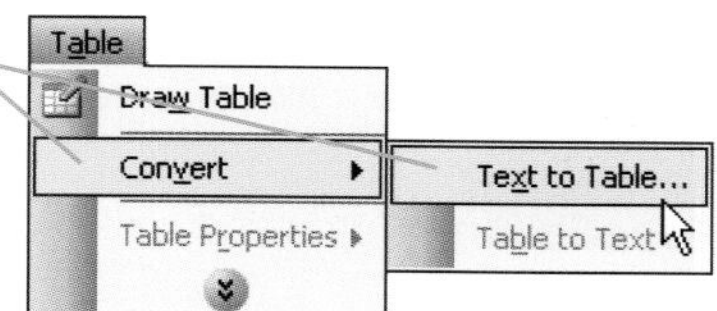

3 Specify the separator character e.g. commas and click OK. The table is created with the number of columns defined by the row with the most separator characters. Cell sizes are adjusted to best fit the text:

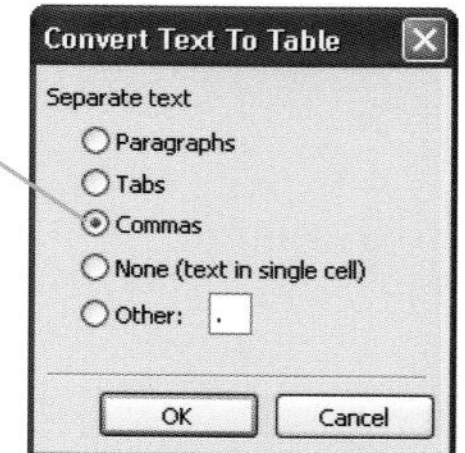

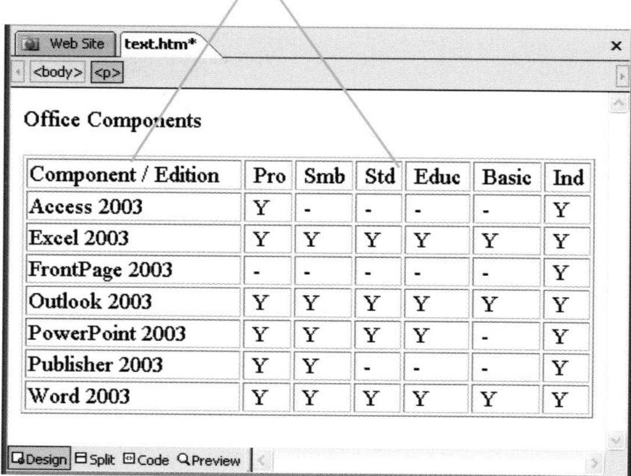

Office Components

Component / Edition	Pro	Smb	Std	Educ	Basic	Ind
Access 2003	Y	-	-	-	-	Y
Excel 2003	Y	Y	Y	Y	Y	Y
FrontPage 2003	-	-	-	-	-	Y
Outlook 2003	Y	Y	Y	Y	Y	Y
PowerPoint 2003	Y	Y	Y	Y	-	Y
Publisher 2003	Y	Y	-	-	-	Y
Word 2003	Y	Y	Y	Y	Y	Y

Tables within tables

You can perform the following additional operations. You can:

- *adjust the entries in an existing table*
- *split a single cell into several rows or columns*
- *remove lines to combine cells*
- *insert a whole table within a cell*

1 Click in the first row and click the Insert Row button on the Table toolbar to add a row above the selected row.

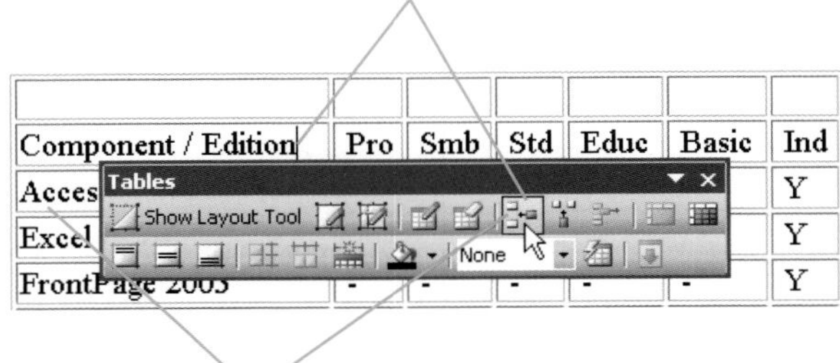

2 Click in the next row, and click the Insert Row button again, to put another row into the table, following the original first row.

If you select Table, Insert Rows or Columns, you can choose to insert above or below the selected cell, and you can specify how many rows you want.

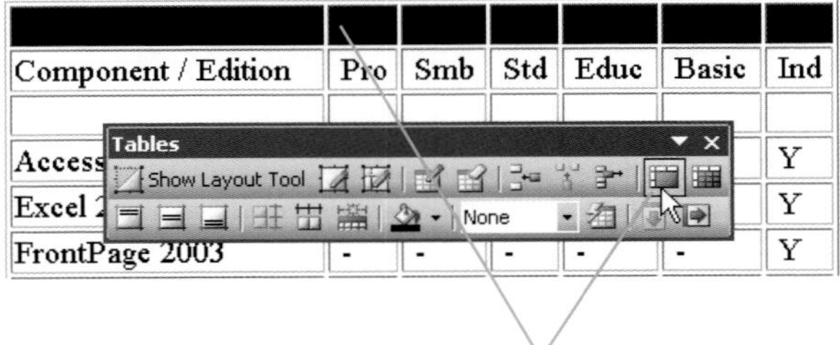

3 Highlight the whole of the first new row and click the Merge Cells button, to combine them all into one wide cell.

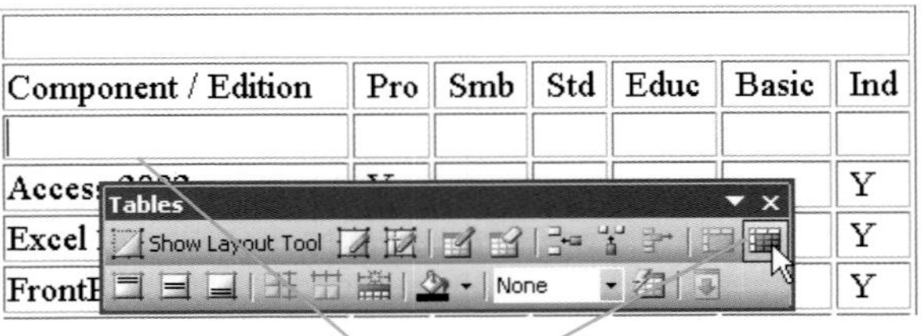

4 Select the first cell in the second new row, click the Split cells button, and choose Split into columns, setting the number as 2.

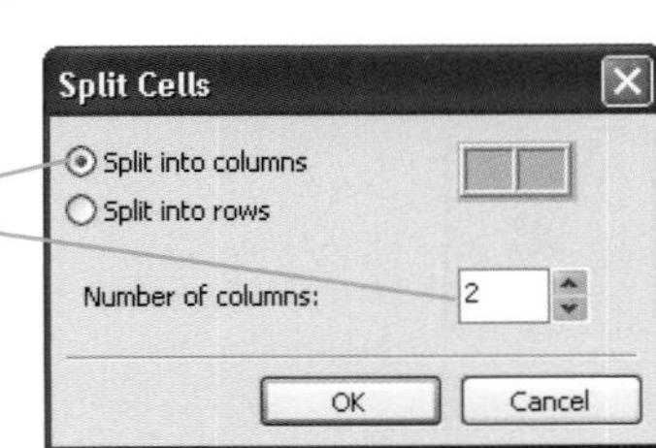

5 Select all the cells except the first cell in the second new row, which is now row three in the table.

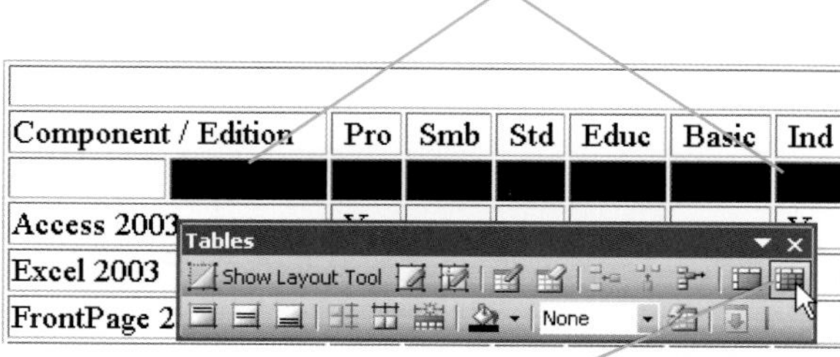

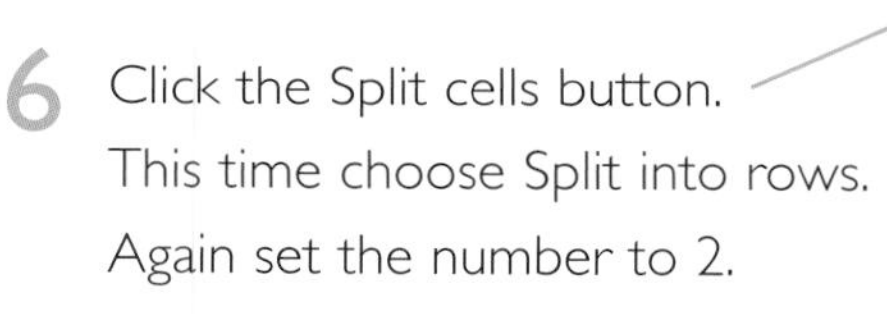

6 Click the Split cells button. This time choose Split into rows. Again set the number to 2.

You can also select Tables from the menu bar and choose Split cells to display this panel to define how you want to split the selected cell or cells.

7 Enter the title, center it, and enter the subtitles and data values.

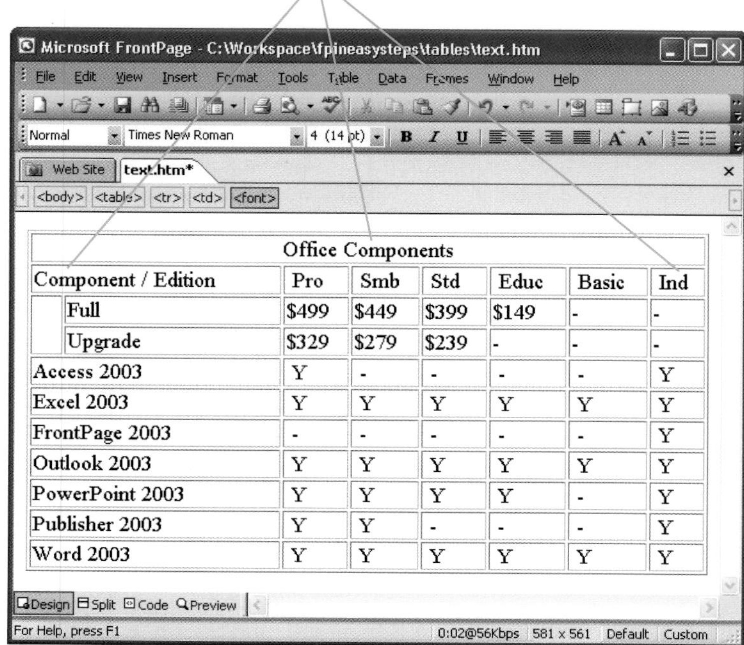

Office Components						
Component / Edition	Pro	Smb	Std	Educ	Basic	Ind
Full	$499	$449	$399	$149	-	-
Upgrade	$329	$279	$239	-	-	-
Access 2003	Y	-	-	-	-	Y
Excel 2003	Y	Y	Y	Y	Y	Y
FrontPage 2003	-	-	-	-	-	Y
Outlook 2003	Y	Y	Y	Y	Y	Y
PowerPoint 2003	Y	Y	Y	Y	-	Y
Publisher 2003	Y	Y	-	-	-	Y
Word 2003	Y	Y	Y	Y	Y	Y

If there's a student or teacher in the house, the special Student and Teacher edition of Office 2003 makes a very economical choice.

Image maps and hotspots

You can associate a hyperlink with a section of a graphic, so that when you click that part of the image, it switches you to the specified URL. If the image has several distinct areas, you may want a different hyperlink for each. Each activated area is known as a hotspot, and an image with one or more hotspots defined is known as an image map.

See page 34 for more details about defining hyperlinks and creating bookmarks on the page.

This link will be the default for the image, and will be associated with any area of the picture not separately defined as a hotspot.

Before defining hotspots, you may want to specify a default hyperlink for the parts of the image not otherwise defined.

1 Select Insert, Picture, From File, to add the image onto the page. Click the image to select it, showing the picture handles.

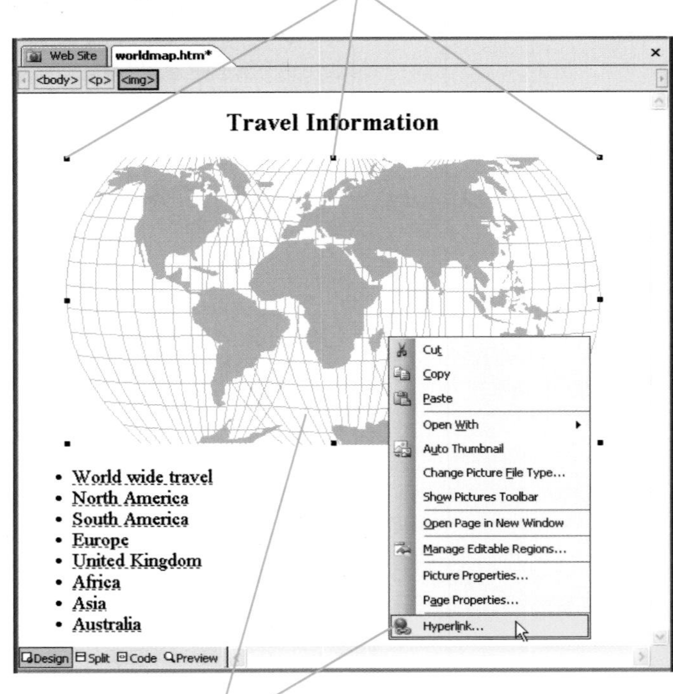

2 Right-click the image and select Hyperlink from the menu. Define the URL for a Web page or for a bookmark to a location on the current page.

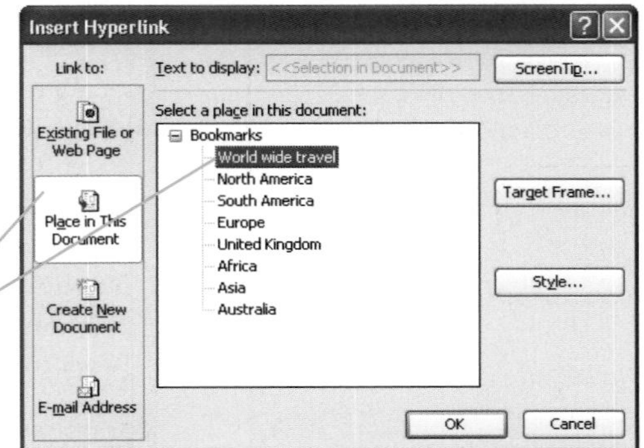

You can define a rectangle, circle or polygon shape. For a close fit, choose the polygon and take a series of small steps.

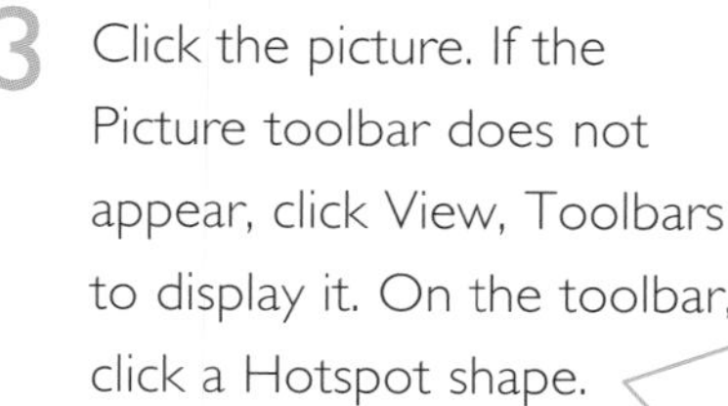

3 Click the picture. If the Picture toolbar does not appear, click View, Toolbars to display it. On the toolbar, click a Hotspot shape.

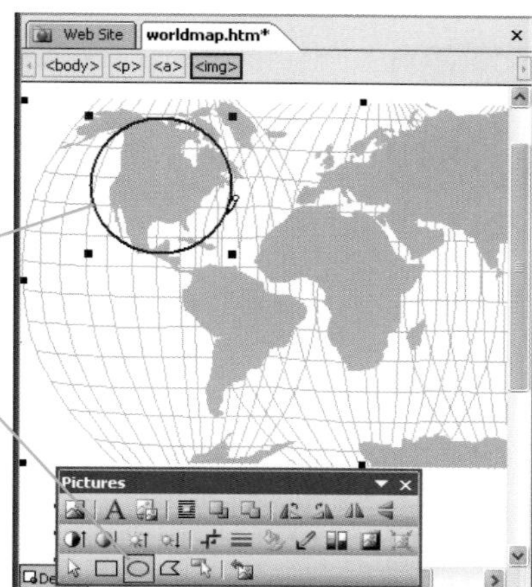

4 Draw the shape onto the image. When you release the mouse button, the Insert Hyperlink panel appears.

Any parts of the image not covered by a hotspot will take on the default hyperlink address.

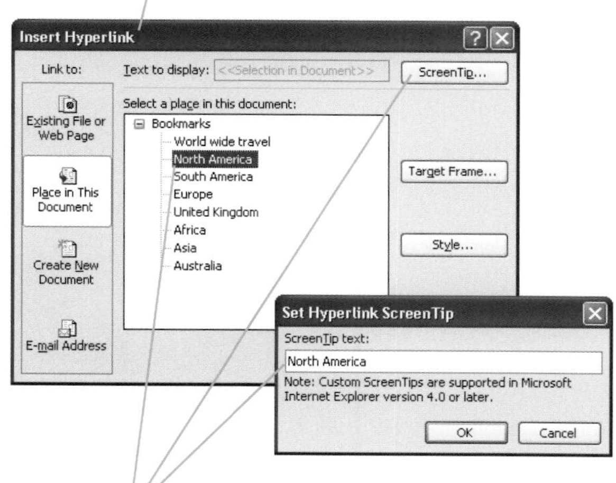

5 Enter the URL or select a bookmark for the hotspot. Click the Screen Tip button to add a text prompt to alert visitors.

6 As you'll find in Preview, the hotspot is hidden, but a hyperlink flag shows when you move the mouse over it, and the screen tip is shown.

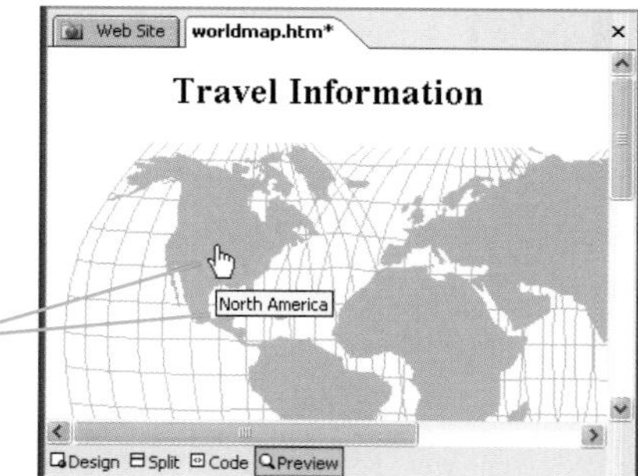

Repeat the drawing and hyperlink definition for each hotspot region, until the map is completely defined.

Text hotspots

A text hotspot is a string of text that you place on the image and assign a hyperlink.

1 Select the picture, and click the Text button from the Picture toolbar.

2 Click the image, and type the desired entry in the text box.

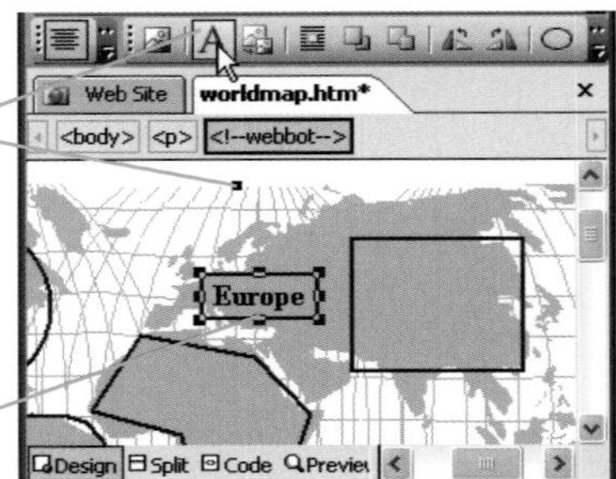

If the image type is in a different format, a GIF format version will be created.

3 Double-click the edge of the text box to display the Insert Hyperlink screen, and add the link and screen tip.

4 Only the text hotspots (and the screen tips) will be visible in Preview or when the page is viewed in the browser.

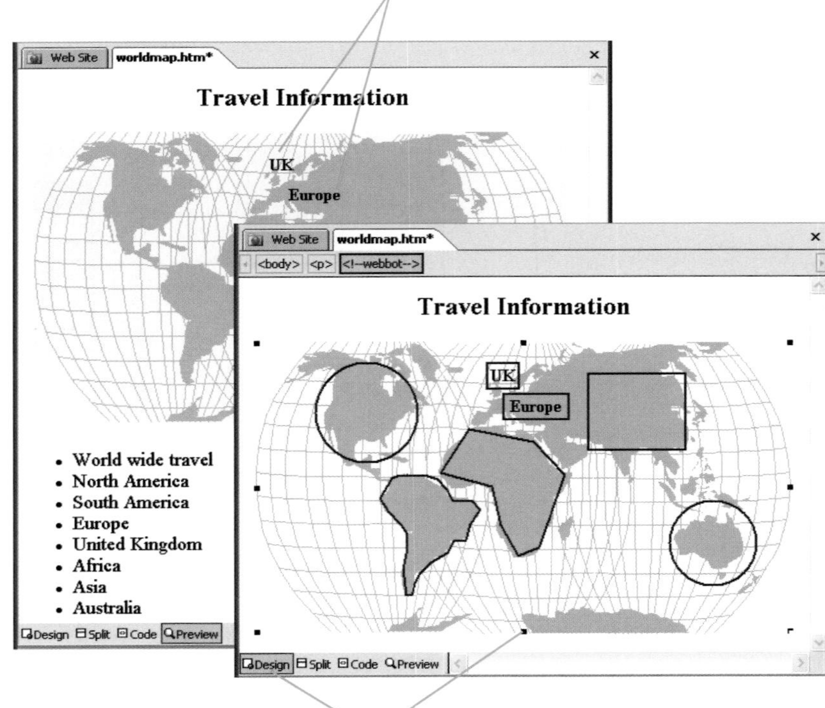

In this example, the image hotspots link to bookmarks in a collapsible list.

5 Select Design view and click the image to see the hotspot areas.

SharePoint Services

SharePoint Services provide most of the features found in FrontPage Extensions, but they support database access using XML rather than ASP.

Windows SharePoint Services are used to build and manage SharePoint Team Sites that contain Web Part Pages. These define page layouts that display data stored in the form of lists. For example, you could have announcements, event listings, member lists or any other list type that you want to define. SharePoint Team sites can also be used to manage discussions and document libraries.

To create a SharePoint Team site:

1. Open FrontPage and select File, New, then click the link for More Web site templates, to create a new Web site.

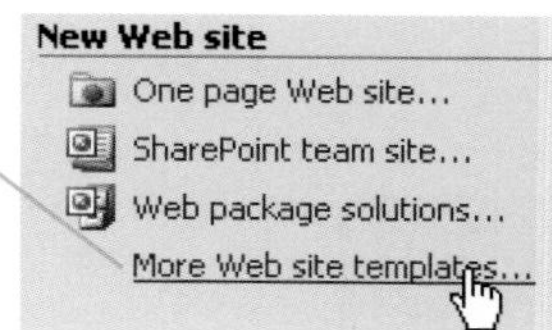

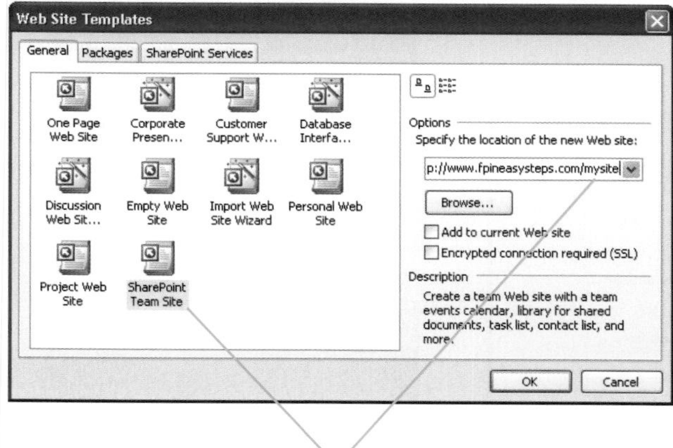

The SharePoint Team Site template will create a team Web site which will include an events calendar, a library for shared documents, a task list and a contacts list.

2. Click the SharePoint Team Site template, and specify the location of the planned site (URL with site name).

3. This Web site must be created on a server such as Interkey.net that runs SharePoint Services. FrontPage will detect if these are not present, and issue a warning message.

Microsoft Office FrontPage

This Web site must be created on a server that is running SharePoint Services from Microsoft. Please choose another location.

If you do not have a Web site hosting service, find one that supports FrontPage or Windows SharePoint Services by using the Web Presence Provider search page.

Click here to learn more.

OK

When FrontPage recognizes that the server supports the SharePoint services, it allows the Web site to be created.

4 If the server is running the SharePoint Services, the Team Web site will be created.

5 The Team Web site components, including a home page and folders for shared documents and lists, will be displayed in FrontPage.

Although it looks like a simple one page Web site, there are many files and folders hidden inside:

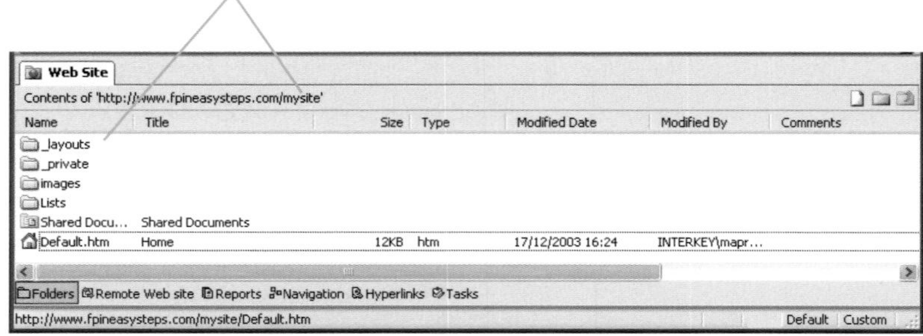

6 Open the home page Default.htm (note the capital letter in the files name), to display the page structure.

The Web pages in the SharePoint Team Site contain special elements used by SharePoint Services, so you should avoid making changes to these pages, other than to the appearance, so that the underlying structure does not get altered.

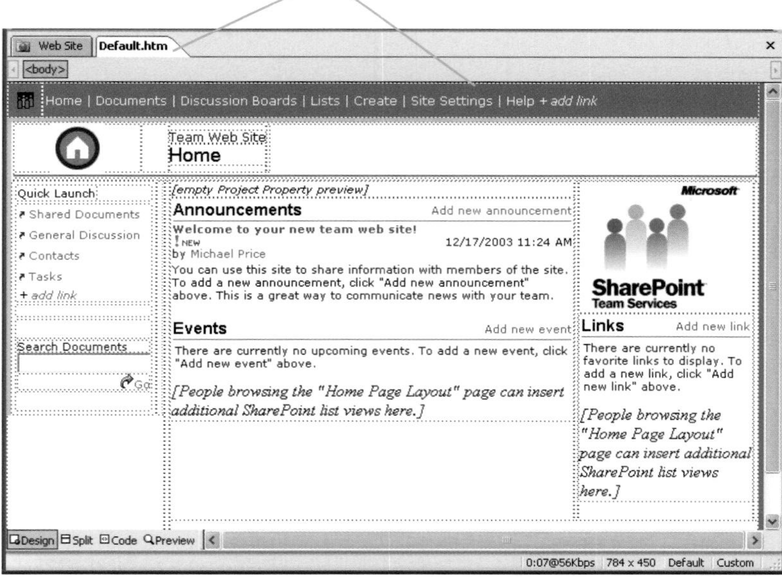

Using the Team Site

1 Open the Web site in the browser, by typing the full URL and Web site name used to create the site.

The menu bar at the top of the screen shows all the features of the Web site:

- Home
- Documents
- Discussion Boards
- Lists
- Create
- Site Settings
- Help

The Quick Launch bar on the left gives access to the most used components:

- Shared Documents
- General Discussion
- Contacts
- Tasks

You can add, remove or rearrange the Web Parts that are displayed for specific users.

2 Click the Add new announcement link to add an entry to the Announcements list, from within the browser.

Anyone with the appropriate user name and password can sign into the Team Web site over the Internet using the browser, and make changes to the data lists that are stored there, so the Team Website provides an easy way for groups to share data and to collaborate on projects.

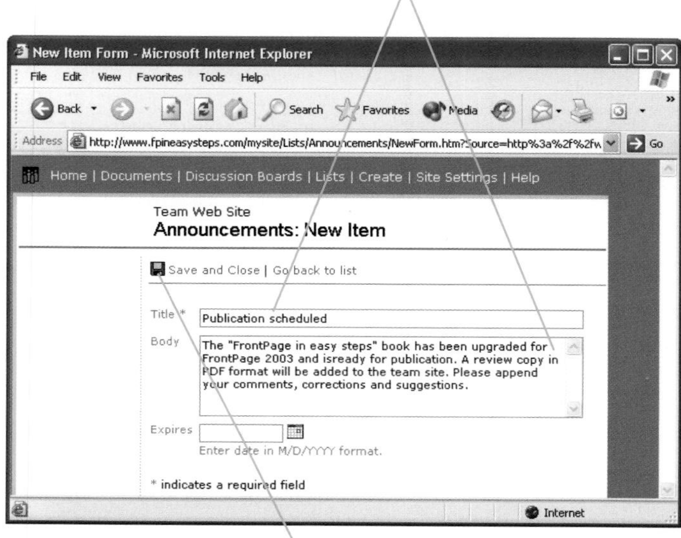

3 Click Save and Close, to save the change and return to the list.

Select Site Settings from the menu to make changes to the Web site, to add new users and to give levels of permission to work with the site.

4 Before the Web site gets updated, you are asked to enter the user name and password to authorize the change.

5 The Web page is redisplayed with the updated component showing.

Select Help from the menu to get information about using and managing the Team site.

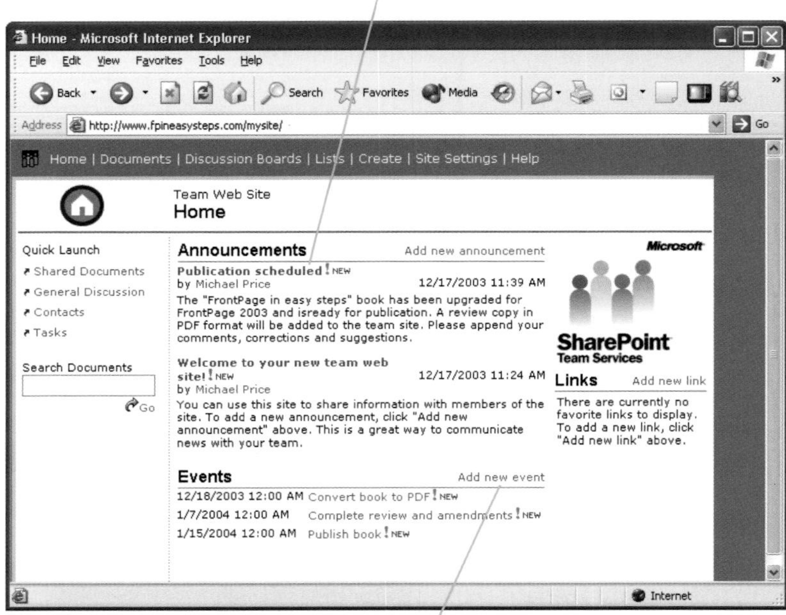

6 Click Add New Event, to add details of forthcoming events to the Events list. Note that you cannot backdate items since the date must be current or in the future.

7 You can export the contents of a list, for example to a spreadsheet program. In Excel, the exported list is a Web Query which stays updated with changes to the original list in your team Web site.

Sources of help

There is a wealth of information about Web site design on the Internet: from Microsoft, from other hardware and software suppliers and from interested groups such as universities. You'll find free, demo or trial add-ins for FrontPage that make the design task easier.

Covers

Chapter Twelve

FrontPage help

FrontPage provides lots of ways to invoke the help system, and takes into account the status of your Internet connection, when it starts up.

FrontPage also supports the Office Assistant. This is normally disabled. Click Help, Start the Office Assistant if you want it.

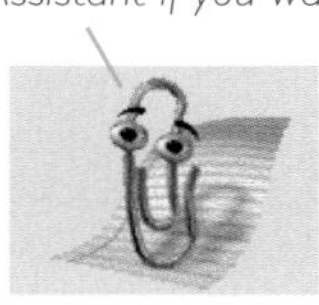

1. To display the Help task pane, press F1, or select Help, FrontPage Help or click the Help button, or click the task pane down arrow and select Help.

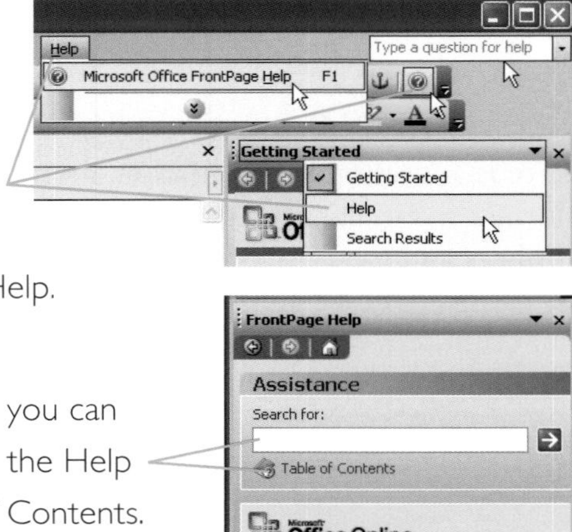

2. From the Help task pane you can enter a query and search the Help files, or click the Table of Contents.

3. If you are disconnected from the Internet, FrontPage displays an off-line copy of the Contents list.

If you type a query in the Ask a Question box and press Enter, the Help task pane will be displayed with the results of your query already showing.

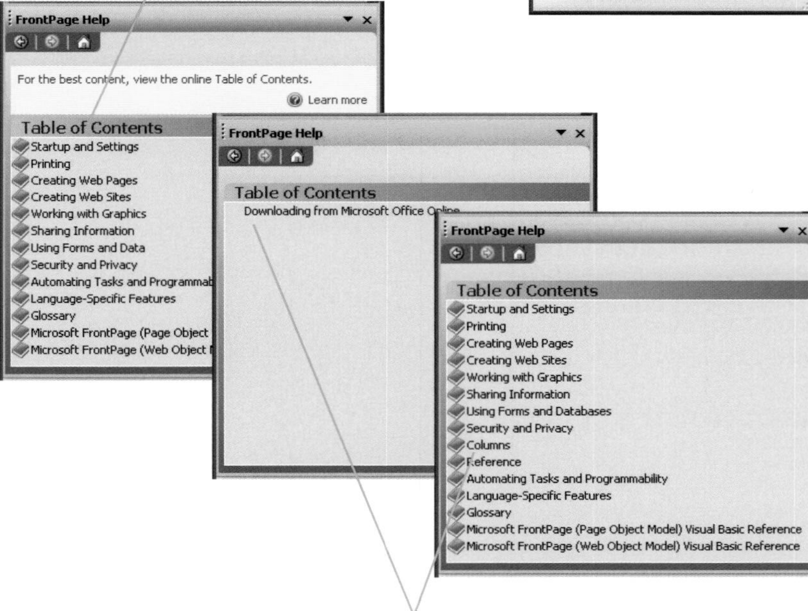

The online copy of the table of contents has additional topics and gives you the latest version of the Help information.

4. If your Internet connection is active, FrontPage downloads the latest Contents list from the Office Online Web site.

Office Online

In addition to the Web page references, there is also a link to help on the Internet, via the Office Update facility.

1 Select Help, Office Online, with an active Internet connection, to display the Home page for Office Online.

Help
Microsoft Office FrontPage Help F1
Show the Office Assistant
Microsoft Office Online
Microsoft FrontPage Developer Resources
Contact Us
Activate Product...
Customer Feedback Options...
About Microsoft Office FrontPage

2 This provides a variety of features for Office applications, FrontPage included.

The contents of these pages will change on a regular basis, so the pages that you see when you select Office on the Web will be different.

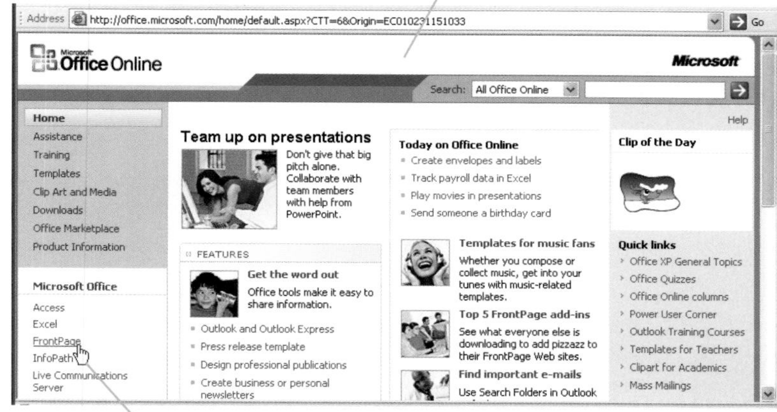

3 Click the FrontPage link to display the Assistance page for FrontPage 2003, and other versions of FrontPage.

There is a direct link to the FrontPage Assistance center on the FrontPage Help Task Pane.

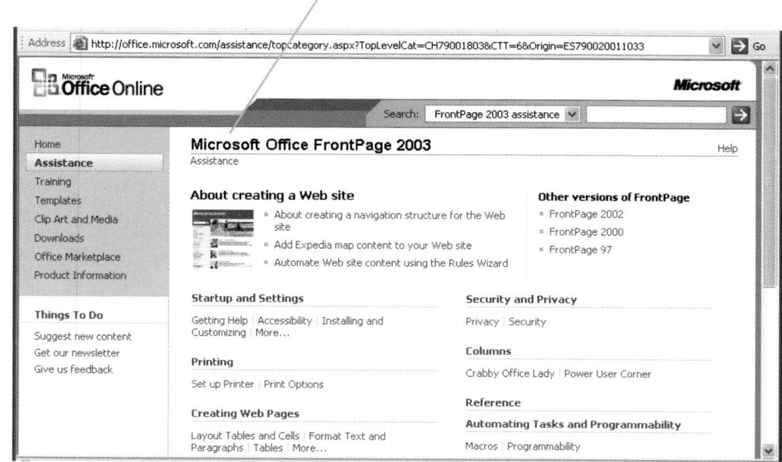

Office Update

Office Update will identify any updates that may be required for any of your installed Office applications, including FrontPage 2003.

1 Click Downloads on the Office Online sidebar (or at the Help task pane), and click the Check for Updates link.

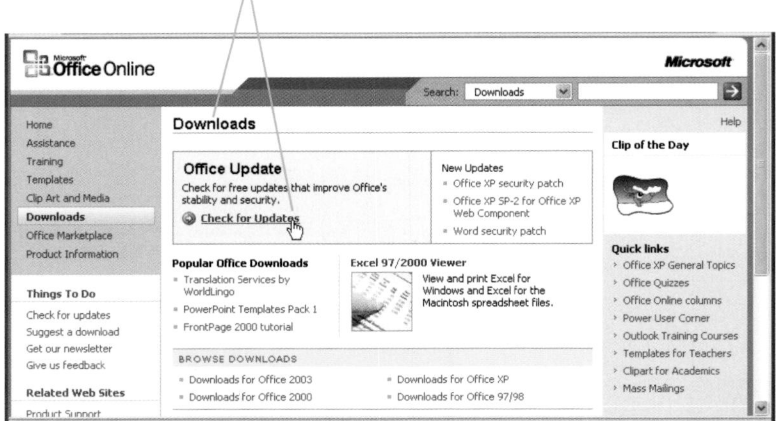

2 Click Start Installation to download and install any critical fixes that may be available for Office 2003.

Click the More Information link to get details of any of the selected updates.

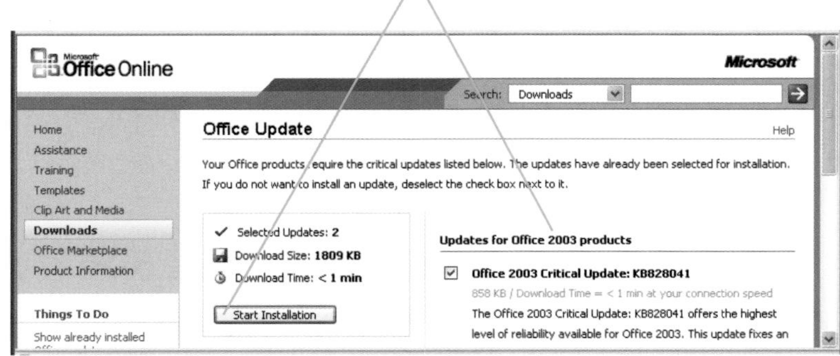

If you chose to save a copy of the installation files on your hard disk when you installed Office, the CD may not be required.

Confirm the terms and conditions when prompted, then the updates will be applied. You may be asked to insert your Office installation CD, so have it available just in case.

You may need to restart your system to complete the installation.

Downloads

The items offered for download will vary as the FrontPage 2003 system evolves, so check the Web site periodically to see what new features have become available.

1 From the Office Online Downloads, click Browse Downloads for Office 2003.

BROWSE DOWNLOADS
- Downloads for Office 2003
- Downloads for Office 2000

2 Click the link for FrontPage 2003 downloads. Initially there were no entries, but as downloads become available, they will be listed here.

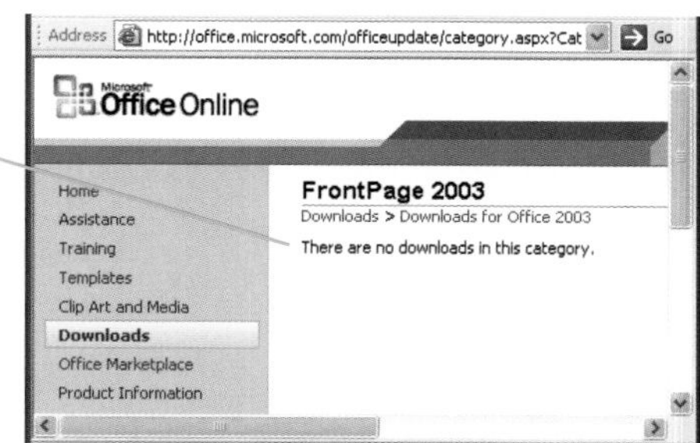

The specific products and options listed will vary from time to time, but you should expect to find downloads at one or other of these two resource centers.

3 You'll find more downloads at the FrontPage Add-in Center, at http://www.microsoft.com/frontpage/downloads/addin/.

See page 178 to search for and download add-ins for FrontPage.

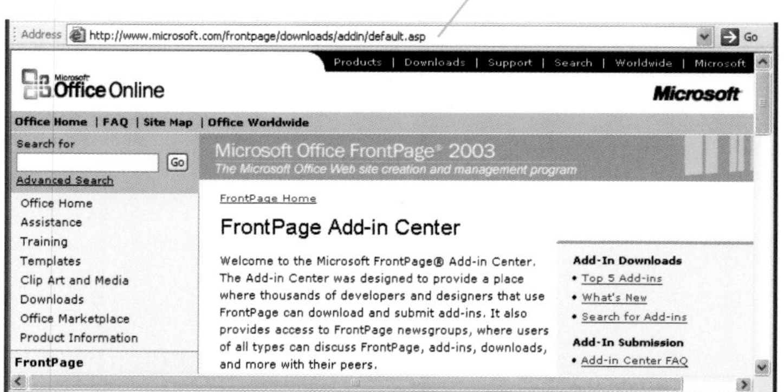

FrontPage Add-ins

1 Click the Search for Add-ins link and click the Go button to display all the registered add-ins.

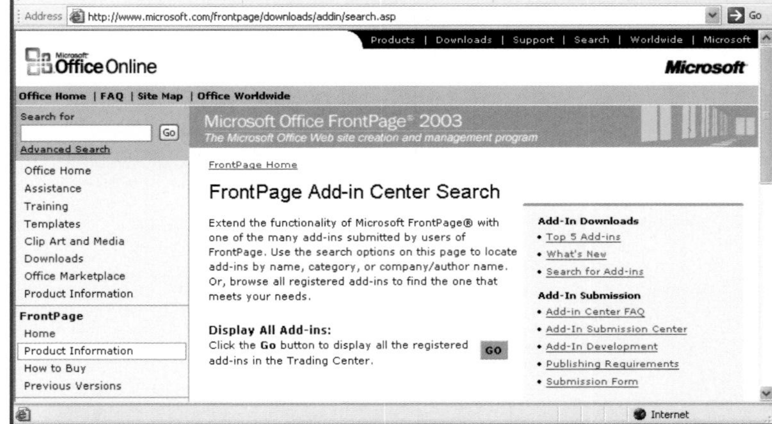

There's no way to search explicitly for products that support FrontPage 2003. You have to scroll through the list and check the descriptions. However, the What's New list is likely to be mainly for FrontPage 2003. At the time of writing, it shows 28 new items, all designed for FrontPage 2003.

2 This finds, at the time of writing, about 250 results, listed in groups of 25. Of course these are for various versions of FrontPage, and not all products work with FrontPage 2003.

3 Refine the search, by specifying the add-in name, the company or the product category, or search for What's New .

There's also a link that will list the top five add-ins, measured by the number of downloads.

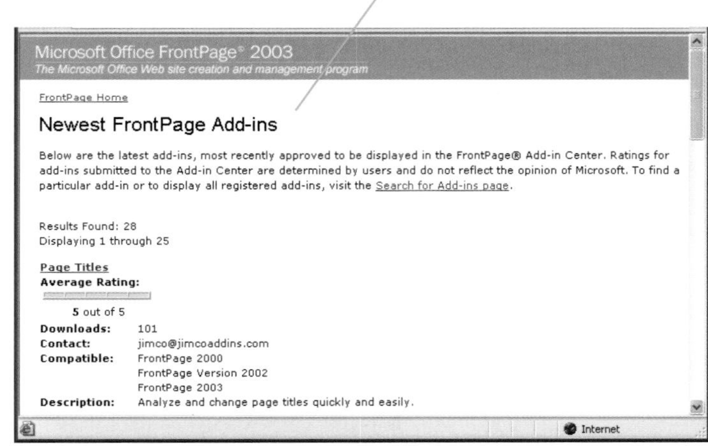

Download Add-in

Case Changer is a small but useful application that converts all file and folder names within the Web site to lower case.

1 To download an add-in from the FrontPage Add-in Center, locate the file and click the title.

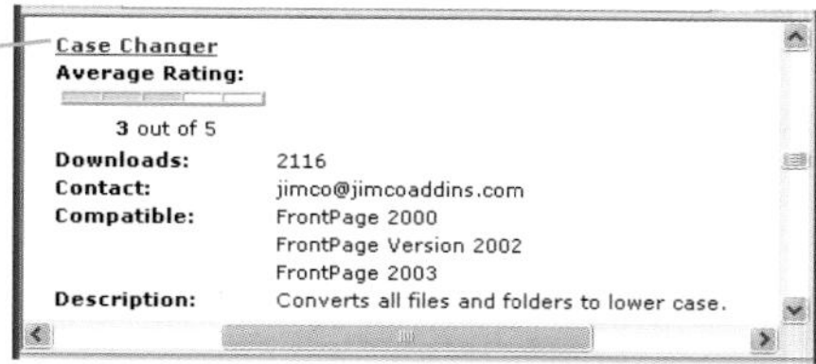

2 Click the Download Now! link and save the file to your hard disk. Follow the installation instructions. In this case, you run the downloaded file to expand it, then double-click the .msi install file that results.

3 The installation program sets up the downloaded application as a FrontPage add-in.

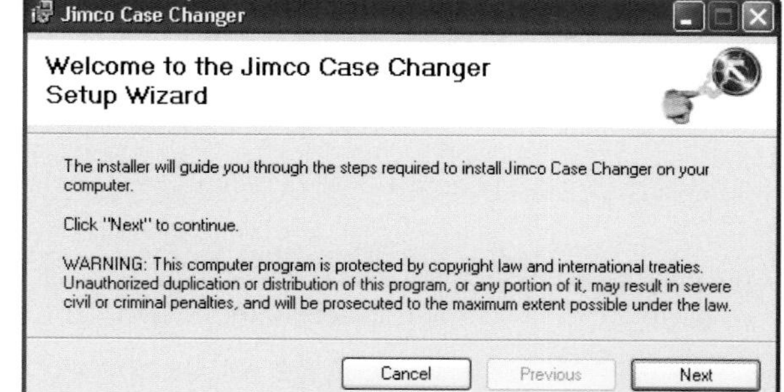

Some add-ins install themselves completely, while others require you to complete the installation by displaying the list of add-ins then clicking Add to select the new program.

4 To check that the application has been installed, select Tools, Add-ins to see a list of installed add-in programs. Case Changer will be added to the list.

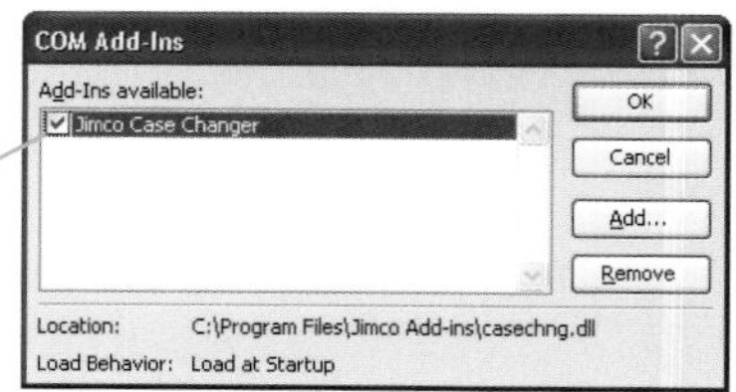

Using Case Changer

Having upper, or mixed case file names may cause problems, especially with non-Windows web servers.

1 Suppose you have a Web site where files have capitals in their names, and you wish to change them to lower case.

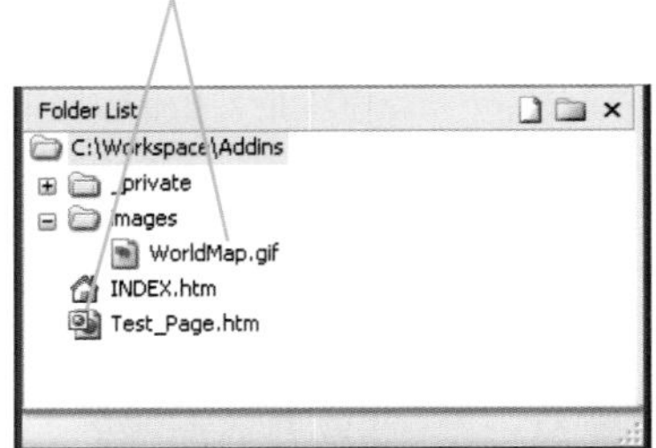

2 Open the Web site with the inappropriate file names and select Tools, Jimco Add-ins, and then Case Changer.

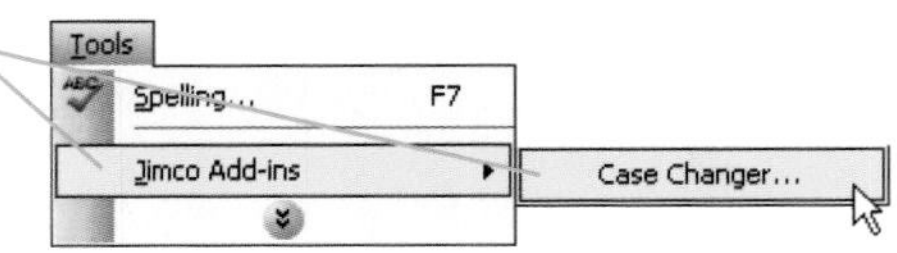

3 Click Yes to run the Case Changer for the files and folders inside the current Web site. A message appears as soon as the changes are completed.

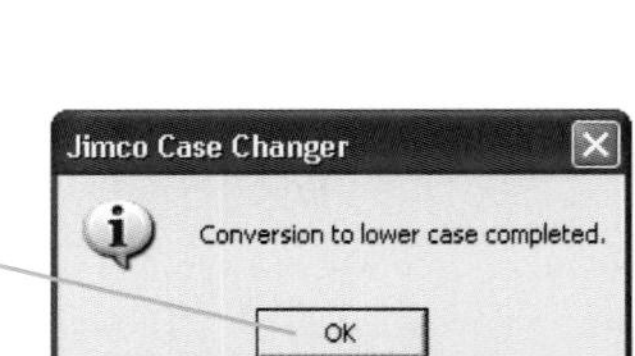

Select Preview or Preview in Browser, to check all the links work as expected.

4 You'll see that all the files and folders within the Web site have their names converted to lower case. The change will be applied to hyperlink references in the Web pages also.

More information from MS

There's a lot more detail on FrontPage offered from the main Microsoft Web site.

You will find many Web pages devoted to FrontPage at various Microsoft Web sites, providing information at various levels, ranging from new user to FrontPage developer.

1 For basic product information, visit the FrontPage home page, at http://www.microsoft.com/frontpage/.

There are links to support pages and related products, and also a link to the Assistance Center and Office Update (see page 175).

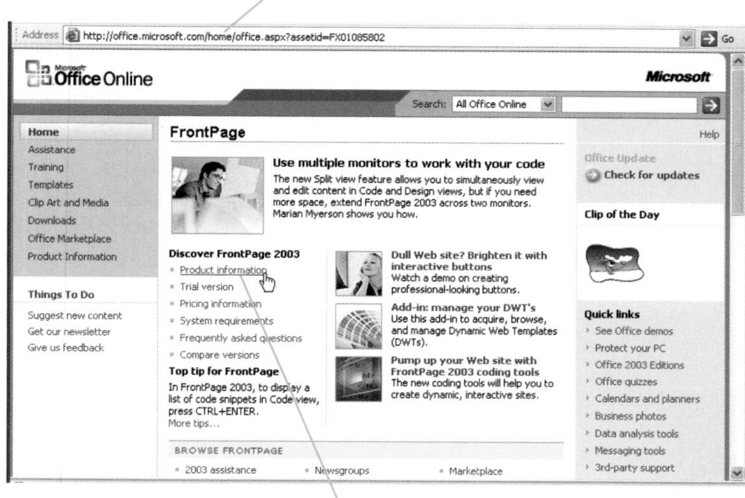

2 For more details, click Product Information. This includes an in-depth information section with a product guide and white papers.

In Product Information you will also find news and reviews, case studies and frequently asked questions.

FrontPage Insider

The Microsoft FrontPage Insider is a bi-monthly publication that can help you with ideas for creating and managing Web sites.

1 From the FrontPage home page, click the link to Get Our Newsletter, to see descriptions of all the Microsoft Office newsletters, including the FrontPage Insider.

When you register for the regular FrontPage Insider from Microsoft you can select a plain text or HTML format. It will be sent as an email message to the email address that you specify.

2 Click Register, and sign in with your Microsoft Passport ID. If you do not already have a Passport, you'll be asked to register and provide your details, including your email address.

You must have a Passport ID in order to complete the registration, and you must sign on in order to make any changes to your profile.

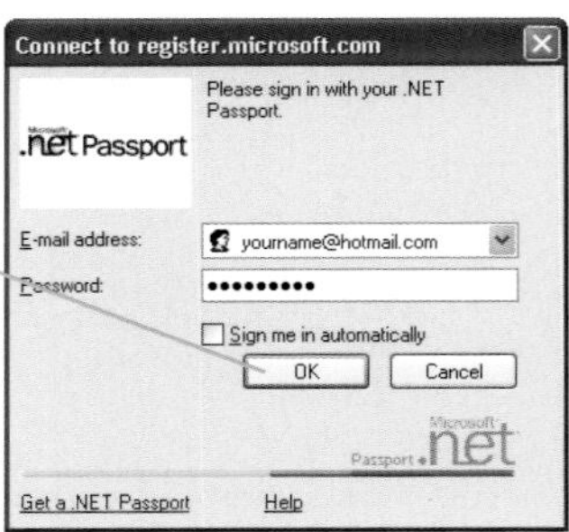

3 Choose the newsletters that you wish to receive, and click Update at the bottom of the screen.

There are similar regular newsletters for other Microsoft products or for special interest groups such as developers.

4 You'll receive a copy of the FrontPage Insider at the email address you specified, in HTML or plain text format.

Back issues of the Bulletin and the FanZine, the newsletters that preceded the Insider, may be found at www.microsoftfrontpage.com/bulletin/archive/index.html. However, this Web site is no longer being updated. If it becomes unavailable, try a Google search for "Microsoft FrontPage Bulletin".

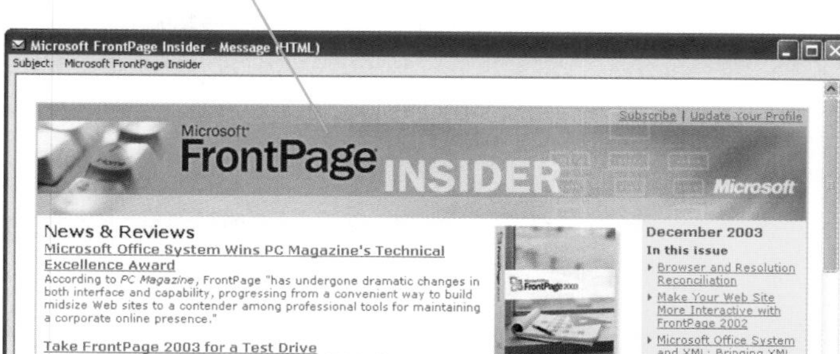

5 Click the Gallery of FrontPage Sites, to get information about the latest examples of Web sites built using FrontPage.

Every month, several Web sites are picked to showcase the use of FrontPage. Visit them to help you identify practices that you admire (or ones that you would prefer to avoid).

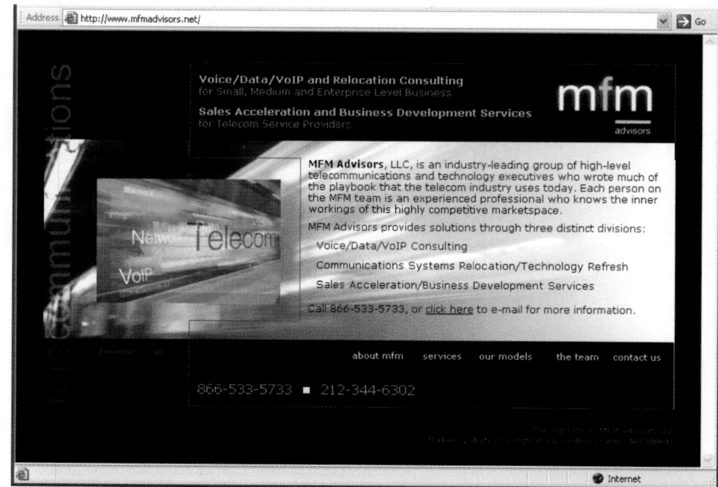

You can save parts of the example Web site to help you build or extend your own Web site, though you should use hyperlinks rather than full copies to share another site with your visitors.

6 If you wish, you can select File, Save As to save the contents of the Web page, HTML code and images to your hard disk.

FrontPage Web sites

The World Wide Web is a very dynamic environment so don't be surprised if the URLs you see mentioned here have been renamed or removed by the time you visit them.

A search for FrontPage 2003 using www.google.com or similar search engines should give you a wide range of related sites.

1 For a variety of FrontPage 2003 related news, information, tips and tricks, tools and templates, visit http://www.outfront.net.

2 If you want ideas for Web site design and Internet marketing, e-commerce and affiliates, visit http://www.frontpageworld.com.

Click the link <u>What's New</u> for a list of recent additions to the FrontPage World Web site, or click <u>Tips</u> for a shortcut to the Tips and Tricks section.

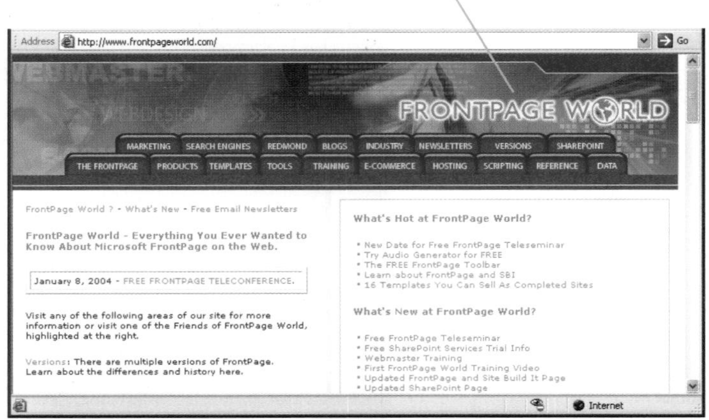

3 You can sign up for a free newsletter at this site. You'll also find numerous links to other FrontPage 2003 related sites.

Design guides

When you view any design guides on the Internet, be sure to check the date created or last updated. You will find documents of all ages. The earlier guides are likely to be overtaken by the advances in Web site or HTML features.

There are many Web sites that are provided to share information and experiences in designing Web sites. For example, view the Web page at: http://webdesign.about.com/mbody.htm.

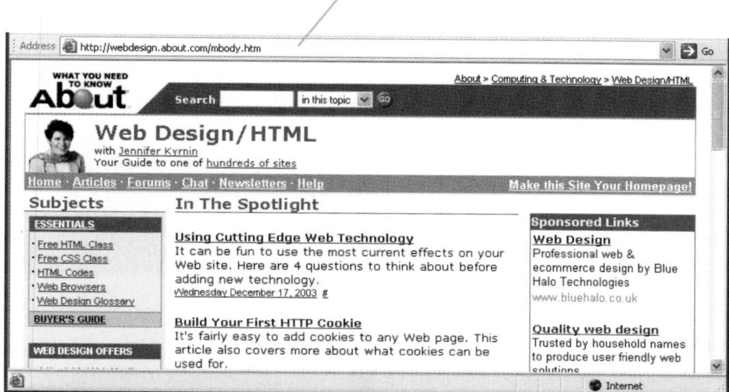

If it is programming the Web site that concerns you, there's a guide to all the HTML tags used by Netscape and Internet Explorer at http://www.werbach.com/barebones, to view online or download.

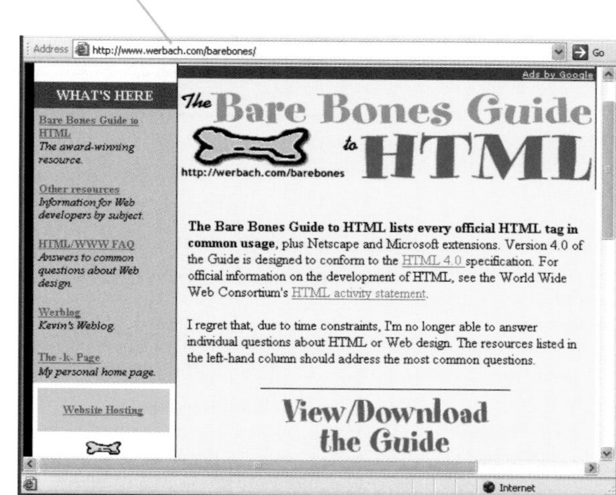

You'll also find Web design help at the Microsoft Web sites. For example, select Help, Developer Resources to visit the MSDN Web site at http://msdn.microsoft.com/office/understanding/frontpage, where you'll find information about planning, coding, building, deploying, and migrating FrontPage–based solutions.

Microsoft® Office Developer Center

Jakob Nielsen's Usability Web site at http://www.useit.com covers general Web site writing guidelines and practices, emphasizing the different characteristics of printed and screen-based text. In particular, you should review the papers at: http://www.useit.com/papers/webwriting/.

FrontPage user groups

Visit the Web sites of FrontPage user groups. Even if they are too far away for you to attend meetings, you can still pick up ideas for making the best use of FrontPage.

Meeting topics can include general Web site authoring overviews, hands-on demonstrations, Web site usability, search engine optimization, moving businesses to the Web site, and replacing graphics with Macromedia Flash!

The Boston FrontPage Web Developer Group, to be found at http://www.bostonfrontpage.com has interesting demonstrations and useful resources freely available at their Web site.

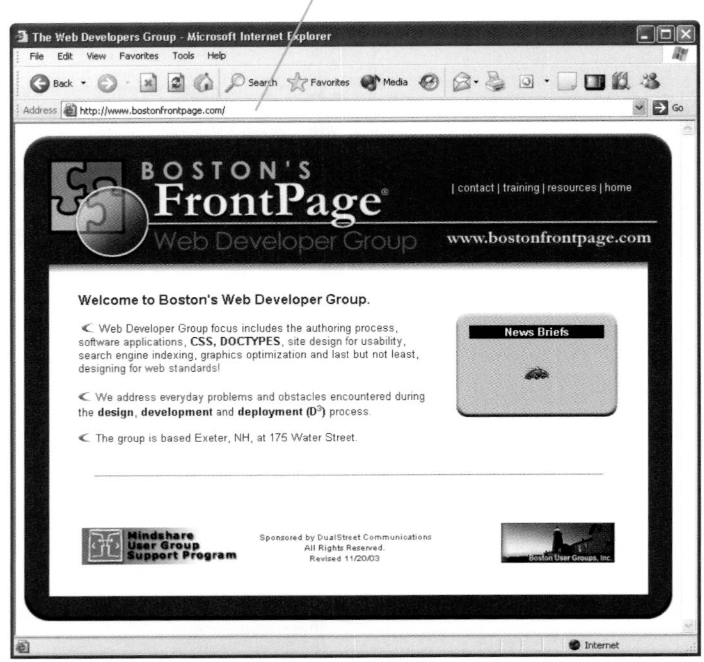

The FrontPage User Group of New York emphasizes "Plain English" design and technical information. Their Web site at http://www.fpug-ny.com has morphed, as they put it, into the Macromedia Flash Web Designers Group (MFWDG).

Join FPUG-NY's extended community of users at Yahoo! Groups. All you need is your Yahoo! Groups sign-on.

However, there's still an active FrontPage User Group forum at http://groups.yahoo.com/group/fpug where you may be able to get your queries answered.

Index

F

G

H

I

J

K

L

M

N

T

U

V

W